trees
of Pennsylvania

trees
of Pennsylvania
the atlantic states and the lake states

Hui-lin Li

University of Pennsylvania Press
Philadelphia

Library of Congress Catalog Number: 72–80376
ISBN: 0–8122–1064–6

Complete design by
Cypher Associates, Inc.

Printed in the United States of America

CONTENTS

ACKNOWLEDGEMENTS

The line drawings for this work were prepared by my wife, C. Y. Hsu Li, in close collaboration with me. I am grateful for her help, interest, and encouragement. I wish to express my appreciation to several persons who have helped in typing or have otherwise assisted in the preparation of the manuscript: Mrs. S. H. Chen Hsiao, Mrs. Margaret Yaeger, Mrs. Josephine Beck, Mrs. Patricia Abrams, and our daughters June and Anne Li. Thanks are also due to contributors of photographic material used as illustrations. The greater part of the photographs are from the Morris Arboretum collections. The Arnold Arboretum contributed two (p. 77, p. 94) and the New Crops Division of USDA one (p. 100). Credits for the Morris Arboretum photographs are as follows: Dr. John M. Fogg, Jr. (p. 29 bottom, p. 30, p. 42, p. 43, p. 44 bottom, p. 45, p. 46, p. 50, p. 58 bottom, p. 68, p. 73, p. 92, p. 98, p. 121, p. 123 top, p. 125, p. 126, p. 128, p. 129, p. 146 bottom, p. 147, p. 150, p. 152, p. 156, p. 164, p. 166, p. 170, p. 178, p. 179, p. 180, p. 184, p. 186, p. 190, p. 194 top, p. 210 top, p. 211, p. 217, p. 218, p. 226, p. 230, p. 238, p. 240, p. 246 bottom, p. 247, p. 255 top); the late Richard C. Chillas, Jr. (p. 65, p. 67, p. 90, p. 96, p. 125 bottom, p. 138, p. 236, p. 250, p. 255 bottom); Dr. Ju-Ying Hsiao (p. 22, p. 24, p. 29 top, p. 48, p. 58 top, p. 66, p. 78, p. 79 top, p. 91 top, p. 123 bottom, p. 124, p. 127 top, p. 134, p. 168, p. 188, p. 194 bottom, p. 199, p. 209, p. 210 bottom, p. 228, p. 246 top); Dr. Patricia Allison (p. 146 top); Elizabeth Orzatti (p. 44 top, p. 91 bottom, p. 140); and others, including some by myself.

LIST OF PHOTOGRAPHS

trees

of Pennsylvania
the atlantic states and
the lake states

INTRODUCTION

The name Pennsylvania, "Penn's Woods," indicates a land of luxuriant and varied tree growth. Nearly all species of trees native to temperate eastern North America grow in the state. This unusual variety arises from the intersection, in Pennsylvania, of the geographic ranges of many species typical of the northern temperate zone with those of many southern species. Since the trees of Pennsylvania are representative of the eastern part of the country, this handbook will be equally valuable in other states along the Atlantic coastline and inland to the Great Lakes.

This book has been designed for people who want to be able to identify the native trees of their state and of the region. Students will find an introduction to classification and terminology. The growing numbers of tree lovers should find it useful in their search to improve our environment through the preservation and cultivation of trees.

Altogether 118 species are described and illustrated: all trees native to Pennsylvania as well as a few introduced species that are extensively naturalized in this area. Since the distinction between trees and shrubs is sometimes arbitrary, most of the large shrubs are included. Commonly introduced culti-vated species are mentioned briefly, in connection with the native genera.

As a guide to the identification of the trees, two sets of keys to the genera are provided, one based on summer and the other on winter characteristics. The descriptions of most of the genera containing more than one species are accompanied by two keys for the identification of these species. Those interested in nature and forest studies should find the use of these keys helpful in learning the categories of tree characteristics. However, readers will generally be able to identify trees from the illustrations and descriptions, without resorting to the keys.

Each species description gives the significant characteristics of the tree, together with brief notes on its cultivation. The illustrations show many of these features in detail, as an especial aid to those who wish to study these trees in greater depth. Technical detail and technical terms have been kept to a minimum, however, since this book was not written for botanists alone. There is an extensive glossary defining those terms which do appear. Those who seek a more complete knowledge of these trees can consult the larger manuals listed in the bibliography.

THE STUDY AND IDENTIFICATION OF TREES

The first step in the study of trees is recognition of the types of their structural elements, for example, different leaf conformations. Identification of families, genera and species depends largely upon such recognition, although it is aided by knowledge of other characteristics such as range and habitat.

This book constructs identification keys and species-descriptions using both structural features and growth characteristics. Each description covers habit, bark, stems, winter-buds, flowers, fruit, distribution and habitat. The range of variation for these criteria and the terms used are summarized below.

HABIT. The habit or form of a tree refers to its overall shape and depends primarily on the growth of the trunk and its primary branches. A plant that has several main stems often branching close to the ground is usually a shrub. Trees nearly always have one main trunk, either short or tall, which can be of two types. In the first, the trunk is straight and upright, does not divide, and bears lateral secondary branches resulting in a pyramidal crown. This is typical of most conifers. In the second, common in broad-leaved trees, the main trunk divides into several large branches resulting in a broad, spreading crown.

There are all kinds of variations within these two major types. Each species generally has a mode of branching different even from others in the same genus. Individual trees within species vary in habit, chiefly due to environmental conditions. Trees growing in the open tend to have wider crowns than those in a forest. Injuries received by a tree during its development may modify its natural form. Age changes the habit, and trees become broader and more spreading as they grow older.

BARK. The characteristics of the bark, which covers the trunk and older branches, are useful for identification throughout the year. Bark varies in thickness, color and texture. It can be close and smooth, deeply or shallowly furrowed, or peeling off in various fashions. All these qualities may change with age, however, so that a young tree will perhaps look different from an old one and a young branch look different from an old trunk.

STEMS. When the buds develop into young branchlets, these may be stout or slender, even-surfaced or grooved, smooth or variously hairy, with or without a bloom and of different colors. The appearance of the branchlets may change in the following season or later, but

3

these changes are often quite specific and provide good guides for identification.

The *pith,* the soft central part of the stem, may be quite large and readily recognizable. It varies in color in different species. While the pith usually extends continuously inside the branch, in some plants it is distinctively *chambered.*

The surface of the stem may be covered by *lenticels,* small corky openings in the outer layer of cells used for the exchange of gases. Species differ in the shape, size, color, distribution and relative abundance of their lenticels, which are especially used for winter identification.

Stems are also distinguished by different kinds of scars. *Leaf-scars* are left by the fall of the leaves, and vary in size, shape, color and position relative to the buds. Also important are the size, number and distribution of *bundle-scars,* caused within the leaf-scars by the vascular bundles. (Vascular bundles are the strand-like portion of the conductive system of the plant.) *Stipule-scars* are sometimes left on plants with stipulate leaves—leaves that bear a pair of appendages or stipules at the base of their stalks. The length of the scar left by deciduous stipules varies from an inconspicuous dot to a long line encircling the stem.

WINTER-BUDS. The location and number of buds on the stem—whether leaf-buds or flower-buds—are especially useful for winter identification. Buds may be arranged alternately, oppositely, or in whorls or clusters, and they are named according to their position on the stem. *Lateral buds* form along the sides of the branches. *Terminal buds,* usually larger but sometimes absent altogether, form at the tip of the branch. *Axillary buds* are located in the axil of the leaves along the stem (the node) and generally occur singly; buds on the stem above them are known as *superposed buds.*

Buds vary in size, shape, color, hairiness, and number of scales. They are usually covered by at least one *bud-scale,* which is a modified leaf serving as protection and which also varies in number, size, shape, arrangement, color and hairiness. Buds without scales are known as *naked buds.*

LEAVES. The first feature usually used to identify a tree is whether its leaves die every fall (deciduous) or persist for several years (evergreens). Other important characteristics of leaves are: 1) their arrangement on the stem (alternate, opposite, or whorled); 2) whether they are simple, pinnate-compound, or palmate-compound; 3) with or without stipules, (stipulate or exstipulate); 4) with or without a stalk (petiolate or sessile); 5) the size, shape, texture and color of the blade; 6) the amount and character of hairs (pubescence); 7) the arrangement of veins (pinnate or palmate); and 8) the character of the margin. The accompanying diagrams illustrate the basic shapes of leaves and the forms of their tips and margins.

FLOWERS. Flowers are present for only a short time each year, but they provide the most critical criteria for the classification and interrelationships of plants. Vegetative features, because of variation within species and similarity between species, may be an inadequate basis for definite identification, and flowers must then form the conclusive evidence.

Flowers occur singly (solitary flowers) or in clusters. The *inflorescence* of a plant which bears flowers in clusters is determined by the particular arrangement of the flowers on an axis. The type of inflorescence is frequently a basic characteristic in the classification of a genus or a family.

The basic parts of a flower are calyx (sepals), corolla (petals), stamens, and pistil; their number, arrangement, color and detailed structure are all important

Figure 1 **LEAF FORMS**

1. Lanceolate	2. Oblanceolate	3. Ovate	4. Obovate	5. Elliptic
(lance-shaped)	(inversely lanceolate)	(egg-shaped)	(inversely ovate)	(ellipse-shaped)

6. Oblong	7. Cordate	8. Orbicular	9. Linear	10. Spatulate
(broad-elliptic)	(heart-shaped)	(circular)	(line-like)	(spoon-like)

Figure 2 **LEAF MARGINS**

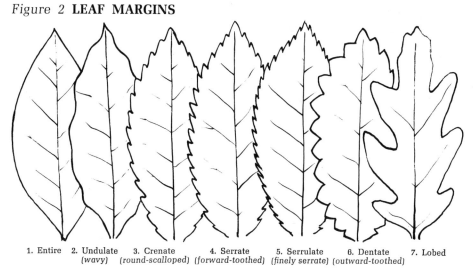

1. Entire	2. Undulate	3. Crenate	4. Serrate	5. Serrulate	6. Dentate	7. Lobed
	(wavy)	(round-scalloped)	(forward-toothed)	(finely serrate)	(outward-toothed)	

Figure 3 **LEAF APICES**

1. Acuminate	2. Acute	3. Obtuse	4. Emarginate	5. Mucronate
(sharply long-pointed)	(sharply pointed)	(bluntly pointed)	(notched)	(fine-pointed)

5

Figure 4 PARTS OF A FLOWER

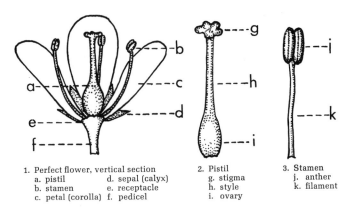

1. Perfect flower, vertical section
   a. pistil   d. sepal (calyx)
   b. stamen   e. receptacle
   c. petal (corolla) f. pedicel

2. Pistil
   g. stigma
   h. style
   i. ovary

3. Stamen
   j. anther
   k. filament

characteristics. Especially significant are their presence or absence, union, fusion, and difference in their sizes resulting in a change in the symmetry of the flower.

The stamen, the male organ of the plant, consists of the filament and the anther. The pistil, the female organ, consists of the style, the stigma and the ovary, which produces ovules. A flower bearing both stamens and pistils is called a *perfect flower*. Flowers with organs of only one sex are unisexual: either *staminate*, with stamens, or *pistillate*, with pistils. When both staminate and pistillate flowers are present on the same tree, the plant is *monoecious*. When staminate and pistillate flowers are found on different trees, the plant is *dioecious*. A plant is *polygamous* when it bears both unisexual and bisexual flowers.

Pollen grains, produced in the anther, contain the male cells or nuclei and are carried to the pistil by wind or insects. One male cell fuses with the egg contained in the ovule, and after fertilization, the egg begins to develop into an embryo and the ovule into a seed. At the same time, the ovary is developing into the fruit.

Figure 5 TYPES OF INFLORESCENCES

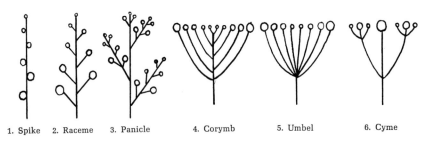

1. Spike   2. Raceme   3. Panicle   4. Corymb   5. Umbel   6. Cyme

FRUIT. Fruits and their seeds vary greatly in trees from minute, light forms to large, heavy ones. They are adapted for several different means of dispersal, chiefly wind and animals. Fruits are either dehiscent (opening to emit the contents) or indehiscent. Some of the major types are:

Follicle. A dry dehiscent fruit opening only on the front suture, derived from 1 pistil.

Achene. A small dry indehiscent 1-seeded fruit.

Capsule. A dry fruit developed from a several-celled ovary, dehiscing along one or more lines.

Nut. An indehiscent, 1-celled, 1-seeded hard and bony fruit.

Legume. A simple fruit dehiscing on both sutures, derived from a 1-celled ovary.

Samara. An indehiscent winged fruit.

DISTRIBUTION AND HABITAT. Every species has a geographical range where it occurs naturally. It may grow in one locality only or extend over a continent, but within its range the plant is usually limited to those situations favorable for its survival. These situations are determined by specific requirements in topography, altitude, soil type, moisture, exposure, etc.

THE CLASSIFICATION
AND NAMING
OF TREES

The classificatory system is a hierarchical system of categories or *taxa* (singular, *taxon*). The basic unit of classification for plants (and animals) is the *species*, which may be defined simply as a group of organisms that actually or potentially interbreed. The Sugar Maple is a species, the Black Oak is a species, the Paper Birch is a species. Their individual members derive their structure from common ancestors and maintain their characteristic features generation after generation. Minor variations in type within a species are called *varieties* or *forms*. (These occur especially in cultivated plants.)

The scientific name of a species consists of two Latin words. The generic name comes first and is capitalized, followed by a lowercase epithet designating the species. After the Latin terms is the name of the man who first named and described the species: the scientific name of the White Pine, for example, is *Pinus strobus* Linnaeus.

A *genus* (plural, *genera*) comprises a group of closely related species. White Pine, Red Pine, Pitch Pine and Jack Pine all differ among themselves yet they possess features in common that indicate their close relationship and that allow them to be grouped as members of the genus *Pinus*. The characteristics

important for classification are not necessarily the resemblances seen at first glance but features such as the position of the ovary in the flower and the number of its chambers and ovules. A group of closely related genera is called a *family*. The Pine Family includes pines *(Pinus)*, spruces *(Picea)*, firs *(Abies)*, hemlocks *(Tsuga)*, larches *(Larix)* and others. The scientific names of most families end in *aceae:* Salicaceae (Willow Family), Juglandaceae (Walnut Family), Magnoliaceae (Magnolia Family), Rosaceae (Rose Family).

A group of related families constitutes an *order,* whose scientific name ends in *ales.* At successively more comprehensive levels, the taxa above orders are *classes* and *divisions.* All the trees and shrubs known to us in the temperate zone belong to the Division Tracheophyta (the vascular plants), the subdivision Pteropsida, and either the class Gymnospermae or Angiospermae. Thus the White Pine is classified as follows:

Division: Tracheophyta
Subdivision: Pteropsida
Class: Gymnospermae
Order: Pinales
Family: Pinaceae
Genus: *Pinus*
Species: *strobus*

For practical use in classifying and identifying plants, the most frequently used taxa are families, genera, and species. The various species of trees in Pennsylvania are described here and illustrated individually and the characteristics of the genera summarized, but only the names of the families are given. Descriptions of these families are readily available in all general manuals and floras or in textbooks on plant classification. A list of the tree species described in this handbook arranged according to family appears on pp. 19–20. The sequence of families is that used by most standard references including *Gray's Manual* and Rehder's *Manual of Cultivated Trees and Shrubs* (see bibliography).

THE USE OF
THE KEYS

As an aid to identification of plants, this work provides two sets of keys with classificatory units that will guide you in singling out the proper name of the plant in question. The first set contains keys to the genera: one for summer identification when leaves are present and another for winter identification. In the main body of the text under the description of each genus that contains more than one native species, there is a second set of keys for the identification of the species, in most cases also one for summer and one for winter.

These keys are called artificial keys because they group together plants on the basis of arbitrarily selected characteristics, i.e., characteristics that are conveniently observed and useful for identification. They do not necessarily indicate natural relationships between the plants that are placed together. For example, *Cornus* and *Chionanthus* are grouped together under the criterion of opposite simple unlobed leaves, but they are not actually related genera (See the previous section for the meaning and system of Natural Classification).

The keys are constructed dichotomously and are used by the process of successive elimination. Each entry consists of two statements marked with the same letter of the alphabet set at the same distance from the left margin of the page. These statements give diametrically opposed characteristics and are the only choices possible. The accepted statement may be followed by the name of a plant but is more often followed by further alternatives. The process of elimination continues until the name of a genus or species appears at the end of the statement.

As an example, the following simple key is constructed for the identification of only five genera, all with oppositely arranged leaves.

A. Leaves simple.
  B. Leaves palmately lobed.   **Acer**
  B. Leaves not lobed.
    C. Leaves toothed on margin.
                    Viburnum
    C. Leaves entire on margin. **Cornus**
A. Leaves compound.
  B. Leaves palmately compound.
                    Aesculus
  B. Leaves pinnately compound.
                    Fraxinus

When the name of a genus or species is reached from the keys, consult the generic description or the species description and illustration carefully. If the description fits the plant, the identification is most probably correct. If there are discrepancies, then you may have made a misjudgment in the choice of one or more of the parallel statements, and you should go over the key again to discover where uncertainty about a characteristic may have led to choosing the wrong branch of the key.

The section "The Study and Identification of Trees" as well as the glossary can be consulted about the meaning of terms and the nature of plant structures used as criteria in the keys.

SUMMER KEY
TO THE GENERA

A. Coniferous trees: leaves needle-like, awl-like or scale-like, evergreen, rarely deciduous *(Larix)*; flowers without perianth; cone-bearing trees with exposed seeds (Gymnosperms).
  B. Leaves long and narrow, needle-like, spirally arranged on stems, sometimes fascicled; cones elongated, the scales and bracts distinct.
    C. Leaves solitary, not fascicled or clustered.
      D. Branches smooth or nearly so, not roughened by persistent leaf-scars. **Abies**
      D. Branches roughened by persistent distinctly raised leaf-scars.
        E. Leaves sessile. **Picea**
        E. Leaves narrowed into a short distinct stalk. **Tsuga**
    C. Leaves in fascicles or clusters of 2 or more, solitary only on terminal shoots.
      D. Leaves deciduous, many clustered on short thick spur branches. **Larix**
      D. Leaves evergreen, in fascicles of 2–5, sheathed at base by thin, dry, membranaceous bud-scales. **Pinus**
  B. Leaves minute, awl-like or scale-like, opposite or in whorls of 3's; cones small, globose or conical.
    C. Branch systems in flattened sprays, frond-like; leaves smaller, to 3 mm long. **Chamaecyparis**
    C. Branch systems not in flattened sprays; leaves larger, 3–6 mm long.
      D. Cones conical, woody. **Thuja**
      D. Cones globose, fleshy, berry-like. **Juniperus**

A. Broad-leaved trees: leaves broad, flat, usually deciduous, sometimes evergreen; flowers with perianth; fruit-bearing trees with enclosed seeds (Angiosperms).
  B. Leaves opposite or whorled, 2–3 at a node.
    C. Leaves simple.
      D. Leaves palmately lobed. **Acer**
      D. Leaves not lobed.
        E. Leaves toothed on margin. **Viburnum**
        E. Leaves entire on margin.
          F. Leaves mostly 3 at a node. **Catalpa**

  F. Leaves 2 at a node.
   G. Leaves with curving primary veins; base of petioles enlarged, encircling stems.   **Cornus**
   G. Leaves with spreading primary veins; base of petioles not encircling stems.   **Chionanthus**
 C. Leaves compound.
  D. Leaves palmately compound.   **Aesculus**
  D. Leaves pinnately compound.
   E. Leaflets 3.   **Acer**
   E. Leaflets 5–11.   **Fraxinus**
B. Leaves alternate, only one at a node.
 C. Leaves persistent, leathery.
  D. Leaves armed with spiny teeth on margin.   **Ilex**
  D. Leaves not spiny.
   E. Leaves white silky beneath; flowers solitary.   **Magnolia**
   E. Leaves yellowish green to scurfy beneath; flowers in clusters.
    F. Leaves yellowish green beneath; corolla with 10 pouches receiving the anthers.   **Kalmia**
    F. Leaves scurfy beneath; corolla without pouches for the anthers.   **Rhododendron**
 C. Leaves deciduous, thinner, not leathery.
  D. Leaves simple.
   E. Leaves, all or some, lobed.
    F. Fruit an acorn.   **Quercus**
    F. Fruit not an acorn.
     G. Lobes of leaves entire on margin.
      H. Leaves all lobed, truncate at apex.   **Liriodendron**
      H. Leaves lobed or unlobed on same tree, of various shapes, not truncate at apex.   **Sassafras**
     G. Lobes of leaves toothed on margin.
      H. Leaves longer than broad, pinnately veined, irregularly lobed; lobed and unlobed leaves found on the same tree.
       I. Branches thorny; sap not milky.   **Crataegus**
       I. Branches unarmed; sap milky.   **Morus**
      H. Leaves as broad as long, palmately veined; all leaves lobed.
       I. Margins of leaf-lobes densely and evenly fine-toothed.   **Liquidambar**
       I. Margins of leaf-lobes sparsely and unevenly coarse-toothed.   **Platanus**
   E. Leaves all unlobed.
    F. Leaves entire or wavy on margin.
     G. Leaves rounded or heart-shaped.   **Cercis**
     G. Leaves ovate to obovate to lanceolate.
      H. Branches spiny; fruit large, orange-like.   **Maclura**
      H. Branches unarmed; fruit small, not orange-like.
       I. Fruit an acorn.   **Quercus**
       I. Fruit not an acorn.
        J. Leaves large, mostly over 12.5 cm long.
         K. Stipules present, the scars encircling stems; flowers greenish or yellowish.   **Magnolia**
         K. Stipules absent; flowers reddish purple.   **Asimina**
        J. Leaves smaller, mostly under 12.5 cm long.
         K. Leaves thick, not clustered at tip of branchlets, short-pointed, shiny above; veins not parallel.

L. Leaves 10–15 cm long, long-pointed.   **Diospyros**
L. Leaves 5–12 cm long, abruptly short-pointed.   **Nyssa**
  K. Leaves thin, clustered at tip of branchlets, long-pointed, not shiny above, with prominent parallel veins.   **Cornus**
F. Leaves toothed along margin.
  G. Branches thorny.   **Crataegus**
  G. Branches unarmed.
    H. Leaves with decidedly oblique base.
      I. Leaves ovate to ovate-oblong, rough above.
        J. Leaves thin, simply toothed on margin.   **Celtis**
        J. Leaves thick, doubly toothed on margin.   **Ulmus**
      I. Leaves rounded or heart-shaped; smooth above.   **Tilia**
    H. Leaves with symmetrical base.
      I. Leaves coarsely toothed, 5 mm or more per tooth.
        J. Leaves smooth on both surfaces.
          K. Leaves very shiny beneath, the teeth short, straight.   **Fagus**
          K. Leaves dull beneath, the teeth stout, incurved.   **Castanea**
        J. Leaves hairy at least beneath.
          K. Leaves oblong-lanceolate to obovate, over 10 cm long; fruit an acorn.   **Quercus**
          K. Leaves broadly ovate to almost circular, less than 10 cm long; fruit a very small capsule.   **Populus**
      I. Leaves finely toothed, 4 mm or less per tooth.
        J. Leaf-stalk laterally compressed.   **Populus**
        J. Leaf-stalk rounded, not laterally compressed.
          K. Leaves doubly toothed on margin; fruit not fleshy.
            L. Leaves with slender sharp incurved teeth on margin; nut small, without involucre.   **Betula**
            L. Leaves with very sharp straight teeth on margin; nut with a leaf-like or bag-like involucre.
              M. Involucre of the fruit flat, leaf-like, 3-lobed.   **Carpinus**
              M. Involucre of the fruit a bladder-like closed bag.   **Ostrya**
          K. Leaves simply toothed on margin.
            L. Leaves very slender, the blade at least 3 times as long as broad.
              M. Leaves decidedly sour; flowers in racemes. **Oxydendrum**
              M. Leaves not sour; flowers not in racemes.
                N. Branchlets brittle; fruit a very small capsule.   **Salix**
                N. Branchlets tough; fruit a drupe.   **Prunus**
            L. Leaves broader, the blade not more than twice as long as broad.
              M. Leaf-blades about twice as long as broad.
                N. Lenticels conspicuous; buds ovoid.   **Prunus**
                N. Lenticels inconspicuous; buds narrowly conical.
                      Amelanchier
              M. Leaf-blades almost as broad as long.
                N. Leaves scattered, downy beneath; sap milky.   **Morus**
                N. Leaves crowded on short, spur-like branchlets, smooth beneath; sap not milky.   **Malus**
D. Leaves compound.
  E. Leaves bipinnate or tripinnate, some if not all.
    F. Leaves not prickly, once- or twice-pinnate; leaflets of even number; prickly or unarmed trees.
      G. Leaves pinnate or bipinnate on same tree; leaflets crenulate on

margin; prickly tree. **Gleditsia**

   G. Leaves all bipinnate; leaflets entire on margin; unarmed tree.

Gymnocladus

  F. Leaves prickly; twice- or thrice-pinnate; leaflets of odd number; stems very prickly. **Aralia**

E. Leaves all once-pinnate.

  F. Leaflets with entire margins.

   G. Stem thorny. **Robinia**

   G. Stems not thorny. **Rhus**

  F. Leaflets with toothed margins.

   G. Large trees; leaflets large, 2.5–12.5 cm broad.

    H. Leaflets 5–11; pith homogeneous. **Carya**

    H. Leaflets 11–23; pith chambered. **Juglans**

   G. Small or medium-sized trees; leaflets small, less than 2.5 cm broad.

    H. Leaflets 13–41, the margins with a few coarse glandular teeth near base. **Ailanthus**

    H. Leaflets 7–17, the margins finely and evenly toothed.

     I. Plants with milky sap. **Rhus**

     I. Plants with clear sap. **Sorbus**

WINTER KEY
TO THE GENERA

A. Coniferous trees: leaves needle-like, awl-like or scale-like, evergreen, rarely deciduous *(Larix);* cone-bearing trees with exposed seeds (Gymnosperms).

  B. Leaves long, needle-like, spirally arranged on stem, sometimes fascicled; cones elongated, the scales and bracts distinct.

    C. Leaves evergreen.

      D. Leaves solitary, not fascicled or clustered.

        E. Leaves sessile.

          F. Branches smooth or nearly so, not roughened by persistent leaf-scars.   **Abies**

          F. Branches roughened by persistent distinctly raised leaf-scars.   **Picea**

        E. Leaves narrowed into a short distinct stalk.   **Tsuga**

    C. Leaves deciduous, many clustered on short thick spur branches.   **Larix**

  B. Leaves minute, awl-like or scale-like, opposite or in whorls of 3's; cones small, globose or conical.

    C. Branch systems in flattened sprays, frond-like; leaves smaller, to 3 mm long.   **Chamaecyparis**

    C. Branch system not in flattened sprays; leaves larger, 3–6 mm long.

      D. Cones conical, woody.   **Thuja**

      D. Cones globose, fleshy, berry-like.   **Juniperus**

A. Broad-leaved trees: leaves broad, flat, usually deciduous, sometimes evergreen; fruit-bearing trees with enclosed seeds (Angiosperms).

  B. Branches or trunk armed with stiff, sharp prickles, thorns or spines.

    C. Spines or thorns often branched.   **Gleditsia**

    C. Spines or thorns unbranched.

      D. Spines short, numerous, scattered all over the internodes of the stem.   **Aralia**

      D. Spines or thorns long, one or two at each node.

        E. Spines in pairs at each node; lateral buds superposed.   **Robinia**

        E. Spines one at each node; lateral buds not superposed.

          F. Spines or thorns less than 1.5 cm long; fruit large, orange-like.   **Maclura**

F. Spines or thorns much exceeding 1.5 cm long; fruit a small pome.
　　　　　　　　　　　　　　　　　　　　　　　　　　Crataegus
B. Branches or trunk unarmed.
　C. Leaf-scars opposite, 2 at a node; sometimes whorled, 3 at a node.
　　D. Leaf-scars 2 or 3 at a node.　　　　　　　　　　**Catalpa**
　　D. Leaf-scars all 2 at a node.
　　　E. Winter-buds more or less hairy.
　　　　F. Winter-buds long, covered by 2 scales, slender, the scales rusty-hairy on the back.　　　　　　　　　　　　　　**Viburnum**
　　　　F. Winter-buds short, ovoid, covered with about 5 pairs of scales, the scales fringed with hairs on the back.　　**Chionanthus**
　　　E. Winter-buds smooth; rarely, slightly hairy toward apex.
　　　　F. Terminal buds 1.5–3.5 cm long, usually resin-coated; branchlets very stout.　　　　　　　　　　　　　　　　**Aesculus**
　　　　F. Terminal buds are over 1.5 cm long, not resin-coated; branchlets not stout.
　　　　　G. Leaf-buds with 1 pair of scales visible.　　**Cornus**
　　　　　G. Leaf-buds with 2 or more pairs of scales visible.
　　　　　　H. Leaf-scars crescent-shaped, with numerous bundle-scars arranged in a curved line.　　　　　　**Fraxinus**
　　　　　　H. Leaf-scars V-shaped, with 3 distinct bundle-scars.　**Acer**
　C. Leaf-scars alternate, one at a node.
　　D. Terminal buds usually absent.
　　　E. Stipule-scars absent.
　　　　F. Buds hairy.
　　　　　G. Leaf-scars broadly heart-shaped, with 3 to 5 scattered raised bundle-scars.　　　　　　　　　　　　　**Gymnocladus**
　　　　　G. Leaf-scars U-shaped, partly encircling bud, with many bundle-scars.
　　　　　　H. Bundle-scars arranged in a curved line.　　**Ailanthus**
　　　　　　H. Bundle-scars arranged in a few clusters.　　**Rhus**
　　　　F. Buds smooth; rarely, slightly hairy toward apex.
　　　　　G. Buds somewhat flattened and appressed; pith with reddish longitudinal streaks.　　　　　　　　　　　　　**Cercis**
　　　　　G. Buds not flattened nor appressed; pith without reddish streaks.
　　　　　　H. Buds usually with 3 visible scales.　　　　**Tilia**
　　　　　　H. Buds with 4 or more visible scales.　　**Oxydendrum**
　　　E. Stipule-scars present.
　　　　F. Stipule-scars encircling the stem; leaf-scars nearly surrounding the bud.　　　　　　　　　　　　　　　　**Platanus**
　　　　F. Stipule-scars not encircling the stem; leaf-scars not surrounding the bud.
　　　　　G. Bud-scales only 1 visible.　　　　　　　　**Salix**
　　　　　G. Bud-scales 2 or more.
　　　　　　H. Lateral buds close or appressed to the branchlets.
　　　　　　　I. Pith chambered; buds smooth.　　　　**Celtis**
　　　　　　　I. Pith not chambered; buds more or less hairy.　**Ulmus**
　　　　　　H. Lateral buds divergent.
　　　　　　　I. Buds with 3–4, sometimes to 8 visible scales, the scales smooth.
　　　　　　　　J. Bundle-scars 3.　　　　　　　　　**Betula**
　　　　　　　　J. Bundle-scars 4.
　　　　　　　　　K. Buds with 2–3 visible scales; sap not milky.　**Castanea**
　　　　　　　　　K. Buds with 4–8 visible scales; sap milky.　**Morus**
　　　　　　　I. Buds with 8 or more visible scales, the scales longitudinally striated.

J. Bark roughened by flattish scales loose at the ends.   **Ostrya**

J. Bark corrugated, smooth, close-fitting.   **Carpinus**

D. Terminal buds present.

  E. Stipule-scars present.

    F. Bundle-scars 3.

      G. Basal (first) scale of lateral buds on outside, directly in front.   **Populus**

      G. Basal (first) scale of lateral buds not directly in front, but to one side of the center of the leaf-scar.

        H. Leaf-scars elliptic in outline.   **Prunus**

        H. Leaf-scars broadly U-shaped.   **Sorbus**

    F. Bundle-scars 4 to many.

      G. Stipule-scars encircling the stem.

        H. Buds smooth.   **Liriodendron**

        H. Buds hairy.   **Magnolia**

      G. Stipule-scars not encircling the stem.

        H. Buds very slender, cylindrical, sharply long-pointed.   **Fagus**

        H. Buds broadly ovoid, more or less bluntly pointed.   **Quercus**

  E. Stipule-scars absent.

    F. Bundle-scars 1–3.

      G. Bundle-scar only 1.

        H. Buds covered with 2 shiny smooth scales; bark thick squarish, separates into blocks.   **Diospyros**

        H. Buds covered with several hairy scales; bark smooth or fissured, not separating into squarish blocks.

          I. Leaf-scars elliptic to broadly triangular; bark smooth.   **Ilex**

          I. Leaf-scars semielliptic; bark fissured into flat ridges.   **Sassafras**

      G. Bundle-scars 3.

        H. Buds bright to dark red.

          I. Bark deeply furrowed separating into broad scaly ridges, often with corky-winged projections.   **Liquidambar**

          I. Bark smooth or fissured, without corky projections.

            J. Branches bearing many short, spur-like branchlets; buds bright red, conical with 4–8 visible scales.   **Malus**

            J. Branches without short, spur-like branchlets; buds dark red, ovoid, with 3–5 visible scales.   **Nyssa**

        H. Buds brownish to gray.

          I. Pith chambered; buds hairy.   **Juglans**

          I. Pith not chambered, buds smooth.

            J. Buds slender, conical, 3–4 times as long as broad, with 5–8 visible scales.   **Amelanchier**

            J. Buds ovoid, 2–3 times as long as broad, with 2–3 scales.   **Cornus**

    F. Bundle-scars 4 to many.

      G. Bundle-scars numerous, more than 12, scattered over the leaf-scars; buds smooth.   **Carya**

      G. Bundle-scars 12 or less, arranged in a line in groups; buds hairy.

        H. Bundle-scars more than 5; branchlets covered with numerous conspicuous lenticels.   **Rhus**

        H. Bundle-scars 5; branchlets covered with a few fine lenticels.   **Asimina**

LIST OF SPECIES ARRANGED ACCORDING TO FAMILIES

Pinaceae
Abies
  1. *A. balsamea*
Tsuga
  2. *T. canadensis*
Picea
  3. *P. rubens*
  4. *P. mariana*
Larix
  5. *L. laricina*
Pinus
  6. *P. strobus*
  7. *P. rigida*
  8. *P. resinosa*
  9. *P. echinata*
 10. *P. virginiana*
 11. *P. pungens*
 12. *P. banksiana*
Cupressaceae
Thuja
 13. *T. occidentalis*
Chamaecyparis
 14. *C. thyoides*
Juniperus
 15. *J. virginiana*
Salicaceae
Populus
 16. *P. deltoides*
 17. *P. tremuloides*
 18. *P. grandidentata*
 19. *P. heterophylla*
Salix
 20. *S. bebbiana*
 21. *S. nigra*
 22. *S. lucida*
 23. *S. discolor*

Juglandaceae
Juglans
 24. *J. cinerea*
 25. *J. nigra*
Carya
 26. *C. cordiformis*
 27. *C. glabra*
 28. *C. ovalis*
 29. *C. ovata*
 30. *C. tomentosa*
 31. *C. laciniosa*
Betulaceae
Betula
 32. *B. populifolia*
 33. *B. lenta*
 34. *B. lutea*
 35. *B. nigra*
 36. *B. papyrifera*
Carpinus
 37. *C. caroliniana*
Ostrya
 38. *O. virginiana*
Fagaceae
Fagus
 39. *F. grandifolia*
Castanea
 40. *C. dentata*
Quercus
 41. *Q. phellos*
 42. *Q. imbricaria*
 43. *Q. alba*
 44. *Q. macrocarpa*
 45. *Q. stellata*
 46. *Q. prinoides*
 47. *Q. bicolor*
 48. *Q. montana*

 49. *Q. muehlenbergii*
 50. *Q. marilandica*
 51. *Q. ilicifolia*
 52. *Q. falcata*
 53. *Q. velutina*
 54. *Q. palustris*
 55. *Q. coccinea*
 56. *Q. borealis maxima*
Ulmaceae
Ulmus
 57. *U. americana*
 58. *U. fulva*
Celtis
 59. *C. occidentalis*
Moraceae
Morus
 60. *M. rubra*
Maclura
 61. *M. pomifera*
Magnoliaceae
Magnolia
 62. *M. tripetala*
 63. *M. acuminata*
 64. *M. virginiana*
Liriodendron
 65. *L. tulipifera*
Annonaceae
Asimina
 66. *A. triloba*
Lauraceae
Sassafras
 67. *S. albidum*
Hamamelidaceae
Liquidambar
 68. *L. styraciflua*

Platanaceae
Platanus
  69. P. occidentalis
Rosaceae
Crataegus
  70. C. mollis
  71. C. pedicellata
  72. C. crus-galli
  73. C. punctata
  74. C. calpodendron
Sorbus
  75. S. americana
Malus
  76. M. coronaria
Amelanchier
  77. A. canadensis
Prunus
  78. P. serotina
  79. P. virginiana
  80. P. americana
  81. P. alleghaniensis
  82. P. pennsylvanica
Leguminosae
Gleditsia
  83. G. triacanthos
Gymnocladus
  84. G. dioicus
Cercis
  85. C. canadensis
Robinia
  86. R. pseudoacacia
Simaroubaceae
Ailanthus
  87. A. altissima
Anacardiaceae
Rhus
  88. R. copallina
  89. R. vernix
  90. R. typhina
Aquifoliaceae
Ilex
  91. I. opaca
  92. I. montana
Aceraceae
Acer
  93. A. negundo
  94. A. saccharinum
  95. A. nigrum

  96. A. pennsylvani-
       cum
  97. A. spicatum
  98. A. rubrum
  99. A. saccharum
Hippocastanaceae
Aesculus
  100. A. glabra
  101. A. octandra
Tiliaceae
Tilia
  102. T. americana
  103. T. heterophylla
Nyssaceae
Nyssa
  104. N. sylvatica
Araliaceae
Aralia
  105. A. spinosa
Cornaceae
Cornus
  106. C. florida
  107. C. alternifolia
Ericaceae
Rhododendron
  108. R. maximum
Kalmia
  109. K. latifolia
Oxydendrum
  110. O. arboreum
Ebenaceae
Diospyros
  111. D. virginiana
Oleaceae
Fraxinus
  112. F. nigra
  113. F. americana
  114. F. pennsylvanica
Chionanthus
  115. C. virginicus
Bignoniaceae
Catalpa
  116. C. bignonioides
Caprifoliaceae
Viburnum
  117. V. lentago
  118. V. prunifolium

20

Manual of genera and species

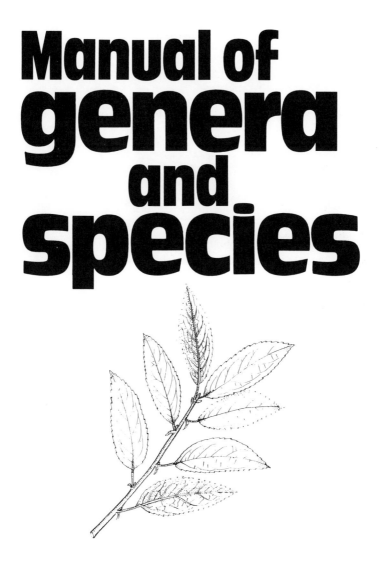

FIRS
Abies *(Pinaceae)*

Balsam Fir *(Abies balsamea)*

There are about 40 species in the genus *Abies,* distributed in the northern hemisphere and on high mountains south to North Africa, the Himalayas, and Central America. Ten of the species are found in North America but only one is native to Pennsylvania.

The species of the Fir genus are evergreen trees of compact pyramidal habit. The branchlets are smooth or sometimes grooved, marked by circular unraised leaf-scars and with resinous buds. The leaves are linear and usually 4-sided, spirally arranged on the branches and persisting for several years. They are usually marked by 2 white stomatiferous bands beneath and in some species also above. The unisexual flowers are borne on the same tree. The staminate flowers are pendent, consisting of many anthers. The pistillate flowers are upright, consisting of many 2-ovuled imbricate scales. The fruiting cone is ovoid to oblong, with imbricate thin leathery scales subtended by narrow exserted or enclosed bracts. At maturity the scales fall from the persistent cone-axis, freeing the large winged seeds.

Besides the widely distributed Balsam Fir, *Abies balsamea,* there occurs in the mountains of Virginia, North Carolina and Tennessee the Southern Fir or She-Balsam, *A. fraseri* (Pursh) Poiret. It resembles the Balsam Fir in its general features, but differs in that the leaves are mostly notched at the apex, the cones are ovoid instead of cylindrical, and the bracts are with a slender recurved awn much longer than the scales.

A number of introduced species are widely planted. Among these the Colorado Fir, *Abies concolor* (Gordon) Engelmann of the western United States, is doing especially well in the East. The leaves of this species are relatively flat and stomatiferous on both sides.

Balsam Fir
Abies balsamea *(Linnaeus)* Miller

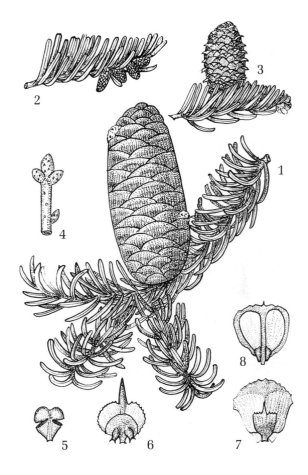

1. Abies balsamea
1. Fruiting branch with a cone, x 1.
2. Branch with staminate flowers, x 1.
3. Branch with pistillate flowers, x 1.
4. Branch with winter-buds, x 1.
5. Staminate scale, outer view, enlarged.
6. Pistillate scale, inner view, enlarged.
7. Cone-scale, outer view with bract, x 1.
8. Cone-scale, inner view with seeds, x 1.

HABIT. A tree 10–25 m with a slender symmetrical crown, becoming broader when old.

BARK. Bark reddish brown and scaly on old trees; smooth, thin, close and grayish brown on young trees.

STEMS. Young branchlets slender, yellowish green and hairy at first, becoming grayish brown and smooth.

WINTER-BUDS. Buds terminal, clustered, ovoid to spherical, about 3 mm long, orange-green, very resinous.

LEAVES. Leaves linear, flat, spreading upward, pectinate below, 1.5–2.5 cm long, rounded and slightly notched at apex, dark green and shiny above and often with a few stomatiferous lines near the apex, pale and with narrow whitish bands beneath.

FLOWERS. May–June. Staminate flowers oblong-cylindrical, 5 mm long, yellow. Pistillate flowers oblong-cylindrical, 2.5 cm long, purple.

FRUIT. Cones maturing at the end of first season, oblong-cylindrical, 5–8 cm long, dark purple, violet purple before maturity; cone-scales 1.5 cm wide; bracts enclosed or sometimes exserted. Seeds winged, about 5 mm long, borne on cone-scales.

DISTRIBUTION. Labrador west to Alberta, south to Pennsylvania and Minnesota and along the mountains to Virginia.

HABITAT. Usually inhabits low swampy ground and well-drained hillsides.

CULTIVATION NOTES. The Balsam Fir is commonly used as a Christmas tree. The tree prefers cool, moist, rich soil.

HEMLOCKS
Tsuga *(Pinaceae)*

Eastern Hemlock *(Tsuga canadensis)*

There are about 10 species in the Hemlock genus distributed in temperate North America and eastern Asia; one of the 4 American species is native to Pennsylvania.

The species of *Tsuga* are evergreen trees with horizontal, often drooping branches, forming an irregular pyramidal crown. The branchlets are marked with prominent leaf-cushions and with nonresinous buds. The leaves are spirally arranged and often somewhat 2-ranked, usually linear and flattened with 2 stomatiferous bands beneath.

The flowers are unisexual and solitary. The staminate and pistillate flowers are borne on the same tree. The staminate flowers are axillary and globose. The pistillate flowers are terminal on lateral shoots and consist of persistent woody scales subtended by short bracts. The seeds, 2 under each scale, are small and winged.

Besides the common native species, several other species of the genus have been introduced into the eastern states, but their cultivation is limited.

Eastern Hemlock
Tsuga canadensis *(Linnaeus)* Carriére

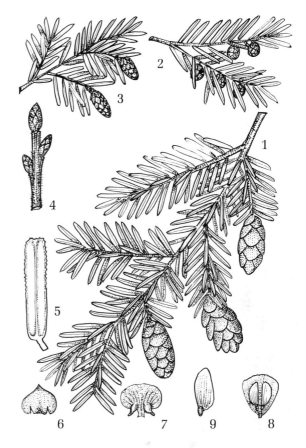

2. Tsuga canadensis
1. Fruiting branch with cones, x 1.
2. Branch with staminate flowers, x 1.
3. Branch with pistillate flowers, x 1.
4. Branch with winter-buds, x 1.
5. Leaf, x 3.
6. Staminate scale, outer view, enlarged.
7. Pistillate scale, inner view, enlarged.
8. Cone-scale, inner view with seeds, x 1.
9. Seed, x 2.

HABIT. A tree 20–30 m, with long, slender, often drooping branches forming a broad pyramidal crown.

BARK. Bark thick, reddish brown or grayish brown, deeply fissured into narrow rounded ridges which are covered with close scales.

STEMS. Young branchlets yellowish brown, somewhat hairy; later smooth, grayish brown; leaf-scars small, rounded, raised on decurrent projections of bark.

WINTER-BUDS. Buds ovoid, 5 mm long, bluntly pointed, reddish brown, not shiny, very resinous.

LEAVES. Leaves 2-ranked, jointed to short persistent stalk, linear, flat, 8–18 mm long, rounded or rarely notched at apex, shiny, dark green and slightly grooved above, dull beneath, with 2 narrow white bands on each side of the midrib.

FLOWERS. April–May. Staminate flowers short-stalked, light yellow, roundish, 5–10 mm long. Pistillate flowers terminal, oblong-cylindrical, pink-tinged pale green, 5 mm long.

FRUIT. Cones small, maturing at end of the first season, usually persisting during first winter, short-stalked, ovoid, 1.5–2.0 cm long, with roundish obovate scales.

DISTRIBUTION. Nova Scotia south to Pennsylvania and on the mountains to Georgia and northern Alabama, west to Minnesota.

HABITAT. Scattered among hilly or rocky woods, especially along northern banks of rivers and streams.

CULTIVATION NOTES. The Eastern Hemlock is a timber tree of some importance, and the bark is used for tannin. It is a handsome tree, much used for ornamental purposes. It is rather slow growing. Shade-loving and not very wind-firm, it grows best in groves or in dense forest structure.

SPRUCES
Picea *(Pinaceae)*

There are about 40 species in the Spruce genus distributed in the cooler and temperate regions of the northern hemisphere and on high mountains of the warm temperate regions. Two of the 12 species in North America are native to Pennsylvania.

The Spruces are evergreen trees with whorled branches giving a pyramidal form. The branchlets are grooved, and they bear prominent leaf-cushions prolonged into a peg-like stalk bearing the leaf. The leaf-cushions remain as distinct raised leaf-scars when the leaf falls. The spirally arranged leaves are linear, usually 4-angled and stomatiferous on all sides, or flattened and stomatiferous on one side only. The flowers are unisexual, and the staminate and pistillate flowers occur on the same tree. The staminate flowers are axillary and catkin-like, consisting of numerous spirally arranged anthers. The pistillate flowers are terminal, consisting of numerous 2-ovuled bracted scales. The fruiting cone is pendulous or upright, with persistent scales subtended by small bracts and bearing 2 small winged seeds.

In addition to the two widely distributed species described below, there is a northern species which extends southward through New England to northeastern New York, the White Spruce, *Picea glauca* (Moench) Voss, a handsome tree resembling the Balsam Fir, *Abies balsamea*. It differs from the other species of spruces mentioned here in that the branchlets and buds are smooth, and the longer cylindrical cones bear thin pale scales.

Many introduced species are cultivated in northeastern North America. The most common is the Norway Spruce, *Picea abies* (Linnaeus) Karsten, of northern and central Europe, which is planted as an ornamental tree as well as for shelters and windbreaks. In the northeastern states, it is occasionally escaped. Many horticultural varieties are in cultivation. Other widely cultivated ornamental species include the Colorado Spruce, *Picea pungens* Engelmann, and the Engelmann Spruce, *P. engelmanni* (Parry) Engelmann from the western states. The two native species can be distinguished from these introduced ones by their terminal winter-bud which has a ring of conspicuous subulate scales at base.

PICEA
Key to the species

A. Leaves dark yellowish green, 10–15 mm long, usually sharply pointed; cones green when young, falling off soon after maturity, the scales entire or slightly fine-toothed along margins. **P. rubens**

A. Leaves dull bluish green, 6–13 mm long, usually bluntly pointed; cones purple when young, persisting for several years, the scales fine-toothed along margins. **P. mariana**

Red Spruce
Picea rubens Sargent

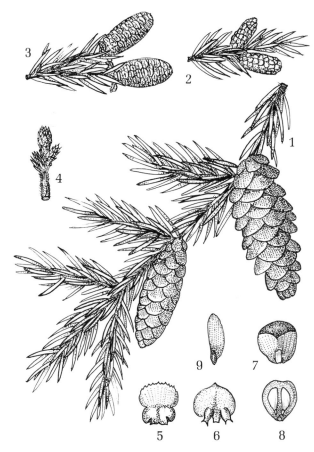

3. Picea rubens
1. Fruiting branch with cones, x 1.
2. Branch with staminate flowers, x 1.
3. Branch with pistillate flowers, x 1.
4. Branch with winter-buds, x 1.
5. Staminate scale, outer view, enlarged.
6. Pistillate scale, inner view, enlarged.
7. Cone-scale, outer view with bract, x 1.
8. Cone-scale, inner view with seeds, x 1.
9. Seed, x 2.

HABIT. A tree to 30 m, with lateral branches horizontal in the middle, ascending above and pendulous below, forming a narrow pyramidal crown.

BARK. Bark reddish brown, fissured and covered by irregular, thin, close scales.

STEMS. Young branchlets rough, slender, brown, covered with pale to dark hairs.

WINTER-BUDS. Terminal buds ovoid, sharply pointed, 6–8 mm long, with sharply pointed scales; lateral buds smaller.

LEAVES. Needle-shaped, usually slender, 4-sided, 10–15 mm long, usually sharply pointed, shiny, dark to yellowish green, with about 6 stomatic lines above and 3 below.

FLOWERS. April–May. Staminate flowers nearly sessile, ovoid, reddish. Pistillate flowers cylindrical, about 2 cm long, with rounded scales.

FRUIT. Cones short-stalked, maturing at the end of the first season, oblong, 3–4 cm long, clear brown or reddish brown, green or purplish green before maturity; cone-scales rounded, rigid, the margins entire or slightly fine-toothed.

DISTRIBUTION. Newfoundland to Pennsylvania, and south along the mountains to North Carolina and Tennessee.

HABITAT. Chiefly on mountain slopes and well-drained upland areas, also found on margins of swamps and streams and sometimes on mountain tops.

CULTIVATION NOTES. This is an important tree for the manufacture of paper pulp. The tree requires a cool and moist climate. A handsome tree of narrow pyramidal habit, it deserves to be used more as an ornamental tree where conditions are favorable.

Black Spruce
Picea mariana *(Miller)* B.S.P.

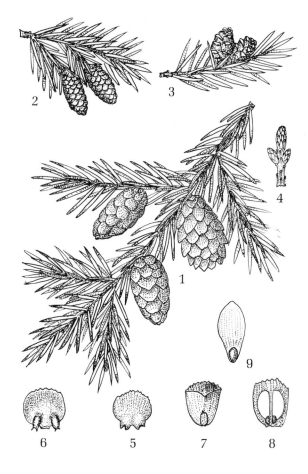

4. Picea mariana
1. Fruiting branch with cones, x 1.
2. Branch with staminate flowers, x 1.
3. Branch with pistillate flowers, x 1.
4. Branch with winter-buds, x 1.
5. Staminate scale, outer view, enlarged.
6. Pistillate scale, inner view, enlarged.
7. Cone-scale, outer view with bract, x 1.
8. Cone-scale, inner view with seeds, x 1.
9. Seed, x 2.

HABIT. A small tree to 18 or occasionally to 30 m, with slender often pendulous lateral branches forming a narrow, frequently irregular conical crown.

BARK. Bark grayish brown, fissured and covered by irregular, thin, close scales.

STEMS. Young branchlets rough, stout, brown to yellowish brown, covered with pale to dark hairs.

WINTER-BUDS. Terminal buds ovoid, 6–9 mm long, with sharply pointed scales; lateral buds smaller.

LEAVES. Needle-shaped, straight or slightly curved, 4-sided, 6–13 mm long, rounded at apex, dull dark or bluish green, with the stomatic bands broader above than beneath.

FLOWERS. May. Staminate flowers in roundish clusters, about 12 mm long, dark red. Pistillate flowers in oblong-cylindrical clusters, with broad purple scales.

FRUIT. Cones short-stalked, maturing at the end of the first season, ovoid, 2.0–3.5 cm long, dull grayish brown, dark purple before maturity; cone-scales rigid, rounded or narrowed at apex, finely toothed on margin.

DISTRIBUTION. Labrador to Alaska, south to Wisconsin, Michigan, northern New Jersey and northern Pennsylvania and in the mountains south to Virginia.

HABITAT. Chiefly on cold slopes, bogs, and swamps, or on lake shores.

CULTIVATION NOTES. The tree grows best on moist alluvial soil and is very tolerant of shade. However, it is not recommended for forestry use except in extremely swampy locations nor for ornamental planting as there are other species of spruce more suitable for this purpose.

Red Spruce *(Picea rubens)*

Black Spruce *(Picea mariana)*

LARCHES
Larix *(Pinaceae)*

American Larch *(Larix laricina)*

There are about 12 species in the Larch genus with 3 native to North America, one of which extends to Pennsylvania.

The Larches are deciduous trees with spreading branches forming a pyramidal crown. The leaves are soft, linear, flattened and arranged spirally on terminal long shoots and clustered on lateral short spur-branchlets. The flowers are unisexual, solitary and terminal, with the staminate and pistillate occurring on the same tree. The staminate flowers are roundish to oblong, consisting of numerous spirally arranged anthers. The pistillate flowers are roundish to oblong, consisting of few to many 2-ovuled scales subtended in the axils of large reddish bracts. The fruiting cones are roundish to oblong, maturing the first year, and with 2 winged seeds under each of their scales.

The Larches are highly ornamental trees and widely cultivated. Even more commonly planted than the American Larch is the European Larch, *Larix decidua* Linnaeus, which grows in the northeastern states better than the native species. It is a rapid grower and thrives in both moist and dry situations. It resembles the native species but has stouter stems, more yellowish branchlets and slightly larger leaves and cones.

American Larch
Larix laricina K. Koch

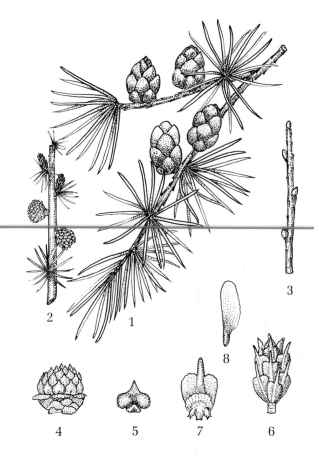

5. Larix laricina
1. Fruiting branch with cones, x 1.
2. Branch with staminate and pistillate flowers, x 1.
3. Branch with winter-buds, x 1.
4. Staminate flower, x 2.
5. Staminate scale, outer view, enlarged.
6. Pistillate flower, x 2.
7. Pistillate scale, inner view, enlarged.
8. Seed, x 2.

HABIT. Tree 10–20 m, sometimes to 35 m, with slender, straight, slightly ascending branches forming a pyramidal crown.

BARK. Bark reddish brown, with small thin roundish scales.

STEMS. Young branchlets slender, smooth, yellowish, bloomy at first, becoming dull brown.

WINTER-BUDS. Terminal bud of long branchlets about 8 mm long, shiny; lateral buds shorter, blunter.

LEAVES. Leaves deciduous, linear, 2.5–3.5 cm long, rounded above, keeled below, soft, bright green, occur scattered along terminal branchlets or in fascicles on short spur-like lateral branches.

FLOWERS. May. Staminate flowers sessile, roundish, yellow. Pistillate flowers short-stalked, oblong, reddish purple.

FRUIT. Cones globose-ovoid, 1.5–2.0 cm long, blunt at apex; cone-scales 12–20 cm, almost circular, smooth, the margins minutely crenulate; bracts one-quarter as long as scales. Seeds about 2 mm long, winged.

DISTRIBUTION. Alaska to Newfoundland, south to Pennsylvania, Illinois and Minnesota.

HABITAT. Found mostly in moist locations, in swamps, along lake shores and river banks, but also on well-drained hillsides.

CULTIVATION NOTES. This is one of the most northern trees of the eastern conifers, extending north beyond the Arctic Circle. In Pennsylvania it occurs naturally in some parts and can be artificially grown in other parts. The tree is adapted to wet situations and should not be planted in dry locations.

31

PINES
Pinus *(Pinaceae)*

There are about 80 species in the Pine genus distributed throughout the northern hemisphere. Of the 34 species found in North America, 7 are native to Pennsylvania.

The Pines are readily recognized by their foliage characteristics. They are evergreen trees with spreading branches and furrowed or scaly bark. The buds are conspicuous with many imbricate scales. The needle-like leaves are borne in clusters of 2–5 on short spur-branchlets, surrounded at the base of sheaths of bud-scales. The flowers are unisexual, and the cone-like staminate and pistillate flowers are borne on the same tree. The staminate flowers are axillary, consisting of numerous spirally arranged 2-celled anthers. The pistillate flowers are lateral or subterminal, consisting of numerous spirally arranged 2-ovuled scales, each subtended by a small bract. The fruiting cone is composed of woody scales with a thickened apex. The exposed part (apophysis), rhombic in outline, is transversely keeled in the middle usually with a prominent boss or umbo with or without a terminal spine. The seeds are usually winged.

In the identification of species, the structure of the needles is often of importance. The needles contain either 1 or 2 vascular bundles and usually 2 or more resin ducts which are situated either beneath the epidermis (marginal),

in the tissue of the leaf (medial), or close to the vascular bundle (internal). These can be observed by cutting a thin cross section and examining it under a microscope.

The Pines are classified into two groups: Haploxylon, Soft Pines, and Diploxylon, Pitch Pines. The Soft Pines have needles with 1 vascular bundle and a deciduous sheath, and soft wood with little resin. The Pitch Pines have needles with 2 vascular bundles and a persistent sheath, and hard, resinous wood.

Besides the species described below, there are a few southern species that extend their range northward to limited areas in the eastern states. The Longleaf Pine, *Pinus australis* Michaux f. extends from Florida north to southeastern Virginia. It is a tree with very long leaves (20–45 cm) in 3's, crowded at the tip of very scaly branches. The cones are large, cylindric, 15–25 cm long, with thick scales bearing a short recurved spine. The Loblolly Pine, *P. taeda* Linnaeus, is also a southern tree extending north to southwestern Tennessee and along the coast to southern New Jersey. It is a large tree with long light green leaves (12–25 cm) in 3's, sometimes in 2's. The cones are slenderly conical, 6–12 cm long, with scales tipped with a stout triangular spine with concave sides. The Pond Pine, *P. serotina* Michaux f., inhabits the Coastal Plain north to southern New Jersey. It is a slender tree similar to the Pitch Pine but has long leaves (12–28 cm) with characteristically long sheaths (1.0–2.5 cm). The cone-scales bear a depressed or flattish umbo tipped with a delicate, early deciduous prickle.

A large number of introduced species have been cultivated for ornamental or reforestation purposes. The most commonly planted species in the northeastern states (all with many horticultural varieties) are:

1. Austrian Pine, *Pinus nigra* Arnold. A species originally of southern and central Europe and Asia Minor, the Austrian Pine is now widely cultivated. It is a tall tree with dark gray bark and a pyramidal head. The long, dark, stiff needles grow in 2's.

2. Scotch Pine, *Pinus sylvestris* Linnaeus. The Scotch Pine is not only widely planted, it is sometimes also naturalized in eastern North America. It is a tall tree with reddish brown bark and a pyramidal crown becoming round-topped and irregular when old. The stiff needles, also in 2's, are shorter and bluish green.

PINUS
Key to the species

A. Needles 5 in a fascicle.   **P. strobus**
A. Needles 2–3 in a fascicle.
  B. Needles 3 in a fascicle.   **P. rigida**
  B. Needles 2 in a fascicle (sometimes 3 in *P. echinata*).
    C. Needles 12–17 cm long; cone-scales unarmed.   **P. resinosa**
    C. Needles less than 12 cm long; cone-scales unarmed or with spines or prickles.
      D. Needles mostly 7–12 cm long, slender, straight; cones deciduous.   **P. echinata**
      D. Needles 2–8 cm long, stout, twisted; cones persistent.
        E. Young branchlets white-bloomy; needles 4–8 cm long.   **P. virginiana**
        E. Young branchlets not bloomy.
          F. Needles 4–8 cm long; cones large, symmetrical; cone-scales with stout and hooked spines.   **P. pungens**
          F. Needles 2–4 cm long; cones small, curved; cone-scales unarmed.   **P. banksiana**

White Pine
Pinus strobus Linnaeus

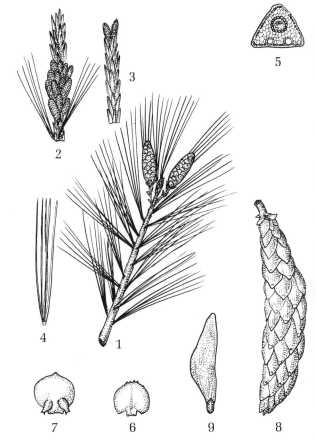

6. Pinus strobus
1. Branch with young cones, x ½.
2. Branch with staminate flowers, x ½.
3. Branch with pistillate flowers, x ½.
4. Fascicle of leaves, x ½.
5. Cross section of leaf, x 15.
6. Staminate scale, outer view, enlarged.
7. Pistillate scale, inner view, enlarged.
8. Cone, x ½.
9. Seed, x 1.

HABIT. A large tree, to 30 m or more, forming a broad, symmetrical pyramidal crown.

BARK. Bark thick, dark gray, deeply fissured into broad longitudinal scaly ridges.

STEMS. Young branchlets yellowish green, becoming light brown, hairy at first, soon smooth.

WINTER-BUDS. Terminal buds oblong-ovoid, 6–12 mm long, sharply pointed, slightly resinous, brown.

LEAVES. Needle-shaped, in fascicles of 5, slender, soft, flexible, 6–14 cm long, finely toothed, tipped with a short abrupt point, bluish green; resin ducts 2, dorsal, marginal.

FLOWERS. May–June. Staminate flowers ovoid in clusters, yellow, about 1.5 cm long. Pistillate flowers in roundish, long-stalked clusters, about 6 mm long, pinkish purple.

FRUIT. Cones maturing in 2 seasons, pendent, narrow-cylindrical, often curved, 8–20 cm long, brown; cone-scales thin, slightly thickened at apex, unarmed. Seeds winged, about 6 mm long, reddish brown, mottled with black spots.

DISTRIBUTION. Newfoundland to Manitoba, south to Georgia, Illinois and Iowa. In Pennsylvania, common in the mountainous portion of the state.

HABITAT. Prefers a light, moist, fertile loam, but also grows well on dry sandy soils and gravelly slopes. Common on banks of streams, river flats and ravines.

CULTIVATION NOTES. An important timber tree widely planted for reforestation and also for shade and ornament. In old age, the tree is usually broad and often very picturesque. It is a rapid grower and adapts itself to a great variety of soil conditions. Seedlings are readily transplanted.

Pitch Pine
Pinus rigida Miller

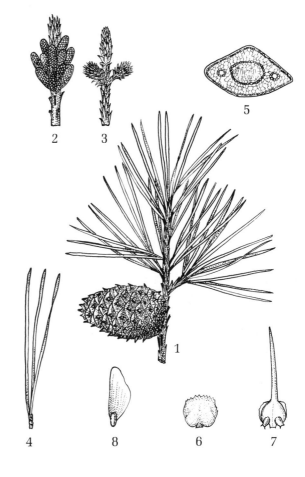

7. Pinus rigida
1. Branch with a cone, x ½.
2. Branch with staminate flowers, x ½.
3. Branch with pistillate flowers,
   x ½.
4. Fascicle of leaves, x ½.
5. Cross section of leaf, x 15.
6. Staminate scale, outer view,
   enlarged.
7. Pistillate scale, inner view,
   enlarged.
8. Seed, x 1.

HABIT. Tree to 25 m, with horizontal branches forming an open, wide, irregular crown.

BARK. Bark reddish brown, deeply fissured into flat scaly ridges which separate into thin scales.

STEMS. Branchlets stout, bright green at first, soon turning bright brown the first winter and becoming dark grayish brown after a few years.

WINTER-BUDS. Terminal bud ovoid or oblong-ovoid, 5–10 mm long, with loose, brown, shiny, imbricate scales; lateral buds smaller.

LEAVES. Needle-shaped, in fascicles of 3, stout, rigid, spreading, 7–12 cm long, light green at first, becoming dark green, dull-pointed, sharply toothed along margin; resin ducts 2–7, medial and internal.

FLOWERS. April–May. Staminate flow-ers cylindrical, 1–2 cm long. Pistillate flowers solitary or clustered, green at first, with spiny scales.

FRUIT. Cones maturing in 2 seasons, often clustered, conical-ovoid, symmetrical, 4–10 cm long, sessile or short-stalked, light brown, shiny; cone-scales thickened at apex, ending in a sharp slender prickle. Seeds winged, black.

DISTRIBUTION. New Brunswick to Ontario, south to Georgia and west to Kentucky.

HABITAT. Grows on dry and rocky soil.

CULTIVATION NOTES. Because of the numerous spreading, gnarled and drooping branches, old trees are often very picturesque. It is useful as an ornamental tree as well as for reforestation. The tree is widely adaptable and valuable for planting in poor soil.

Red Pine
Pinus resinosa Aiton

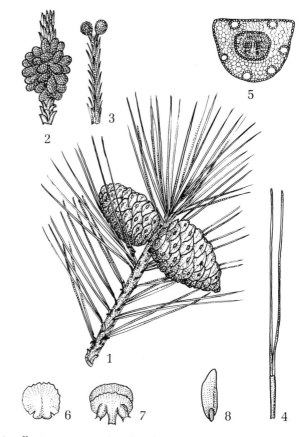

8. Pinus resinosa
1. Fruiting branch with cones, x ½.
2. Branch with staminate flowers, x ½.
3. Branch with pistillate flowers, x ½.
4. Fascicle of leaves, x ½.
5. Cross section of leaf, x 15.
6. Staminate scale, outer view, enlarged.
7. Pistillate scale, inner view, enlarged.
8. Seed, x 1.

HABIT. A tree to 25 m, occasionally to 50 m; branches stout, spreading, sometimes pendulous, forming a broad, more or less irregular crown.

BARK. Bark thick, reddish brown, shallowly fissured into broad flat ridges peeling off in thin scales.

STEMS. Young branchlets pale brown to orange-brown, stout, becoming slightly roughened with the persistent bases of bud-scales.

WINTER-BUDS. Terminal bud ovoid, sharply pointed, to 2 cm long, resinous, with thin, light brown scales fringed on the margin; lateral buds smaller.

LEAVES. Needle-shaped, in fascicles of 2, 12–17 cm long, slender, flexible, dark green, sharply pointed; resin ducts many, marginal and/or medial.

FLOWERS. April–May. Staminate flowers in dense cylindrical clusters, about 12 mm long, dark purple. Pistillate flowers in roundish clusters, scarlet, the stalk stout, covered with pale brown bracts.

FRUIT. Cones maturing the following autumn, falling the third year, subsessile, conical-ovoid, symmetrical, 4–6 cm long, nut-brown; cone-scales conspicuously keeled, slightly thickened at apex, unarmed.

DISTRIBUTION. Nova Scotia to Manitoba, south to Pennsylvania and west to Michigan and Minnesota. In Pennsylvania found only in the northern part of the state.

HABITAT. Usually found on sandy plains and dry, gravelly ridges, mixed with other trees.

CULTIVATION NOTES. The Red Pine is attractive and picturesque and deserves to be used more widely as an ornamental tree. It is adapted to variable conditions and easy to grow. It is a valuable timber tree and as a prolific seeder, regenerates naturally. The tree is also known by the misleading name Norway Pine. It is not, however, cultivated in Norway, and the name is said to be after the town of Norway, Maine.

Short-leaf Pine
Pinus echinata Miller

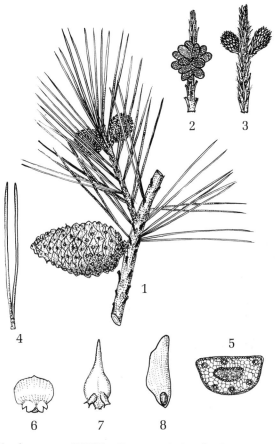

9. Pinus echinata
1. Fruiting branch with young and mature cones, x ½.
2. Branch with staminate flowers, x ½.
3. Branch with pistillate flowers, x ½.
4. Fascicle of leaves, x ½.
5. Cross section of leaf, x 15.
6. Staminate scale, outer view, enlarged.
7. Pistillate scale, inner view, enlarged.
8. Seed, x 5.

HABIT. Tree 30–40 m, with slender, often pendent branches in regular whorls, forming a wide pyramidal or rounded crown.

BARK. Bark light cinnamon red, broken by distinct fissures into large scaly plates.

STEMS. Young branchlets at first green and bloomy, later dark reddish brown and scaly.

WINTER-BUDS. Terminal bud oblong-ovoid, brown, dull-pointed, covered with sharply pointed brown scales; lateral buds smaller.

LEAVES. Needle-shaped, in fascicles of 2–3, sometimes 3–4, slender, flexible, 7–12 cm long, dark bluish green, surrounded on base by persistent sheaths; resin ducts 3–6, medial.

FLOWERS. April–May. Staminate flowers nearly sessile, pale purple. Pistillate flowers usually 2–4 in a whorl, pale rose colored.

FRUIT. Cones maturing in 2 seasons, short-stalked or subsessile, conical-ovoid, 4–6 cm long, dull brown; cone-scale slightly thickened, the ends slightly enlarged, ending with a short prickle. Seeds small, nearly triangular but full and rounded on the sides, 4–5 mm long, pale brown, mottled with black dots.

DISTRIBUTION. Southeastern New York to northern Pennsylvania, south to Florida, west to Illinois and southeastern Texas.

HABITAT. A tree of the plains and foot-hills, usually on poor, dry or sandy soil.

CULTIVATION NOTES. This is essentially a southern species that extends north into Pennsylvania. It is a handsome tree with a broad crown and can be planted, in favorable situations, anywhere in Pennsylvania as an ornamental tree. It is also useful for reforestation.

Virginia Pine
Pinus virginiana Miller

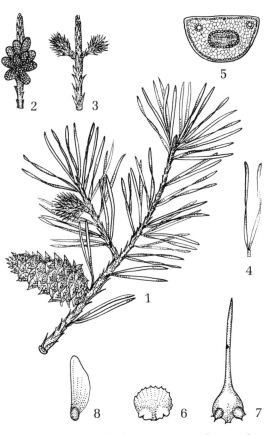

10. Pinus virginiana
1. Fruiting branch with young and mature cones, x ½.
2. Branch with staminate flowers, x ½.
3. Branch with pistillate flowers, x ½.
4. Fascicle of leaves, x ½.
5. Cross section of leaf, x 15.
6. Staminate scale, outer view, enlarged.
7. Pistillate scale, inner view, enlarged.
8. Seed, x 1.

HABIT. A bushy tree 10–15 m or sometimes to 30 m, with long slender horizontal or pendulous branches in widely spaced irregular whorls, forming a flat-topped conical crown.

BARK. Dark reddish brown, shallowly fissured into small, scaly scales, smooth on the branches.

STEMS. Young branchlets slender, flexible, greenish purple and bloomy, later becoming light grayish brown.

WINTER-BUDS. Terminal buds oblong, 6–12 mm long, sharply pointed, dark brown, very resinous, with sharply pointed appressed scales.

LEAVES. Needle-shaped, in fascicles of 2, with persistent sheath, rather stout, rigid, usually twisted, 4–8 cm long, sharply thick-pointed, toothed along margins; resin ducts usually medial.

FLOWERS. April or May. Staminate flowers oblong, 8–25 mm long. Pistillate flowers long-stalked, roundish, solitary or few in a whorl, with tapering sharp scales.

FRUIT. Cones persisting for 3–4 years, usually sessile, conical-ovoid to oblong, symmetrical, 5–7 cm long, reddish brown, shiny, dehiscent at maturity; cone-scales thin, flat, thickened at apex, ending in a slender prickle. Seeds rounded, 7–8 mm long, pale brown.

DISTRIBUTION. New York and Pennsylvania south to Georgia and Alabama, west to Ohio and Kentucky. In Pennsylvania throughout the southern and central part of the state.

HABITAT. Common on light, sandy, or poor rocky soils.

CULTIVATION NOTES. This small tree is very common in abandoned fields of central and southern Pennsylvania and useful for reclamation of exhausted farm lands. Although little used, it is valuable as an ornamental tree because of its picturesque shape and ease of growth on poor soil.

Table Mountain Pine
Pinus pungens Lambert

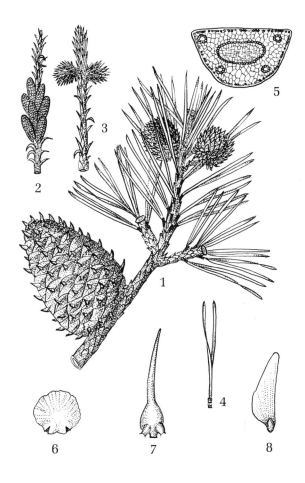

11. Pinus pungens
1. Fruiting branch with young and mature cones, x ½.
2. Branch with staminate flowers, x ½.
3. Branch with pistillate flowers, x ½.
4. Fascicle of leaves, x ½.
5. Cross section of leaf, x 15.
6. Staminate scale, outer view, enlarged.
7. Pistillate scale, inner view, enlarged.
8. Seed, x 1.

HABIT. Trees to 10, occasionally to 20 m, with stout spreading branches forming a broad, open crown.

BARK. Bark reddish brown, thick, fissured into scaly irregular plates.

STEMS. Young branchlets stout, rather brittle, light orange and smooth at first, becoming rough and dark brown.

WINTER-BUDS. Terminal buds oblong, bluntly pointed, 12–20 mm long, dark chestnut-brown, resinous; lateral buds smaller.

LEAVES. Needle-shaped, in fascicles of 2, sometimes 3, stout, rigid, very sharply pointed, more or less twisted, 4–8 cm long, dark green, surrounded by persistent sheaths; resin ducts 2–5, medial.

FLOWERS. April–May. Staminate flowers in long loose clusters, yellow. Pistillate flowers in whorls of 2–7, short and stout-stalked, the scales prolonged into a pointed triangle.

FRUIT. Cones persistent for many years, short-ovoid, symmetrical or oblique at base, 6–9 cm long, light brown; cone-scales much thickened, ending in a stout curved spine.

DISTRIBUTION. Pennsylvania and New Jersey and south along the mountains to Tennessee and northern Georgia.

HABITAT. An upland tree, commonly found on dry rocky and gravelly slopes.

CULTIVATION NOTES. This rather small tree is primarily southern in distribution, extending north to Pennsylvania. It spreads aggressively and is well adapted for regeneration of exhausted fields and for protection of rocky slopes from erosion.

Jack Pine
Pinus banksiana Lambert

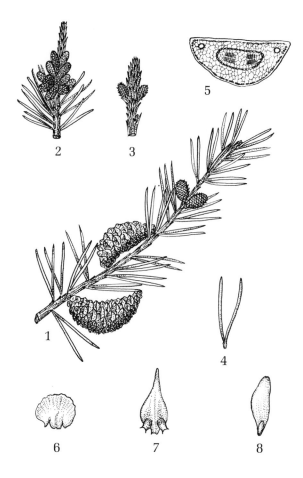

12. Pinus banksiana
1. Fruiting branch with young and mature cones, x ½.
2. Branch with staminate flowers, x ½.
3. Branch with ovulate flowers, x ½.
4. Fascicle of leaves, x ½.
5. Cross section of leaf, x 15.
6. Staminate scale, outer view, enlarged.
7. Pistillate scale, inner view, enlarged.
8. Seed, x 1.

HABIT. Tree to 25 m, but usually about 5–10 m, sometimes shrubby, with slender spreading branches forming an open, broad crown.

BARK. Bark thin, dark brown, slightly tinged with red, shallowly fissured into narrow ridges covered with thick scales.

STEMS. Young branchlets yellowish green, becoming purplish to yellowish brown, finally dark reddish brown and roughened with the persistent bases of bud-scales.

WINTER-BUDS. Terminal bud 5 mm long, ovoid, with rounded apex, pale brown, very resinous; lateral buds smaller.

LEAVES. Needle-shaped, in fascicles of 2, rigid, curved or twisted, spreading, 2–4 cm long, sharply or bluntly pointed, bright or dark green; resin ducts 0–2, medial.

FLOWERS. May–June. Staminate flowers in cylindrical clusters, 12 mm long, yellow. Pistillate flowers in roundish clusters, purplish.

FRUIT. Cones maturing in the 2nd or 3rd year but persistent for 10–15 years on the tree, erect, conical-ovoid, oblique, usually much curved, 3–5 cm long, tawny yellow, shiny; scales thickened at apex, unarmed. Seeds nearly triangular but full and rounded on the sides, 6 mm long, blackish.

DISTRIBUTION. From Hudson Bay to Maine and northern New York, west to the Mackenzie River and Minnesota.

HABITAT. On dry, sandy, sterile soil.

CULTIVATION NOTES. A small slow-growing tree, it is usually stunted, with sprawling habit. It is difficult to transplant.

40

White Pine *(Pinus strobus)*

Pitch Pine *(Pinus rigida)*

Red Pine *(Pinus resinosa)*

Short-leaf Pine *(Pinus echinata)*

Virginia Pine *(Pinus virginiana)*

Table Mountain Pine *(Pinus pungens)*

44

Jack Pine *(Pinus banksiana)*

ARBORVITÆ
Thuja *(Cupressaceae)*

American Arborvitæ *(Thuja occidentalis)*

There are 4 or 5 species in the genus *Thuja* distributed in the temperate regions of North America and eastern Asia. In North America, one species is native to the West and one to the East.

The species of *Thuja* have spreading and erect branches forming a pyramidal head. The branchlets, densely covered by small appressed leaves, are flattened and disposed in horizontal planes. The leaves are scale-like, opposite and 4-ranked, the lateral pair nearly covering the facial ones. The flowers are unisexual, the staminate and pistillate ones occurring on the same tree. The fruiting cones are ovoid, with 8–12 scales which are thickened at ridge or at apex. There are 2–3 seeds under each scale, thin and winged.

Other than the native *Thuja occidentalis,* which is widely cultivated in endless variations, several other introduced species are planted, the most widely cultivated one being the Oriental Arborvitæ, *Thuja orientalis* Linnaeus, of eastern Asia. This species is sometimes placed in a separate genus as *Biota orientalis* (Linnaeus) Endlicher. It differs from the other species of *Thuja* in that the branchlets, instead of being disposed in horizontal planes, are in vertical planes and are thus green on both sides. It has also thick instead of thin cone-scales, and thick, wingless seeds.

American Arborvitæ
Thuja occidentalis Linnaeus

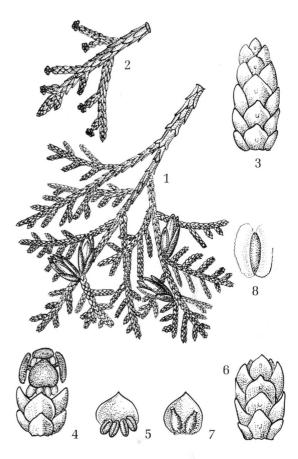

13. Thuja occidentalis
1. Fruiting branch with cones, x 1.
2. Branch with staminate and pistillate flowers, x 2.
3. Tip of branch, x 5.
4. Staminate flower, x 5.
5. Staminate scale, inner view, enlarged.
6. Pistillate flower, x 5.
7. Pistillate scale, enlarged.
8. Seed, x 5.

HABIT. A tree to 20 m, with stout buttressed trunk and spreading branches forming a dense conical crown.

BARK. Bark reddish brown, thin, fissured into narrow ridges covered with elongated scales.

STEMS. Young branchlets yellowish green, flattened but somewhat 4-sided, covered by closely arranged leaves, arranged in fan-shaped clusters.

WINTER-BUDS. Buds not scaly, covered by the closely appressed scale-like leaves.

LEAVES. Scale-like, opposite, closely overlapping, 2–3 mm long, abruptly pointed, dark green above, conspicuously or inconspicuously glandular, of two kinds in alternating pairs, those on the side of the branchlets keeled, those on the face of the branchlets flat.

FLOWERS. April–May. Staminate flowers globose, inconspicuous, yellowish, with 3 pairs of stamens. Pistillate flowers small, ovoid, purplish, with 4–6 pairs of thin ovate scales.

FRUIT. Cone oblong, 8–15 mm long, light or reddish brown, with 6–12 blunt scales 8–12 mm long, usually 4 fertile. Seeds oblong, winged, about 2–3 mm long.

DISTRIBUTION. Nova Scotia to Manitoba, south along mountains to North Carolina and Tennessee, west to Minnesota and Illinois.

HABITAT. Usually found in low swampy situations but sometimes grows on drier ground.

CULTIVATION NOTES. A highly ornamental tree cultivated throughout the state. It is sometimes planted for hedges. There are numerous horticultural forms, mostly shrubby ones. The tree is of rather slow growth.

CYPRESSES
Chamaecyparis *(Cupressaceae)*

White Cedar *(Chamaecyparis thyoides)*

There are 6 species in the *Chamaecyparis* genus distributed in North America, Japan and Formosa. Four species are native to North America, only one of which is found in the northeastern part.

The species are evergreen trees with spreading branches forming a pyramidal crown. The branchlets, densely covered by the leaves, are usually flattened and appear frond-like. The leaves are opposite, minute and scale-like, or needle-like in the juvenile state. The flowers are unisexual, and the staminate and pistillate flowers occur on the same tree. The fruiting cone is globose, ripening the first season. It consists of 6–12 shield-like scales, each fertile scale bearing 1 or 2 winged seeds.

Besides the native White Cedar, several other species are introduced and widely planted. These include Nootka Cypress, *Chamaecyparis nootkatensis* (Lambert) Spach, and Lawson Cypress, *C. lawsoniana* (A. Murray) Parlatore, from western North America; and Hinoki Cypress, *C. obtusa* (Siebold and Zuccarini) Endlicher, and Sawara Cypress, *C. pisifera* (Siebold and Zuccarini) Endlicher, from Japan. All of these species are very variable, and they appear in many garden forms. In the last-named species, the varieties *filifera* Beissner and *plumosa* Beissner are especially extensively planted. *C. pisifera* var. *filifera* is a medium-sized tree of graceful habit with elongated, slender, drooping branches bearing few short lateral branchlets. Variety *plumosa* is of dense conical habit with ascending branches bearing frond-like leathery branchlets.

White Cedar
Chamaecyparis thyoides *(Linnaeus)* B.S.P.

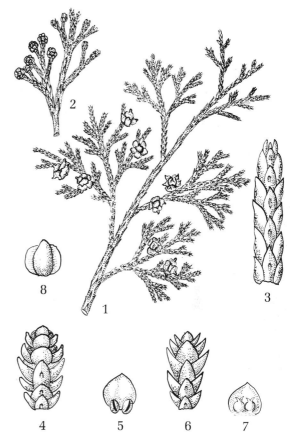

14. Chamaecyparis thyoides
1. Fruiting branch with cones, x 1.
2. Branch with staminate and pistillate flowers, x 2.
3. Tip of branch, x 5.
4. Staminate flower, x 5.
5. Staminate scale, inner view, enlarged.
6. Pistillate flower, x 5.
7. Pistillate scale, inner view, enlarged.
8. Seed, x 5.

HABIT. A small tree 10–25 m, with slender upright spreading or horizontal branches forming a narrow spire-like crown.

BARK. Bark thin and reddish brown, fissured into flat connected ridges and peeling off into long fibrous scales.

STEMS. Young branchlets slender, somewhat flattened, rather irregularly arranged, bluish green, becoming roundish and reddish brown; terminal branchlets often arranged in fan-like clusters.

WINTER-BUDS. Buds very small and inconspicuous, usually covered by the closely overlapping leaves.

LEAVES. Leaves small, scale-like, 4-ranked but appearing compressed, ovate, closely overlapping or on vigorous branchlets spreading at the apex, keeled, conspicuously glandular on the back, dark bluish or light green.

FLOWERS. March–April. Staminate flowers minute, oblong, about 3 mm long, dark brown, with 4–6 pairs of stamens. Pistillate flowers globose, about 2 mm across, with about 6 shield-like scales, each bearing 2 ovules.

FRUIT. Cones globose, small, 6–8 mm across, stalkless on short leafy branch, light green when young, later bluish purplish with a white bloom, finally dark reddish brown; scales of about 3 pairs, tipped with pointed, often reflexed bosses; seeds 1 or 2 to each scale, slightly winged.

DISTRIBUTION. Maine to Florida, west to Mississippi. Native to Pennsylvania, but now appears only as a cultivated tree.

HABITAT. Prefers swamps and marshes.

CULTIVATION NOTES. The tree is the hardiest of all native conifers. It is attractive in form, has beautiful foliage and is extensively planted for ornamental purposes. Many garden varieties are known. It is a moisture-loving plant but will also grow in dry locations.

JUNIPERS
Juniperus *(Cupressaceae)*

Red Cedar *(Juniperus virginiana)*

There are over 40 species in the Juniper genus, widely distributed throughout the northern hemisphere. Over 16 are found in North America, 2 of which are native to Pennsylvania, one being a tree and the other shrubby.

The species of *Juniperus* are evergreen trees or shrubs. The leaves of young plants are needle-like and ternate. On old plants they may be a mixture of needle-like and scale-like, opposite and ternate. The flowers are unisexual and axillary or terminal. The staminate and pistillate flowers occur on the same or different trees. The staminate flowers consist of numerous stamens forming an oblong catkin. The pistillate flowers consist of 3–8 pointed scales, each bearing 1 or 2 ovules. These scales become fleshy and unite together into a berry-like fleshy cone subtended by scaly bracts. The cone contains 1–12 wingless seeds.

The native *Juniperus virginiana* is widely planted in numerous garden varieties. Similarly the shrubby species *Juniperus communis* Linnaeus is also cultivated in innumerable horticultural forms, the species being native to nearly the entire northern regions of Europe, Asia and North America. Among the introduced species, the Chinese Juniper, *J. chinensis* Linnaeus, is the most extensively cultivated. This species is a very hardy plant with both scale-like and needle-like leaves. Of the many varieties in cultivation, *pfizeriana* Spath, a low form with horizontally spreading branches, is the most extensively planted.

Red Cedar
Juniperus virginiana Linnaeus

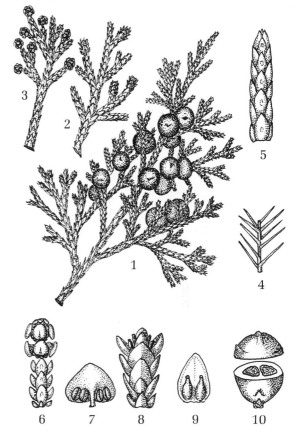

15. Juniperus virginiana
1. Fruiting branch with cones, x 1.
2. Branch with staminate flowers, x 2.
3. Branch with pistillate flowers, x 2.
4. Branch with awl-shaped leaves, x 2.
5. Tip of branch, x 5.
6. Staminate flower, x 5.
7. Staminate scale, inner view, enlarged.
8. Pistillate flower, x 5.
9. Pistillate scale, inner view, enlarged.
10. Cone showing cross section, x 2.

HABIT. A tree usually 10–15 m, sometimes attaining to 30 m or more, with upright or spreading branches forming a narrow or broad pyramidal crown.

BARK. Bark thin, reddish brown, often grooved, shredding in long, narrow strips.

STEMS. Young branchlets very slender, less than 1 mm thick, green at first, soon becoming reddish brown.

WINTER-BUDS. Buds naked, minute, inconspicuous, covered by the leaves.

LEAVES. Leaves of 2 kinds. Scale-like leaves ovate, closely appressed, about 1.5 mm long, rounded or pointed and free at apex, dark bluish green, often with a small gland on back. Awl-shaped leaves often present, 5–6 mm long, opposite or on vigorous shoots and on young plants sometimes in 3's, spiny-pointed, concave and bloomy above.

FLOWERS. April–May. Staminate and pistillate flowers usually on different trees. Staminate flowers with about 6 pairs of stamens. Pistillate flowers small, short-stalked, with about 6 scales, the scales spreading, short-pointed, bluish.

FRUIT. Cones maturing the first or second season, roundish or ovoid, 6 mm long, dark bluish, bloomy. Seeds 1–2, deeply pitted.

DISTRIBUTION. Nova Scotia to Ontario, south to Florida and Texas.

HABITAT. Prefers loamy soil on sunny slopes, swamps or borders of lakes and streams, but also on dry, rocky hillsides.

CULTIVATION NOTES. The Red Cedar is the most widespread species of tree in the northern hemisphere. It is a very variable species divided into geographical varieties and many garden forms with varied color, size and growth forms. Although it will grow in almost any location, it grows best in limestone soil and moist situations. It tolerates shade but will grow best in abundant light.

POPLARS
Populus *(Salicaceae)*

There are about 30 species in the Poplar genus with 19 species native to North America and 4 to Pennsylvania.

The species of the genus *Populus* are deciduous trees with furrowed pale bark of bitter taste and soft light wood. The buds are resinous and the terminal bud is usually present. The alternate leaves are ovate to ovate-lanceolate and long-stalked. The unisexual flowers are found on separate trees, appearing in drooping catkins before the leaves. The flowers are usually borne in the axil of a laciniate bract with a cup-shaped disk at the base, in contrast to the Willow genus, where the bract is entire and the flowers are without a disk. The numerous small seeds, surrounded at the base by long silky hairs, are borne in a dehiscent, 2- to 4-valved capsule.

In addition to the following widely distributed introduced species in the eastern states, there is a northern species which extends along river banks south to New York: the Balsam Poplar, *Populus balsamifera* Linnaeus. The species resembles the Cottonwood, but it is characterized by the large winter-buds which are very resinous and strongly balsam-scented. The terminal buds are covered by 5 scales. The branches, instead of being flattish as in the Cottonwood, *P. deltoides,* are rounded in cross section.

Poplars are rapid-growing trees and readily propagated by cuttings. They are used as timber trees and much planted as ornamental and shade trees. Besides the native species described here, 3 introduced species are very commonly planted in the northeastern United States. The Eurasian species *P. alba* Linnaeus, the White Poplar, is cultivated as an ornamental tree and is frequently naturalized. It can be recognized by the contrasting white-felted undersurface of its leaves. Also commonly cultivated is the European Aspen, *P. tremula* Linnaeus, a species from Europe, North Africa, and Asia, and the Black Poplar, *P. nigra* Linnaeus, originally from Europe and western Asia. The former resembles the American Quaking Aspen, *P. tremuloides* Michaux, differing in the more irregularly sinuate-toothed leaves which are often blunt at the apex. The Quaking Aspen has fine, regular teeth along the leaf margin, and the leaves are sharply short-pointed. The Black Poplar is especially known by its variety *italica* Muenchhausen, the Lombardy Poplar, a striking tree with a distinct fastigate habit, the closely ascending long branches forming a narrow columnar head. It is often planted as an avenue tree.

POPULUS
Summer key to the species

A. Leaves with flattened petioles.
    B. Leaves broadly triangular, abruptly and sharply pointed at apex.
              P. deltoides
    B. Leaves broadly ovate to roundish ovate, usually pointed at apex.
        C. Leaf margins finely toothed; bark greenish white.   **P. tremuloides**
        C. Leaf margins coarsely toothed; bark yellowish gray to black.
              P. grandidentata
A. Leaves with rounded or channeled petioles.   **P. heterophylla**

Winter key to the species

A. Terminal buds 5–25 mm long, resinous.   **P. deltoides**
A. Terminal buds 3–5 mm long, not resinous.
    B. Stems with white pith.
        C. Terminal buds about 5 mm long, smooth, shiny; lateral buds often incurved and closely appressed.   **P. tremuloides**
        C. Terminal buds about 3 mm long, downy, dull; lateral buds straight or widely divergent.   **P. grandidentata**
    B. Stems with orange-colored pith.   **P. heterophylla**

Cottonwood
Populus deltoides Marshall

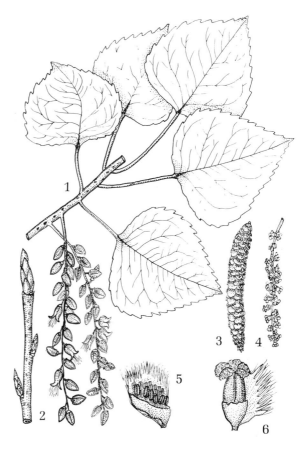

16. Populus deltoides
1. Branch with fruits, x ½.
2. Branch with winter-buds, x ½.
3. Staminate catkin, x ½.
4. Pistillate catkin, x ½.
5. Staminate flower with scale, enlarged.
6. Pistillate flower with scale, enlarged.

HABIT. A large tree 15–25 m, sometimes 30 m high, with upright, spreading branches forming a high, rather broad crown.

BARK. Bark on old trunk thick, ashy gray, deeply fissured into straight furrows with broad, rounded ridges; on upper trunk and stems rather thin, smooth and yellowish green.

STEMS. Young branchlets stout, slightly ridged or nearly round, smooth, yellowish green with 3 bundle-scars; pith white.

WINTER-BUDS. Buds smooth, brownish, large, shiny, the scales numerous, viscid; terminal bud often 5-angled, larger than lateral bud, 5–25 mm long.

LEAVES. Leaves thick, triangular-ovate or broadly ovate, sharply pointed, subcordate to truncate and with 2 or 3 glands at base, coarsely toothed with curved teeth on margin, entire at base and apex, densely ciliate, 7–12 cm long and about as broad, smooth, deep green and shiny above, bright green beneath; petioles laterally flattened.

FLOWERS. March–April. Staminate catkins drooping, 7–10 cm long, densely flowered; scales divided into filiform lobes; stamens 40–60. Pistillate catkins drooping, sparsely flowered, 6–8 cm long; stigmas 3–4.

FRUIT. Capsules short-stalked, 3- to 4-valved in drooping catkins 15–25 cm long. Seeds small, surrounded with a mat of long white hairs.

DISTRIBUTION. Quebec to North Dakota, Kansas, Texas and Florida.

HABITAT. Prefers rich, moist soil, along river banks, river bottoms, and lake shores, but also grows well in drier situations.

CULTIVATION NOTES. The Cottonwood is extensively planted as an ornamental tree because of its rapid growth and luxuriant attractive foliage. The young leaves have a pleasant balsamic odor. As an ornamental tree, it is especially useful in wet locations. It is also a valuable pulpwood tree.

Quaking Aspen
Populus tremuloides Michaux

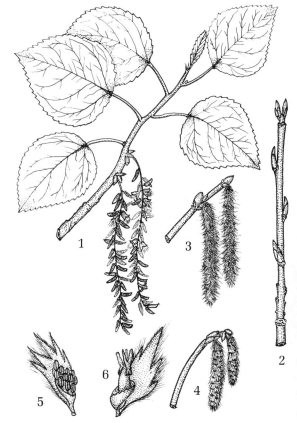

17. Populus tremuloides
1. Branch with fruits, x ½.
2. Branch with winter-buds, x ½.
3. Branch with staminate cat-kins, x ½.
4. Branch with pistillate catkins, x ½.
5. Staminate flower with scale, enlarged.
6. Pistillate flower with scale, enlarged.

HABIT. A small tree 10–15 m, rarely to 30 m high, with a high, narrow, more or less round crown.

BARK. Bark at the base of old trunks thick, deeply fissured and almost black; on upper trunk and stems thin, yellowish green and smooth, often roughened with dark blotches.

STEMS. Young branchlets smooth, very shiny, reddish brown, slender, with reddish yellow lenticels; leaf-scars large, conspicuous, crescent-shaped with 3 simple or compounded bundle-scars; pith white.

WINTER-BUDS. Buds ovoid, about 5 mm long, sharply pointed, slightly viscid; scales 6–7, reddish brown, smooth, shiny.

LEAVES. Leaves thin, ovate to orbicular, pointed, broadly wedge-shaped to heart-shaped at base, finely glandular-toothed on margin, 3–7 cm long, smooth, dark green and shiny above, pale green beneath; petioles laterally flattened.

FLOWERS. March–April. Staminate catkins drooping, 4–7 cm long; stamens 6–12.

Pistillate catkins drooping, 4–7 cm long gradually elongating to 10 cm; stigmas 2, 2-lobed, red.

FRUIT. Capsules oblong-conical, 2-valved light green, on catkins about 10 cm long Seeds light brown, surrounded with a mass of long, soft, white hairs.

DISTRIBUTION. Labrador to Alaska south to Pennsylvania, Missouri, norther. Mexico and lower California.

HABITAT. Prefers sandy soil and grav elly hillsides.

CULTIVATION NOTES. The Quaking Aspen has the widest natural range of any tree in North America, from the Atlantic coast to the Pacific. The tree grows well in all soil conditions and is common in abandoned fields and on cut-over areas. It is a most important tree for pulpwood and useful also as a temporary shelter species for other more valuable trees. The distinctly flattened petioles cause the leaves to flutter in even a light breeze, hence the name Quaking Aspen.

Large-toothed Aspen
Populus grandidentata Michaux

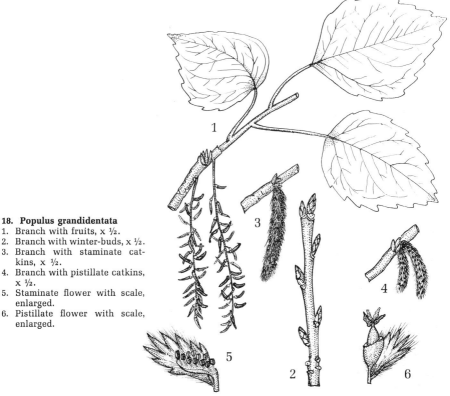

18. Populus grandidentata
1. Branch with fruits, x ½.
2. Branch with winter-buds, x ½.
3. Branch with staminate catkins, x ½.
4. Branch with pistillate catkins,
x ½.
5. Staminate flower with scale,
enlarged.
6. Pistillate flower with scale,
enlarged.

HABIT. A small tree 10–15 m, occasionally to 20 m high, with a rather narrow,
more or less round but usually irregular
crown.

BARK. Bark at the base of old trunks
thick, dark reddish brown or blackish, irregularly fissured, with broad, flat ridges
between fissures; on upper trunk and stems
thin, yellowish and smooth, often roughened
with dark blotches.

STEMS. Young branchlets at first greenish gray, downy, becoming shiny, reddish or
orange-brown and finally greenish gray;
leaf-scars large, conspicuous, crescent-
shaped with 3 simple or compounded
bundle-scars; pith white.

WINTER-BUDS. Buds ovoid, about 3 mm
long, pointed; scales 6–7, brown, downy.

LEAVES. Leaves broad-ovate, sharply
pointed, wedge-shaped to heart-shaped at
base, coarsely toothed on margin, 7–10 cm
long, dark green above, gray hairy beneath
at first, soon becoming smooth; leaves of
short branchlets elliptic, with sharper teeth
than those on long shoots; petioles laterally
flattened.

FLOWERS. March–April. Staminate catkins drooping, 4–7 cm long; scales lobed
and fringed with long hairs; stamens 6–12.
Pistillate catkins drooping, 4–7 cm long;
scales lobed; stigmas 2, 2-lobed.

FRUIT. Capsules 2-valved, conical,
pointed, hairy, 2–3 mm long, borne in
drooping catkins 10–15 cm long. Seeds
minute, dark brown, surrounded with a mat
of brown hairs.

DISTRIBUTION. Nova Scotia to Ontario,
west to Minnesota, south to Pennsylvania,
and along mountains to North Carolina and
Tennessee.

HABITAT. Prefers rich, moist, sandy
soil, usually large along borders of swamps
and river banks, and smaller and scrubby
in dry situations.

CULTIVATION NOTES. The Large-
toothed Aspen is useful as a temporary
shelter for more valuable trees while the
latter are getting established. It aids in
shading out Scrub Oak which is the most
aggressive forest weed. Because of its rapid
growth, it is of value as a soil conserver.

Swamp Cottonwood
Populus heterophylla Linnaeus

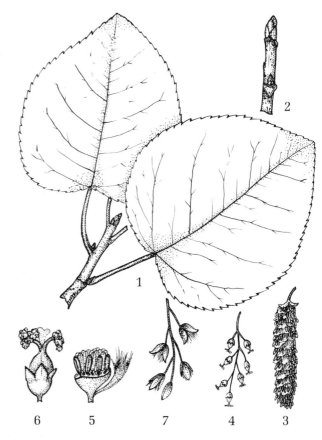

19. Populus heterophylla
1. Branch with leaves, x ½.
2. Branch with winter-buds, x ½.
3. Staminate catkins, x ½.
4. Pistillate catkins, x ½.
5. Staminate flower with scale, enlarged.
6. Pistillate flower with scale, enlarged.
7. Fruits, x ½.

HABIT. A small tree 10–15 m, occasionally to 30 m, but in cultivation often scrubby; crown high, rather narrow, round-topped.

BARK. Bark on old trunks thick, brown, roughened by long fissures in long, narrow plates; on upper trunks and stems thinner, not so rough, with shallower fissures and smoother ridges.

STEMS. Young branchlets stout, light yellow and hairy at first, becoming dull brown or gray; leaf-scars large, elevated, often 3-lobed with 3 conspicuous bundle-scars; pith orange-colored.

WINTER-BUDS. Buds broadly ovate, reddish brown, slightly resinous; the scales 4–7, slightly hairy toward the base.

LEAVES. Leaves broadly ovate, pointed or rounded at apex, rounded or heart-shaped at base, coarsely toothed on margin, 8–18 cm long, dark green above, pale green beneath; petioles rounded, 6–8 cm long.

FLOWERS. March–April. Staminate catkins drooping, 3–6 cm long, densely flowered; stamens 12–20; scales long, slender-lobed. Pistillate catkins drooping, 3–5 cm long, few-flowered; scales fimbriate; stigmas 2–3, thick.

FRUIT. Capsules dark green, 3- to 4-valved, attached to a drooping catkin 10–15 cm long by a slender stalk. Seeds minute, surrounded with a mat of long white hairs.

DISTRIBUTION. Connecticut west to Illinois, south to Georgia and Louisiana.

HABITAT. Found in low and wet situations.

CULTIVATION NOTES. The Swamp Cottonwood, with its heavy limbs and spare crown, is not ornamental and is rarely cultivated. The wood is used for pulpwood along with the Cottonwood.

Cottonwood *(Populus deltoides)*

Quaking Aspen *(Populus tremuloides)*

Large-toothed Aspen *(Populus grandidentata)*

Quaking Aspen *(Populus tremuloides)*

WILLOWS
Salix *(Salicaceae)*

The Willow genus contains over 300 species distributed chiefly in the colder and temperate regions of the northern hemisphere. About 100 species are native to North America and over 15 species to Pennsylvania; most of these are shrubs.

The Willows are deciduous, rarely evergreen, trees or shrubs with soft light wood. The winter-buds have only a single scale and terminal bud is usually lacking. The alternate leaves are long and narrow, mostly lanceolate in shape. The unisexual flowers, borne on separate trees in upright catkins before or after the leaves, are without a disk but with 1 or 2 glands at base and subtended by an entire-margined bract. The numerous small seeds, surrounded by long silky hairs at the base, are produced in 2-valved capsules.

The Willows are rapid-growing trees. Some of the species are important timber trees and many species are highly ornamental. The slender tough branchlets of some species are extensively used in basketry. The bark contains tannic acid and salicin. In cultivation, the trees are readily propagated by cuttings. It is desirable to select only the stamen-bearing trees as they are more ornamental in flower and they do not produce the cottony fruit which is often disagreeable near dwellings.

As the Willow species very closely resemble each other and hybridize among themselves freely, their classification and identification are difficult. Furthermore, since the plants often flower before the leaves are out and since the sexes are found on separate trees, complete material for study is frequently not available. The classification of willows is the task for the specialist. It is impractical to use winter characteristics alone for identification, and the winter key is here omitted.

Besides the more common native species described below, there are two notable species of tree size: a northern species and a southern species. Both resemble the Black Willow, *Salix nigra,* but differ from the latter in that the leaves are whitish beneath. The northern species is the Peach-leaved Willow, *S. amygdaloides* Andersson, which extends southward through New England to New York and Indiana. It is a small tree with yellowish branchlets. The leaves have long petioles (1–3 cm) and minute, deciduous stipules. The southern species is the Ward's Willow, *S. caroliniana* Michaux, extending northward to Maryland, West Virginia and southern Indiana. It is also a small tree but the branchlets are reddish or purplish tinged. The leaves have short petioles (3–7 mm) and large, persistent stipules.

Besides the native species, the most common introduced species of willows, the Crack Willow, *S. fragilis* Linnaeus, is sometimes escaped in the eastern states. It is a tree from Europe and western Asia, characterized by the brittle base of its branchlets. It has rough, thick, brownish bark and upright, spreading branches. The catkins, borne on leafy stalks, are rather long. Other species common in cultivation are the White Willow, *S. alba* Linnaeus from Europe, North Africa to Central Asia, and the Weeping Willow, *S. babylonica* Linnaeus, native to China. The former is recognized by its silky branchlets and young leaves and is planted as a timber tree. The variety *tristis* Gaudichaud, with bright yellow pendulous branches and long, narrowly lanceolate leaves, is widely planted for ornament.

SALIX
Summary key to the species

A. Leaves hairy on both surfaces.   **S. bebbiana**
A. Leaves smooth or nearly so when mature.
  B. Leaves narrowly lanceolate; petioles without glands.   **S. nigra**
  B. Leaves oblong-lanceolate; petioles glandular or not.
    C. Petioles glandular above; capsules smooth.   **S. lucida**
    C. Petioles not glandular; capsules hairy.   **S. discolor**

Beak Willow
Salix bebbiana Sargent *(Salix rostrata Richards)*

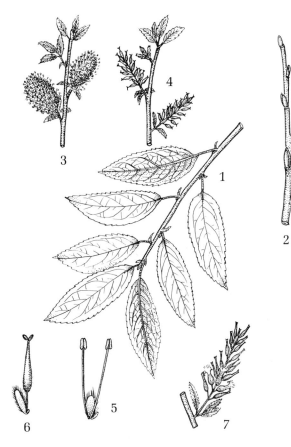

20. Salix bebbiana
1. Leafy branch, x ½.
2. Branch with winter-buds, x ½.
3. Branch with staminate catkins, x ½.
4. Branch with pistillate catkins, x ½.
5. Staminate flower with scale, enlarged.
6. Pistillate flower with scale, enlarged.
7. Branch with fruits, x ½.

HABIT. A shrub or small tree usually 2–3 m, sometimes 8 m, with short trunk and a broad, round-topped crown.

BARK. Bark gray or brown, thin, smooth, sometimes shallowly fissured; usually scaly.

STEMS. Young branchlets purplish to brown, slender, hairy at first, becoming smooth; leaf-scars crescent-shaped, somewhat raised.

WINTER-BUDS. Buds oblong, narrow, about 5 mm long, bluntly pointed, chestnut-brown, covered by a single scale.

LEAVES. Alternate, simple, elliptic to oblong-lanceolate, 3–10 cm long, short-pointed to sharply pointed at apex, rounded to wedge-shaped at base, sparingly toothed or entire on margin, dull green and smooth above, pale green and hairy beneath and prominently veined; petiole 4–12 mm long; stipules slightly heart-shaped, deciduous.

FLOWERS. April–May. Staminate catkins erect, terminal, to 3 cm long; stamens 2; filaments hairy at base. Pistillate catkins to 6 cm long; ovary silky haired, stalked.

FRUIT. Capsule narrowly ovoid, 5–9 mm long, somewhat hairy, beaked and stalked, in lax and open catkins.

DISTRIBUTION. Newfoundland to Alaska, south to Pennsylvania, Illinois, Utah and California.

HABITAT. Prefers moist situations but also grown on dry hillsides; common in swamps and along stream borders.

CULTIVATION NOTES. The Beak Willow is a wide-ranging and variable species and occurs in both moist and dry situations. It is not of any particular ornamental value except that in wet situations it is useful as a soil-binder to prevent erosion.

Black Willow
Salix nigra Marshall

21. Salix nigra
1. Leafy branch, x ½.
2. Branch with winter-buds, x ½.
3. Branch with staminate catkins, x ½.
4. Branch with pistillate catkins,
   x ½.
5. Staminate flower with scale,
   enlarged.
6. Pistillate flower with scale,
   enlarged.
7. Branch with fruits, x ½.

HABIT. A tree to 12 m high, occasionally to 25 m, usually with crooked trunk,
drooping branches, and a wide, open, round-
topped crown.

BARK. Bark dark brown, rough, deeply
furrowed with wide ridges covered with
thick scales.

STEMS. Young branchlets yellowish,
slightly hairy when young; leaf-scars narrow, crescent-shaped, with 3 bundle-scars.

WINTER-BUDS. Buds small, narrow-
conical, 2–3 mm long, pointed, reddish
brown, covered by a single scale.

LEAVES. Alternate, simple, narrowly
lanceolate, 6–12 cm long, long-pointed at
apex, tapering or slightly rounded at base,
finely toothed on margin, usually smooth
and dark green above, pale green and sometimes hairy on the veins beneath; petioles
3–6 mm long; stipules slightly heart-shaped,
persistent.

FLOWERS. March–April. Staminate catkins 3–5 cm long, slender, drooping; stamens
3–7. Pistillate catkins 4–8 cm long, drooping; ovary smooth; stigma subsessile; stalk
much longer than gland.

FRUIT. Capsules ovoid-conical, 2–3 mm
long, reddish brown, smooth. Seeds many,
minute, covered with a dense tuft of long,
silky, white hairs.

DISTRIBUTION. New Brunswick to Florida, west to California.

HABITAT. Prefers moist situations like
banks of streams and lake shores.

CULTIVATION NOTES. The Black Willow is the largest willow tree among the
native species. It is a graceful tree but is
not considered valuable as an ornamental
species. Useful as a soil conserver, the
tree grows well in moist situations and requires plenty of light.

Shining Willow
Salix lucida Muhlenberg

22. Salix lucida
1. Leafy branch, x ½.
2. Branch with winter-buds, x ½.
3. Branch with staminate catkins, x ½.
4. Branch with pistillate catkins, x ½.
5. Staminate flower with scale, enlarged.
6. Pistillate flower with scale, enlarged.
7. Branch with fruits, x ½.

HABIT. A shrub or small tree to 6–8 m, with a short trunk and ascending branches forming a broad, rather symmetrical crown.

BARK. Bark brown to reddish brown, smooth, thin.

STEMS. Young branchlets shiny, yellowish brown, becoming dark brown; leaf-scars crescent-shaped, somewhat raised, with 3 bundle-scars.

WINTER-BUDS. Buds small, ovoid, 5 mm long, pointed, smooth, yellowish brown, covered by a single scale.

LEAVES. Alternate, simple, broadly lanceolate to ovate, 7–12 cm long, long-pointed at apex, tapering or rounded at base, finely glandular-toothed on margin, smooth and green on both sides, paler beneath, smooth or hairy on midrib; petioles 6–12 mm long, glandular; stipules slightly heart-shaped, very glandular, usually persistent.

FLOWERS. April. Staminate catkins 3–6 cm long, densely flowered; stamens usually 5. Pistillate catkins slender, 5–7 cm long, densely flowered; stigmas subsessile.

FRUIT. Capsules narrowly ovoid, 5.0–6.5 mm long, greenish to pale brown or straw-colored, smooth, dull.

DISTRIBUTION. Newfoundland to Manitoba, south to Pennsylvania, west to Kentucky and Nebraska.

HABITAT. Prefers moist situations; low ground, shores, swamps.

CULTIVATION NOTES. The Shining Willow is very common in wet situations throughout Pennsylvania. It is valuable as a soil conserver. The species is an attractive small tree and useful as an ornamental.

Pussy Willow
Salix discolor Muhlenberg

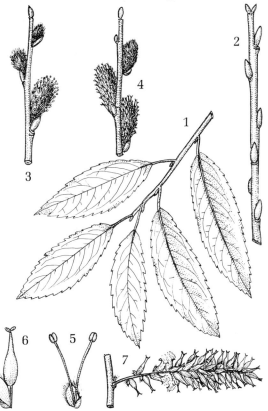

23. Salix discolor
1. Leafy branch, x ½.
2. Branch with winter-buds, x ½.
3. Branch with staminate catkins, x ½.
4. Branch with pistillate catkins, x ½.
5. Staminate flower with scale, enlarged.
6. Pistillate flower with scale, enlarged.
7. Branch with fruits, x ½.

HABIT. A shrub or small tree usually 2–5 m high, but sometimes may reach a height of 7–8 m, with short trunk and stout ascending branches forming a round-topped crown.

BARK. Bark gray or reddish brown, thin, smooth, sometimes scaly.

STEMS. Young branchlets stout, dark green to reddish purple, rather flexible, hairy at first, soon becoming smooth; leaf-scars crescent-shaped, somewhat raised, with 3 bundle-scars.

WINTER-BUDS. Buds somewhat cylindrical, flattened and pointed at apex, about 8–10 mm long, dark reddish purple and shiny.

LEAVES. Alternate, simple, thin, elliptic-oblong to oblong-lanceolate, 4–10 cm long, sharply pointed at apex, pointed to rounded at base, coarsely and irregularly toothed on margin or sometimes nearly entire, hairy when young, smooth at maturity, green above, white-bloomy beneath; petioles 8–25 mm long; stipules slightly heart-shaped, deciduous.

FLOWERS. March. Staminate catkins densely flowered, to 3.5 cm long. Pistillate catkins 2.5–7.0 cm long; style distinct, short, with narrow bifid stigmas; stalk smooth, shorter than the hairy ovary.

FRUIT. Capsule about 7–12 mm long, cylindrical, more or less contracted above the middle into a long beak, light brown, minute pale hairs; stalk much longer than the gland.

DISTRIBUTION. Nova Scotia to Manitoba, south to Virginia and Missouri.

HABITAT. Prefers damp habitats; along streams and lake shores; in swamps and wet situations.

CULTIVATION NOTES. The tree has a handsome form and attractive bark. It is especially valued for its ornamental flowers which appear early in spring before the leaves have unfolded. Although the tree prefers moist situations in its natural habitat, it can be planted in rather dry situations.

Beak Willow (*Salix bebbiana*)

Black Willow (*Salix nigra*)

Shining Willow (*Salix lucida*)

Pussy Willow (*Salix discolor*)

WALNUTS
Juglans *(Juglandaceae)*

Butternut *(Juglans cinera)*

There are about 15 species in the Walnut genus, mainly distributed in the northern hemisphere. Five species are native to North America and 2 to Pennsylvania.

The species of *Juglans* are deciduous trees. The trunk has scaly furrowed bark and the branches are characterized by chambered pith. The alternate, compound leaves are large, aromatic and without stipules. The odd-pinnate leaflets are opposite in arrangement. The unisexual flowers, appearing with or shortly after the leaves, are borne on the same tree. The staminate flowers appear in long drooping catkins and the pistillate ones in few- to many-flowered terminal racemes. The fruit is a large drupe with indehiscent husk and a thick-walled sculptured nut inside.

Besides the native species, the European Walnut or Persian Walnut, *J. regia* Linnaeus, originally of Europe and Asia, is widely planted in the United States as a fruit and ornamental tree. The tree has gray smooth bark and coarsely chambered light brown pith. The pinnately compound leaves consist of 7–9 smooth and almost entire-margined leaflets. The branchlets as well as the buds are smooth.

JUGLANS
Summer key to the species
A. Leaflets 11–17, oblong-lanceolate, viscid-hairy; nut elongated, ovoid.
J. cinerea
A. Leaflets 12–23, ovate-lanceolate, not viscid, hairy; nut globose. **J. nigra**

Winter key to the species
A. Bark gray; pith dark brown; leaf-scar not notched along upper margin, hairy fringe above. **J. cinerea**
A. Bark dark brown; pith light brown; leaf-scar notched along upper margin, no hairy fringe above. **J. nigra**

Butternut
Juglans cinerea Linnaeus

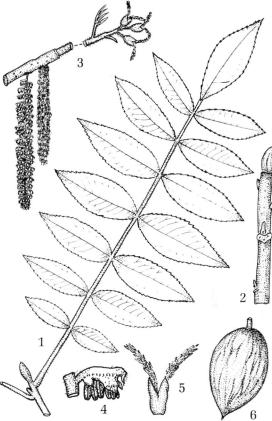

24. Juglans cinerea
1. Branch with leaf, x ¼.
2. Branch with winter-buds, x ½.
3. Branch with staminate catkins and pistillate flowers, x ½.
4. Staminate flower, enlarged.
5. Pistillate flower, enlarged.
6. Fruit, x ½.

HABIT. A small to medium-sized tree 10–15 m tall, occasionally to 30 m, with a short trunk and broad, round-topped, often irregular crown.

BARK. Bark gray, deeply fissured into wide smooth ridges; inner bark light colored.

STEMS. Young branchlets hairy, glandular, becoming smooth, roughened by leaf-scars, bitter to taste; leaf-scar large, 3-lobed, the upper margin straight or convex, not notched, with hairy fringe above leaf-scar, with 3 clusters of bundle-scars each arranged in a U-shaped line; pith chambered, dark brown.

WINTER-BUDS. Terminal bud 1–2 cm long, oblong-conical, somewhat flattened, bluntly pointed, brownish, downy; lateral buds smaller, ovoid, often superposed.

LEAVES. Alternate, compound; leaflets 11–19, oblong-lanceolate, pointed at apex, toothed on margin, 6–12 cm long, finely hairy above, hairy and glandular beneath;

petioles and rachis viscid-hairy.

FLOWERS. May. Staminate flowers in unbranched catkins, 5–8 cm long. Pistillate flowers in 5- to 8-flowered catkins.

FRUIT. Fruit ovoid-oblong, 4.0–6.5 cm long, very viscid-hairy; nut ovoid-oblong, thick-shelled, pointed at one end, 4- to 5-ribbed.

DISTRIBUTION. New Brunswick and Quebec west to Dakota and Minnesota, south to Arkansas and along the mountains to Georgia.

HABITAT. Prefers low, rich woods, river banks and lower fertile hillsides.

CULTIVATION NOTES. The Butternut produces a beautiful wood and delicious fruits, but as a timber tree it is much less valuable than *Juglans nigra*. The nut contains a sweet, edible, very oily kernel. The tree is common in Pennsylvania. It is also planted as an ornamental tree but it seldom attains a large size. It grows best on rich moist soil.

Black Walnut
Juglans nigra Linnaeus

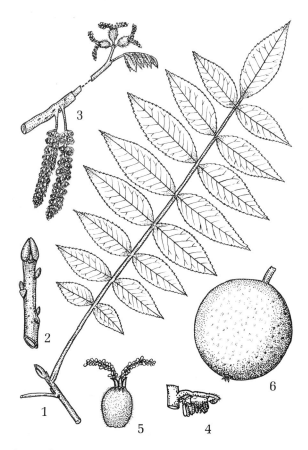

25. Juglans nigra
1. Branch with leaf, x ¼.
2. Branch with winter-buds, x ½.
3. Branch with staminate catkins and pistillate flowers, x ½.
4. Staminate flower, enlarged.
5. Pistillate flower, enlarged.
6. Fruit, x ½.

HABIT. A large tree to 50 m, with straight trunk and a round-topped crown.

BARK. Bark thick, rough and deeply furrowed, dark brown to grayish brown; inner bark light colored.

STEMS. Young branchlets hairy; leaf-scars large, 3-lobed, notched along upper margin, without hairy fringe above leaf-scar, with 3 clusters of bundle-scars each arranged in a U-shaped line; pith chambered, pale brown.

WINTER-BUDS. Terminal bud 7–8 mm long, ovoid, bluntly pointed, slightly flattened, silky hairy; lateral buds smaller, superposed.

LEAVES. Alternate, compound; leaflets 15–23, ovate-oblong to ovate-lanceolate, sharply pointed, rounded at base, irregularly toothed, 6–12 cm long, at first minutely hairy above, becoming nearly smooth and somewhat shiny; hairy and glandular beneath.

FLOWERS. May. Staminate flowers unbranched, the catkins 5–12 cm long; stamens 20–30. Pistillate flowers in 2- to 5-flowered catkins.

FRUIT. Fruit rounded or slightly pear-shaped, 3.5–5.0 cm across, hairy; nut more or less rounded, slightly compressed, 3–4 cm across, strongly and irregularly sculptured.

DISTRIBUTION. New England and New York west to Minnesota and south to Texas and Florida.

HABITAT. Prefers rich bottom lands and fertile hillsides.

CULTIVATION NOTES. The Black Walnut is a highly valued timber tree with beautiful wood. The nut is oily, edible and much prized. As a large tree, it is highly ornamental and desirable. It should be planted in rich moist soil to obtain the best growth.

70

Black Walnut *(Juglans nigra)*

Butternut *(Juglans cinera)*

71

HICKORIES
Carya *(Juglandaceae)*

There are some 20 species in the genus *Carya*, primarily in North America, from eastern North America south to Mexico. Only 1 or 2 little known species are found in eastern Asia. Six species are native to Pennsylvania.

The Hickories are deciduous trees similar in appearance to the Walnuts, but can be distinguished by the solid pith, dehiscent husk of the fruit, and smooth nut. The leaves are large, odd-pinnate and with opposite leaflets. The staminate and pistillate flowers are borne on the same tree, appearing in late spring after the leaves unfold. The staminate flowers are arranged in pendulous catkins and the pistillate ones in few- to many-flowered spikes. The large fruit has a husk splitting into 4 valves when mature and containing a smooth, often angled nut.

There are several species extending into limited areas in the eastern United States. The Pecan, *Carya pecan* (Marshal) Engler and Graebner (*C. illinoensis* K. Koch), extends from Mexico and Texas eastward to Indiana. The species is characterized by 11–17 oblong-lanceolate leaflets, flattened yellowish winter-buds, stalkless staminate catkins and elongated more or less cylindrical fruits. Resembling the Pecan is the Water Hickory, *C. aquatica* (Michaux f.) Nuttall, a swamp-land species of the Coastal Plain, extending north to Virginia. It differs from the former in having fewer leaflets (7–13), reddish brown buds, stalked staminate catkins and more rounded fruits. Another southern species, the Pale Hickory, *C. pallida* (Ashe) Engler and Graebner, extends from Florida upland into North Carolina and Tennessee and along the Coastal Plain to southern New Jersey. It resembles the Sweet Pignut, *C. ovalis*, but with the winter-buds, petioles and the lower surface of the leaves hairy. It is so named because of the pale bark which is very rough.

The Hickories are important timber trees, yielding wood of exceptional quality. Most species of the genus also have edible nuts, and some, such as the Pecan, *C. pecan* and the Shagbark Hickory, *C. ovata,* are planted as fruit trees. The different species are all handsome plants often planted as ornamental trees.

CARYA
Summer key to the species

A. Leaflets 7–11.   **C. cordiformis**
A. Leaflets 5–7, rarely 9.

  B. Branchlets and petioles smooth; husk of fruit thin, splitting tardily into 4 valves.

    C. Leaflets usually 5 (3–7); fruit obovoid, gradually narrowed toward the base, splitting to or near the middle.   **C. glabra**
    C. Leaflets usually 7 (5–7); fruit nearly globose, not narrowed at base, splitting to or near the base.   **C. ovalis**

  B. Branchlets and petioles more or less hairy; husk of fruit thick, splitting freely at the base into 4 valves.

    C. Leaflets mostly 5 (3–7), usually nearly smooth.   **C. ovata**
    C. Leaflets 7 (5–9), usually hairy.

      D. Bark close, rough, with narrow ridges but not shaggy; branchlets stout; leaves 20–30 cm long.   **C. tomentosa**
      D. Bark shaggy, separating into long plates; branchlets not stout; leaves over 30 cm long.   **C. laciniosa**

Bitternut Hickory *(Carya cordiformis)*

Winter key to the species

A. Buds yellow, the scales 4–6, opposite and valvate.   **C. cordiformis**
A. Buds not yellow, the scales 10 or more, usually overlapping.

    B. Buds smaller, the terminal ones 6–12 mm long, their outer scales glandular, dotted; branchlets slender.

        C. Bark close and ridged; terminal bud pointed.   **C. glabra**
        C. Bark soon breaking into small plates or scales; terminal bud blunt.
                                                             C. ovalis

    B. Buds larger, the terminal ones 1–2 cm or more; their outer scales scarcely glandular; branchlets stout.

        C. Bark close, rough, with narrow ridges but not shaggy; nut brownish, with small kernel; outer scales of terminal bud early deciduous.
                                                   C. tomentosa
        C. Bark shaggy; nut white to yellowish, with large kernel; outer scales of terminal bud persistent to tardily deciduous.

            D. Terminal buds about 2.5 cm long; nut dull white and yellowish, pointed at both ends.   **C. laciniosa**
            D. Terminal buds to 2 cm long; nut white, rounded or notched at the base.   **C. ovata**

Bitternut Hickory
Carya cordiformis *(Wangenheim)* K. Koch

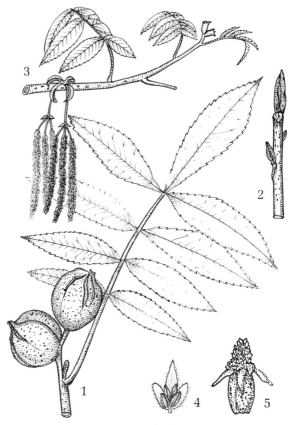

26. Carya cordiformis
1. Branch with fruits, x ½.
2. Branch with winter-buds, x 1.
3. Branch with staminate and pistillate flowers, x ½.
4. Staminate flower, enlarged.
5. Pistillate flower, enlarged.

HABIT. A rather large tree 20–30 m high, with a long trunk and round-topped crown.

BARK. Bark light brown, rather thin, with shallow fissures and narrow ridges, not peeling off or shaggy.

STEMS. Young branchlets rusty hairy at first, finally smooth, shiny and reddish brown, with numerous elongated lenticels; leaf-scars large, conspicuous, raised, somewhat triangular, with many bundle-scars scattered irregularly or arranged in groups of 3; pith brown.

WINTER-BUDS. Terminal bud about 2 cm long, long-pointed, flattish, glandular, yellow; lateral buds smaller, more or less 4-angled, usually superposed.

LEAVES. Alternate, compound, 15–25 cm long; leaflets 7–11, ovate-lanceolate to lanceolate, 8–15 cm long, sharply pointed at apex, toothed on margins, light green and hairy beneath especially along the midrib, becoming nearly smooth.

FLOWERS. May. Staminate flowers in drooping catkins 8–10 cm long, clustered in 3's on a stalk, the scales 3-lobed, hairy; stamens 4, the anthers yellow, bearded. Pistillate flowers in 2- to 5-flowered catkins about 12 mm long, scurfy-hairy.

FRUIT. Fruit obovoid to nearly globose, 2.0–3.5 cm long, 4-winged above the middle, the husk thin, yellowish glandular-dotted, splitting below the middle into 4 valves; nut broadly ovoid to nearly globose, more or less flattened, abruptly short-pointed, gray, small, thin-shelled; kernel very bitter.

DISTRIBUTION. Quebec to Minnesota, south to Florida and Louisiana.

HABITAT. Prefers a rich soil. Grows on low, wet woodlands or along the borders of streams, but also found in high dry uplands.

CULTIVATION NOTES. The Bitternut Hickory produces a valuable wood but the nut is not edible. It is an ornamental tree with a rather broad crown and handsome foliage. The tree stands transplanting better and grows more rapidly than other native species of the same genus. It prefers sunlight and does not tolerate shade very well.

Pignut
Carya glabra *(Miller)* Sweet

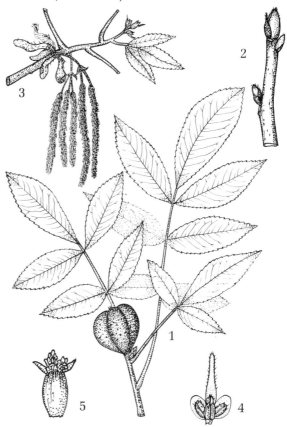

27. Carya glabra
1. Branch with fruits, x ½.
2. Branch with winter-buds, x 1.
3. Branch with staminate and pistillate flowers, x ½.
4. Staminate flower, enlarged.
5. Pistillate flower, enlarged.

HABIT. A tree to 30 m, occasionally to 40 m, with a slender trunk and an oblong crown.

BARK. Bark dark gray, close, fissured shallowly with narrow ridges.

STEMS. Young branchlets smooth or nearly so, slender, yellowish green at first, becoming reddish brown, with numerous elongated lenticels; leaf-scars heart-shaped or more or less 3-lobed, with many bundle-scars scattered irregularly, arranged in a curved line, or grouped in clusters of 3.

WINTER-BUDS. Terminal bud 6–12 mm long, pointed, with the outer scales smooth, reddish brown, deciduous, the inner scales pale, hairy; lateral buds smaller.

LEAVES. Alternate, compound, 20–30 cm long; leaflets 3–7, usually 5, oblong to oblong-lanceolate, 5–8 cm long, sharply pointed at apex, finely toothed along margin, nearly smooth, dark green above, paler beneath; petioles and rachis smooth, green.

FLOWERS. May. Staminate flowers in pendulous catkins in 3's, 8–18 cm long, slender, yellowish green, hairy; scales 3-lobed; stamens 4, the anthers orange. Pistillate flowers in crowded, 2- to 5-flowered catkins, 5–6 mm long, yellow, hairy.

FRUIT. Fruit pear-shaped to obovoid-oblong, 2.5 cm long and 2 cm across, smooth, slightly winged toward apex, the husk splitting to about the middle; nut oblong to oval, brownish, not angled, the shell thick, bony; kernel usually astringent.

DISTRIBUTION. Maine to Ontario, south to Florida and Alabama.

HABITAT. Prefers deep, rich loam. Common on dry ridges and hillsides; rarer in swampy situations.

CULTIVATION NOTES. This is a tall handsome tree, producing a valuable wood. The nut is not edible. Because of the long taproot, the seedlings are difficult to transplant, and nuts should be planted. The tree prefers plenty of sunlight and rich loam, but it grows in any well-drained soil.

Sweet Pignut
Carya ovalis *(Wangenheim)* Sargent

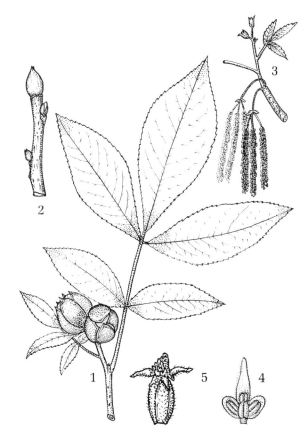

28. Carya ovalis
1. Branch with fruits, x ½.
2. Branch with winter-buds, x 1.
3. Branch with staminate and pistillate flowers, x ½.
4. Staminate flower, enlarged.
5. Pistillate flower, enlarged.

HABIT. A tree to 20 m, occasionally to 40 m, with a slender trunk and a narrowly oblong crown.

BARK. Bark close and furrowed on young trees, breaking into small scales or plates, often shaggy on old trunks.

STEMS. Young branchlets stout, downy at first, soon becoming smooth, with numerous elongated lenticels; leaf-scars heart-shaped or more or less 3-lobed, with many bundle-scars scattered irregularly, grouped in 3's, or arranged in a curved line.

WINTER-BUDS. Terminal bud 1–2 cm long, rather blunt, the outer scales smooth, reddish brown, deciduous, the inner scales pale, hairy; lateral buds smaller.

LEAVES. Alternate, compound; leaflets 5–7, oblong-ovate to oblong-lanceolate or oblong-obovate, 8–15 cm long, finely toothed along margin, yellowish downy while young, becoming smooth; petioles and rachis often reddish.

FLOWERS. May. Staminate flowers in pendulous catkins in 3's, 8–17 cm long, yellowish green, finely short-haired. Pistillate flowers in crowded 2- to 5-flowered catkins, 5–6 mm long, yellow, lepidote.

FRUIT. Fruit globose to ellipsoid, 2–3 cm long, slightly winged, the husk light brown, dull, warty, splitting to base; nut slightly flattened, rounded at apex or sometimes slightly angular, brownish, thin-shelled; kernel sweet.

DISTRIBUTION. Massachusetts to Wisconsin, south to Georgia, Alabama and Mississippi.

HABITAT. Prefers rich woodlands and bluffs.

CULTIVATION NOTES. This species is sometimes treated as a variety of the Pignut, *C. glabra*. It is a tree similar to the latter but with sweet instead of bitter kernel. The fruit is very variable in shape. Its cultivation is similar to that of the Pignut.

Pignut (*Carya glabra*)

Shagbark Hickory (*Carya ovata*)

Mockernut (*Carya tomentosa*)

Big Shell-bark Hickory (*Carya laciniosa*)

Shagbark Hickory
Carya ovata *(Miller)* K. Koch

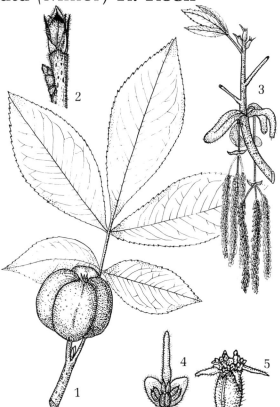

29. Carya ovata
1. Branch with fruits, x ½.
2. Branch with winter-buds, x 1.
3. Branch with staminate and pistillate flowers, x ½.
4. Staminate flower, enlarged.
5. Pistillate flower, enlarged.

HABIT. A large tree 20–25 m, occasionally to 40 m, with a straight trunk and a high oblong-cylindrical crown.

BARK. Bark light gray, shaggy, peeling off in rough strips or plates.

STEMS. Young branchlets downy-hairy at first, usually soon becoming smooth and reddish brown, with many conspicuous elongated lenticels; leaf-scars large, slightly raised, heart-shaped or more or less 3-lobed, with many bundle-scars arranged in 3's or scattered irregularly.

WINTER-BUDS. Terminal bud ovoid, bluntly pointed, 1–2 cm long, usually covered by about 10 bud-scales, the inner scales becoming large and conspicuous when unfolding in spring, yellowish green or reddish, densely downy on outer surface.

LEAVES. Alternate, compound, 20–35 cm long; leaflets 5, rarely 7, elliptic to oblong-lanceolate, 10–15 cm long, sharply pointed, tapering or rounded at base, toothed and densely ciliate along margins, hairy and glandular beneath when young, finally smooth.

FLOWERS. May. Staminate flowers hairy, green in drooping catkins in 3's 10-12 cm long; scales in 3 parts, bristle-tipped; stamens 4, the anthers yellow, bearded. Pistillate flowers in 2- to 5-flowered catkins, 15–17 mm long, brownish, woolly.

FRUIT. Fruit roundish, 3.5–6.0 cm long, the husk thick, splitting into 4 pieces to base; nut white, ellipsoid to broadly obovoid, slightly flattened and ridged, rather thin-shelled; kernel large, sweet.

DISTRIBUTION. Quebec west to Minnesota and south to Florida and Texas.

HABITAT. Prefers light, well-drained, loamy soil. Common on low moist hillsides, along streams and rivers, and on the borders of swamps.

CULTIVATION NOTES. This is an important species for its valuable wood and edible fruit. Next to the Pecan, this species is the best fruit tree of its genus; several varieties are in cultivation. It is more desirable to plant seeds as the tree has a long tap root and is difficult to transplant. It prefers plenty of light.

Mockernut
Carya tomentosa *(Lamarck)* Nuttall

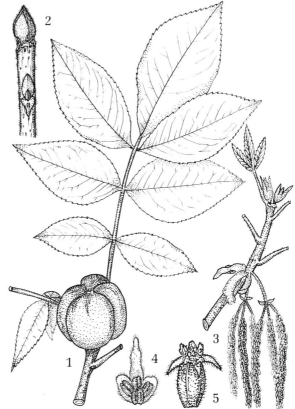

30. Carya tomentosa
1. Branch with fruits, x ½.
2. Branch with winter-buds, x 1.
3. Branch with staminate and
   pistillate flowers, x ½.
4. Staminate flower, enlarged.
5. Pistillate flower, enlarged.

HABIT. A large tree sometimes to 30 m with a straight trunk often swollen at base, and a round-topped crown.

BARK. Bark dark or light gray, rather close, with broad, flat, scaly, round ridges.

STEMS. Young branchlets stout, usually downy, sometimes nearly smooth, reddish brown, with numerous elongated lenticels; leaf-scars large, somewhat raised, heart-shaped or more or less 3-lobed, with many bundle-scars scattered irregularly, grouped in 3's or arranged in a curved line.

WINTER-BUDS. Terminal bud large, ovoid, 1.5–2.0 cm long, densely hairy, bluntly pointed, the outer pair of scales drops off in autumn, exposing the inner overlapping yellowish gray downy scales; lateral buds smaller, reddish brown.

LEAVES. Alternate, compound; leaflets 7–9, oblong to oblong-lanceolate, 8–18 cm long, sharply pointed, toothed along margin, densely hairy and glandular beneath, very fragrant when crushed; petioles and rachis hairy.

FLOWERS. May. Staminate flowers in slender drooping catkins 10–12 cm long, clustered in 3's on a stalk, green; scales 3-lobed, hairy; stamens 4–5, the anthers red. Pistillate flowers in 2- to 5-flowered catkins, hairy.

FRUIT. Fruit globose or pear-shaped, 3.5–5.0 cm long, the husk very thick and hard, splitting to the middle or nearly to the base; nut globose to ellipsoid, light brown, slightly flattened, 4-angled toward apex, thick-shelled; kernel small, sweet.

DISTRIBUTION. Massachusetts to Ontario and Nebraska, south to Florida and Texas.

HABITAT. Prefers rich, moist woodlands.

CULTIVATION NOTES. The Mockernut is a handsome tree producing a valuable wood. The fruit is large but the kernel is rather small. The tree has a long taproot and hence it is difficult to transplant. Planting should be done with seeds rather than seedlings. The tree requires moisture and sunshine, and does not thrive in shady situations.

81

Big Shell-bark Hickory
Carya laciniosa *(Michaux f.)* Loudon

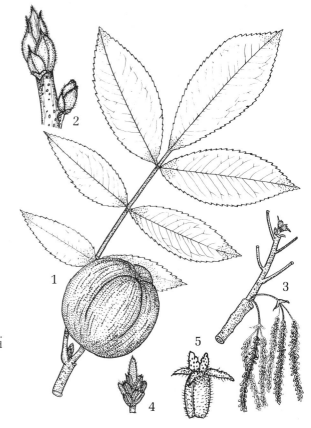

31. Carya laciniosa
1. Branch with fruits, x ½.
2. Branch with winter-buds, x 1.
3. Branch with staminate and pistillate flowers, x ½.
4. Staminate flower, enlarged.
5. Pistillate flower, enlarged.

HABIT. A tree to 40 m tall with a straight trunk and a highly cylindrical crown.

BARK. Bark shaggy, light gray, peeling off in rough strips or plates.

STEMS. Young branchlets hairy at first, later becoming nearly smooth and orange, with many elongated, rather inconspicuous lenticels; leaf-scars large, somewhat raised, heart-shaped or more or less 3-lobed, with many bundle-scars arranged in a line, grouped in 3's or scattered irregularly.

WINTER-BUDS. Terminal bud ovoid, to 2.5 cm long, bluntly pointed, usually covered by about 10 scales, the inner scales becoming large and conspicuous when unfolding in spring, yellowish green or reddish, downy on outer surface.

LEAVES. Alternate, compound; leaflets 7, rarely 5 or 9, oblong-lanceolate, 10–20 cm long, sharply pointed, toothed along margin, hairy beneath; petioles and rachis hairy or smooth, often persistent during winter.

FLOWERS. May. Staminate flowers in slender drooping catkins 12–20 cm long, clustered in 3's on a stalk, yellowish green; scales 3-lobed, hairy; stamens 4, the anthers yellow, hairy. Pistillate flowers in crowded, 2- to 5-flowered catkins, tomentose, light green.

FRUIT. Fruit ellipsoid to roundish, 4–7 cm long, 4-ribbed above the middle, the husk very thick, splitting readily to base; nut ellipsoid or roundish, slightly flattened and obscurely 4-angled, pointed at ends, yellowish or reddish, thick-shelled; kernel sweet.

DISTRIBUTION. New York and Pennsylvania west to Iowa, south to Tennessee and Arkansas.

HABITAT. Prefers deep, rich bottom lands and fertile hillsides.

CULTIVATION NOTES. This is an important timber tree, producing valuable wood and also edible nuts. On account of the long taproot, it is difficult to transplant and needs to be started from seeds.

Mockernut *(Carya tomentosa)*

BIRCHES
Betula *(Betulaceae)*

The genus *Betula* comprises some 40 species in the northern hemisphere. They are deciduous trees or shrubs, essentially of the northern regions. About 15 species are native to North America and 5 to Pennsylvania.

The species of Birch are graceful trees with colorful bark marked by characteristically horizontally elongated lenticels. The buds are sessile and with 3 to several imbricate scales. The leaves are generally ovate, doubly toothed or slightly lobed on margin, with few or many veins. The unisexual flowers, appearing in the spring before or with the developing leaves, are borne on the same tree. The staminate flowers form elongated catkins in autumn and remain naked during winter, becoming long and pendulous when they open in the following spring. There are 3 flowers to a bract, each with a minute calyx and 2 bifid stamens. The pistillate flowers form small slender catkins below the staminate. There are also 3 flowers to each bract but the flowers are without a calyx. The fruit is a small nut, compressed and winged, and attached to a thin, 3-lobed scale which drops together with the nut when mature. These scales are arranged on an axis in a cone-like structure which is known as a strobile.

Besides the species described here there is a lesser known species of northern distribution, the Blue Birch, *Betula caerulea-grandis* Blanchard. This is a species of eastern Canada, extending south through New England to eastern New York. It is a large tree with whitish bark resembling the European White Birch but the branchlets are spreading and not pendulous and the leaf-bases are round and toothed. It has also longer fruiting strobiles, 2.5–5.0 cm long.

Besides the native species, a species commonly planted as a shade and ornamental tree in northeastern United States is the European White Birch, *B. pendula* Roth, originally of Europe and western Asia. The tree has white, exfoliating bark and graceful, more or less drooping branches and smooth branchlets. It resembles the native Paper Birch, *B. papyrifera,* but the latter has more ascending branches with pendulous glandular branchlets.

Some of the Birch species are valued as timber trees. Most of the species are handsome plants useful as ornamentals. They are adaptable to poor dry soil or boggy situations. However, they are relatively short-lived plants.

BETULA
Summer key to the species

A. Leaves with 7 or more pairs of veins.
  B. Leaves light green beneath, the base rounded to heart-shaped.
    C. Leaves triangular in outline, long sharp point at apex. **B. populifolia**
    C. Leaves not triangular in outline, the apex pointed to short and sharply pointed.
      D. Bark close, reddish brown; young branchlets nearly smooth; bracts of strobiles smooth. **B. lenta**
      D. Bark peeling off, yellowish; young branchlets hairy; bracts of strobiles hairy. **B. lutea**
  B. Leaves whitish beneath, the base wedge-shaped. **B. nigra**
A. Leaves with 3–7 pairs of veins. **B. papyrifera**

Winter key to the species

A. Bark peeling off in thin papery layers.
  B. Outer bark white; inner bark orange-yellow. **B. papyrifera**
  B. Outer bark not white, but yellow to reddish brown.
    C. Bark yellow to yellowish gray. **B. lutea**
    C. Bark reddish brown, the inner bark tinged with red. **B. nigra**
A. Bark close, not peeling off in papery layers.
  B. Bark white, with triangular black spots below the branches; small trees, often in clumps. **B. populifera**
  B. Bark reddish brown; large trees. **B. lenta**

Gray Birch
Betula populifolia Marshall

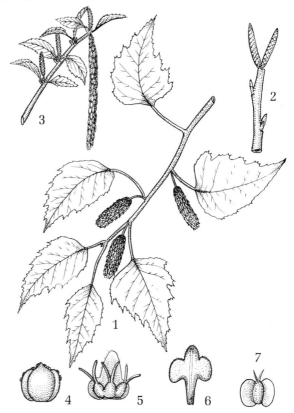

32. Betula populifolia
1. Branch with fruits, x ½.
2. Branch with winter-buds and young staminate catkins, x ½.
3. Branch with staminate and pistillate catkins, x ½.
4. Staminate scale, enlarged.
5. Pistillate flowers with scale, enlarged.
6. Fruiting scale, enlarged.
7. Nut, enlarged.

HABIT. A small tree attaining to a height of 10 m, usually occurring in clumps; trunk slender, the branches ascending with drooping ends, forming a narrow pyramidal crown.

BARK. Bark on old trunks black and roughened with fissures; on young trunks chalky or ashy white, close, smooth, not peeling off into thin film-like layers, with triangular black spots below the branches.

STEMS. Branchlets slender, greenish to brown, densely warty-glandular, covered by raised, pale, horizontally elongated lenticels; leaf-scars small, semi-oval in outline, with 3 small bundle-scars.

WINTER-BUDS. Buds ovoid, pointed, pale chestnut-brown, smooth, about 5–6 mm long.

LEAVES. Alternate, simple, triangular-ovate or triangular, 6–8 cm long, 4–5 cm wide, sharply long-pointed at apex, wedge-shaped at base, coarsely and doubly toothed on margin, shiny above; petioles long, slender, 1.5–3.0 cm long.

FLOWERS. April. Staminate catkins solitary or sometimes in pairs, 5–10 cm long. Pistillate catkins cylindrical, slender, about 12 mm long, stalked.

FRUIT. Fruit a strobile about 1.5–3.0 cm long, slender, cylindrical, blunt at apex, slender-stalked; scales 3-lobed, small, spreading, hairy, the lateral lobes broad, recurving, the terminal lobe straight, narrow. Seeds small, oval, winged, the wings broader than the nutlet.

DISTRIBUTION. Nova Scotia west to Ontario and south to Delaware and southern Pennsylvania.

HABITAT. Grows in both dry and poor and boggy soils.

CULTIVATION NOTES. The Gray Birch is a small tree of little commercial value. It is, however, an attractive tree for ornamental purposes. The tree is of small size and short-lived.

Cherry Birch
Betula lenta Linnaeus

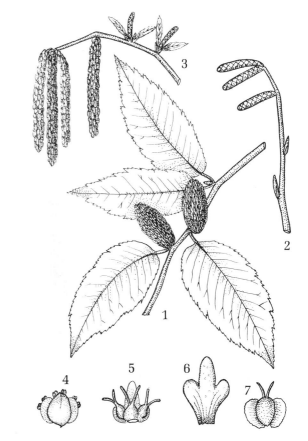

33. Betula lenta
1. Branch with fruits, x ½.
2. Branch with winter-buds and young staminate catkins, x ½.
3. Branch with staminate and pistillate catkins, x ½.
4. Staminate scale, enlarged.
5. Pistillate flowers with scale, enlarged.
6. Fruiting scale, enlarged.
7. Nut, enlarged.

HABIT. A large tree to 25 m in height, with long slender branches forming a wide spreading crown.

BARK. Bark dark reddish brown, peeling off into large, thick irregular plates.

STEMS. Branchlets at first green and hairy, becoming brown and smooth, with wintergreen-like flavor, covered with elongated, horizontal lenticels; leaf-scars small, semi-oval in outline, with 3 small bundle-scars.

WINTER-BUDS. Terminal bud absent; lateral buds about 6 mm long, conical, sharply pointed, somewhat flattened; the scales reddish brown, hairy.

LEAVES. Alternate, simple, ovate, 6–12 cm long, 3.5–6.5 cm wide, sharply pointed at apex, usually heart-shaped at base, toothed on margin, with long silky hairs beneath when young, dark green above, pale green beneath; petioles slender, 1.5–2.5 cm long.

FLOWERS. April. Staminate catkins in clusters of 3, 7–10 cm long, slender, drooping, purplish yellow. Pistillate catkins erect, about 2.0–2.5 cm long, slender, pale greenish, sessile or nearly so.

FRUIT. Fruit a strobile, short-stalked or nearly sessile, 2–3 cm long, 1.5–2.0 cm thick, erect; scales 5–8 mm long, smooth or hairy, with narrow lobes, the middle lobe longer, narrower and more sharply pointed.

DISTRIBUTION. Newfoundland to Florida, west to Ontario, Illinois and Tennessee.

HABITAT. Prefers rich soil, but grows in wet or dry situations.

CULTIVATION NOTES. The Cherry Birch is a valuable timber tree and furnishes one of the best fuel woods in Pennsylvania. It also yields an oil which is used as a substitute for wintergreen. The tree is an ornamental one, pyramidal when young, becoming round-headed when old. It is attractive in early spring with its slender drooping catkins. It is, however, a slow grower and subject to fungi attack when young.

Yellow Birch
Betula lutea Michaux

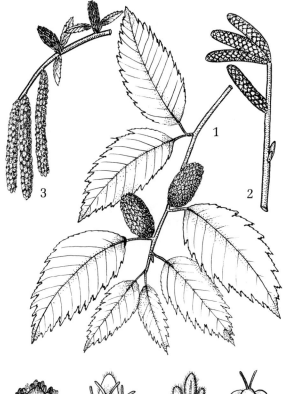

34. Betula lutea
1. Branch with fruits, x ½.
2. Branch with winter-buds and young staminate catkins, x ½.
3. Branch with staminate and pistillate catkins, x ½.
4. Staminate scale, enlarged.
5. Pistillate flowers with scale, enlarged.
6. Fruiting scale, enlarged.
7. Nut, enlarged.

HABIT. A large tree to 30 m in height, with long slender branches forming a wide open crown.

BARK. Bark yellowish or silvery gray, separating into thin papery scales, becoming reddish brown on older trunks; young bark aromatic and somewhat bitter.

STEMS. Branchlets green and hairy when young, becoming brown and smooth, finally dull silvery gray, covered with elongated horizontal lenticels; leaf-scars small, semi-oval in outline, with 3 small bundle-scars.

WINTER-BUDS. Terminal bud absent; lateral buds about 6 mm long, conical, somewhat flattened, pointed, the scales chestnut-brown, more or less hairy.

LEAVES. Alternate, simple, ovate to oblong-ovate, 8–12 cm long, pointed at apex, wedge-shaped or heart-shaped at base, doubly toothed on margin, with long pale hairs on both surfaces, becoming smooth at maturity, dull green above, yellowish green beneath; petioles slender, 1.5–2.5 cm long.

FLOWERS. April. Staminate catkins slender, drooping, to 7.5–10.0 cm long, purplish yellow. Pistillate catkins erect, to 2.5 cm long, sessile or nearly so, the scales pointed, light red and hairy above, green below.

FRUIT. Fruit an erect strobile, ovoid, 2–3 cm long and 1.5–2.0 cm thick, short-stalked or nearly sessile; scales numerous, 5–8 mm long, 3-lobed, hairy; the lobes narrow, upright, the middle one longer. Seeds small, winged, the wings slightly narrower than the nutlet.

DISTRIBUTION. Newfoundland to Manitoba, south to the high mountains of Georgia and Tennessee.

HABITAT. Prefers rich moist uplands, borders of streams and swamps, but grows in wet and dry situations.

CULTIVATION NOTES. The Yellow Birch is a valuable timber tree but not much cultivated as an ornamental tree.

River Birch (Red Birch)
Betula nigra Linnaeus

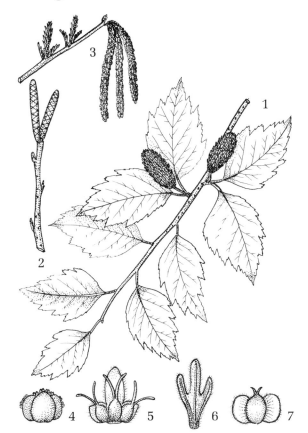

35. Betula nigra
1. Branch with fruits, x ½.
2. Branch with winter-buds and young staminate catkins, x ½.
3. Branch with staminate and pistillate catkins, x ½.
4. Staminate scale, enlarged.
5. Pistillate flowers with scale, enlarged.
6. Fruiting scale, enlarged.
7. Nut, enlarged.

HABIT. A medium-sized tree 20–30 m, with a more or less irregular narrow, oblong crown.

BARK. Bark dark reddish brown on old trunks, separating into irregular scales; on younger trunks reddish brown to greenish brown, peeling off into thin, papery scales.

STEM. Young branchlets slender, greenish and hairy, becoming reddish brown and smooth, covered by pale horizontally elongated lenticels; leaf-scars small, semioval in outline, with 3 small bundle-scars.

WINTER-BUDS. Terminal bud absent; lateral buds ovoid, sharply pointed, smooth or slightly hairy; scales chestnut-brown.

LEAVES. Alternate, simple, ovate, 3–8 cm long, pointed at apex, wedge-shaped at base, doubly toothed on margin, dark green above, pale yellowish green beneath and hairy beneath when young, finally only on the veins.

FLOWERS. April. Staminate catkins in clusters of 3, to 5–8 cm long. Pistillate catkins about 1.5 cm long.

FRUIT. Fruit an erect oblong strobile 2.5–3.5 cm long, slender-stalked; scales numerous, hairy, 3-lobed, with upright, linearoblong lobes, the terminal lobe larger than the laterals. Seeds winged, the wings half to nearly as broad as nutlet.

DISTRIBUTION. Massachusetts to Florida, west to Minnesota and Kansas.

HABITAT. Prefers moist, sandy soil, along banks of streams, lakes and swamps; sometimes found in drier situations.

CULTIVATION NOTES. The River Birch is of little commercial importance but it is attractive as an ornamental tree. It has a graceful appearance with its oblong crown and slender branchlets. Because it is a moisture-loving tree, it is especially desirable for cultivation in very swampy locations and for use in such situations for soil-binding purposes.

Paper Birch *(White Birch, Canoe Birch)*
Betula papyrifera Marshall

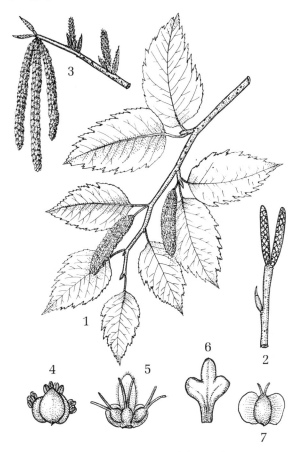

36. Betula papyrifera
1. Branch with fruits, x ½.
2. Branch with winter-buds and young staminate catkins, x ½.
3. Branch with staminate and pistillate catkins, x ½.
4. Staminate scale, enlarged.
5. Pistillate flowers with scale, enlarged.
6. Fruiting scale, enlarged.
7. Nut, enlarged.

HABIT. A large tree to 30 m, occasionally to 40 m in height, usually with ascending branches forming a narrow open crown.

BARK. Bark chalky to creamy white, peeling off in thin yellow-tinged layers.

STEMS. Branchlets stout, hairy and green when young, becoming smooth and reddish brown, eventually whitish, covered with horizontally elongated lenticels; leaf-scars small, semi-oval in outline, with 3 small bundle-scars.

WINTER-BUDS. Terminal bud absent; lateral buds about 6 mm long, ovoid, flattish, pointed at apex, slightly resinous.

LEAVES. Alternate, simple, ovate to narrow-ovate, 4–10 cm long, 4–5 cm wide, sharply pointed at apex, narrowed or rounded at base, coarsely and usually doubly toothed on margin, dark green and smooth above, light green and hairy along the nerves to nearly smooth beneath; petioles stout, 1.5–3.0 cm long, hairy.

FLOWERS. April–May. Staminate catkins clustered in groups of 2–3, to 7–10 cm long, slender, drooping, brownish. Pistillate catkins clustered, about 2.5–4.0 cm long, slender, erect or spreading, the scales greenish, the styles bright red.

FRUIT. Fruit a cylindrical strobile 3–5 cm long, slender-stalked, usually drooping; scales long, with thick lateral lobes and longer middle lobe. Seeds small, winged, the wings wider than the nut.

DISTRIBUTION. Labrador to British Columbia and Washington, south to Pennsylvania, Michigan, Nebraska and Montana.

HABITAT. Prefers rich moist slopes and borders of streams, lakes and swamps; found scattered in drier situations.

CULTIVATION NOTES. The Paper Birch is native only in the northern part of the state. It is widely planted as an ornamental tree. The characteristic white bark, once removed, is never renewed.

Gray Birch (*Betula populifolia*)

Cherry Birch *(Betula lenta)*

Yellow Birch
(Betula lutea)

91

River Birch (*Betula nigra*)

Paper Birch *(Betula papyrifera)*

HORNBEAMS
Carpinus *(Betulaceae)*

American Hornbeam *(Carpinus caroliniana)*

The genus *Carpinus* comprises about 30 species of deciduous trees and shrubs in the northern hemisphere. Only 1 species is native to North America.

The Hornbeams are small to medium-sized trees with a short trunk, smooth or scaly grayish bark and slender branchlets. The buds are pointed, with many imbricate scales. The alternate, simple, toothed leaves are more or less 2-ranked, with straight veins. The unisexual flowers appear on the same tree as catkins at the same time as the leaves in the spring. The staminate catkins, enclosed in the bud during winter, emerge in spring and are pendulous. The flowers are naked, each bearing several bifid stamens. The pistillate catkins are terminal and slender. There are 2 flowers to 1 bract, each flower subtended by 2 bractlets. The flower has a small, toothed perianth and a 2-celled ovary with a short style and 2 stigmas. The fruit is a ribbed nutlet subtended by a large bract.

The Hornbeams are ornamental trees with handsome foliage. The wood is very hard and tough. Besides the native species, the European Hornbeam, *C. betulus* Linnaeus, originally from Europe and western Asia, is commonly cultivated in the eastern states and used sometimes for tall hedges. Several horticultural varieties are in cultivation. It is similar to the American Hornbeam in foliage but the leaves are slightly narrower and thicker in texture, with the veins more impressed on the upper surface. It is a larger tree, with larger buds. The fruiting bracts are 3- to 5-nerved at the base instead of 5- to 7-nerved as in the American species.

American Hornbeam
Carpinus caroliniana Walter

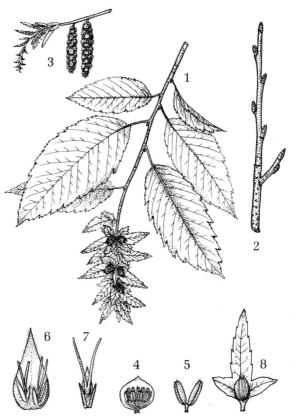

37. Carpinus caroliniana
1. Branch with fruits, x ½.
2. Branch with winter-buds, x ½.
3. Branch with staminate and pistillate catkins, x ½.
4. Staminate flower with scale, enlarged.
5. Stamen, enlarged.
6. Pistillate flowers with scale, enlarged.
7. Pistillate flowers with bracts, enlarged.
8. Nut with involucre, x 1.

HABIT. A small tree or shrub, usually attaining a height of 10–12 m, with a short fluted trunk and ascending branches forming a round-topped crown.

BARK. Bark thin, close, dark-bluish gray, often mottled with lighter or darker patches.

STEMS. Branchlets slender, pale green and silky, becoming smooth, shiny, and dark red, covered with scattered pale lenticels; leaf-scars small, elevated, elliptic, with 3 inconspicuous bundle-scars.

WINTER-BUDS. Buds 3 mm long, narrowly ovoid, pointed, hairy, brownish, covered with 8–12 4-ranked bud-scales.

LEAVES. Alternate, simple, ovate-oblong, 6–12 cm long, 2.5–6.0 cm wide, sharply pointed at apex, rounded or wedge-shaped at base, sharply double-toothed, deep green and smooth above, pale green with scattered hairs along the nerves and axillary tufts of hairs beneath.

FLOWERS. April–May. Staminate catkins 2.5–4.0 cm long, drooping, the scales greenish, saucer-shaped, each bearing 3–20 stamens. Pistillate catkins 1–2 cm long, the scales greenish, hairy, each bearing 2 pistils with long, bright scarlet styles.

FRUIT. Fruit a small nut enclosed by a leaf-like, 3-lobed bract, the nut corrugated, about 8 mm long, the bracts ovate to ovate-lanceolate, 2–3 cm long, with short, broad lateral lobes and a long, pointed terminal lobe, 1- to 2-toothed on margin; bracts arranged in a stalkless strobile 4–5 cm long.

DISTRIBUTION. Nova Scotia to Minnesota, south to Florida and Texas.

HABITAT. Prefers a deep, rich, moist soil along borders of streams and swamps.

CULTIVATION NOTES. A small tree of little economic importance but an ornamental one, with its bushy growth, fluted trunk, slender and often slightly drooping branches and leaves turning beautifully orange and scarlet in autumn. It is a slow-growing tree. While moisture-loving, it will also grow in drier locations, especially in shaded situations.

HOP-HORNBEAMS
Ostrya *(Betulaceae)*

American Hop-Hornbeam *(Ostrya virginiana)*

The genus *Ostrya* comprises some 7 species in the temperate regions of the northern hemisphere, 2 native to North America.

The species of the Hop-Hornbeam genus are deciduous trees with scaly, rough bark and pointed buds with many imbricate scales. The ovate leaves are doubly toothed. The flowers are unisexual, and both the staminate and pistillate ones, appearing with the leaves, occur on the same tree. The staminate flowers are without a perianth and have 3–4 bifid stamens to each bract. They form long, slender, drooping catkins, naked during winter. The pistillate catkins are slender and upright, each bract bearing 2 flowers. The calyx is adnate to the ovary which is enclosed in an open tubular involucre formed by the union of the bract and 2 bractlets. The fruit is a ribbed nutlet enclosed by the characteristic bladder-like involucre. The nutlets and their involucre form imbricately into a short drooping strobile.

The Hop-Hornbeams are ornamental trees with a neat round form and handsome foliage. A few species introduced from Europe and Asia are cultivated in North America.

American Hop-Hornbeam
Ostrya virginiana *(Miller)* **K. Koch**

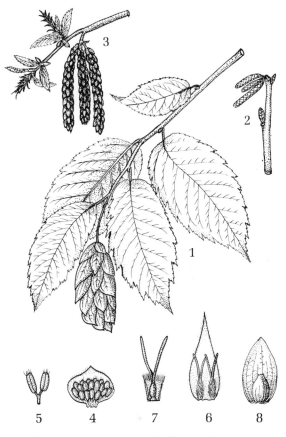

38. Ostrya virginiana
1. Branch with fruits, x ½.
2. Branch with winter-buds and young staminate catkins, x ½.
3. Branch with staminate and pistillate catkins, x ½.
4. Staminate flower with scale, enlarged.
5. Stamen, enlarged.
6. Pistillate flowers with scale, enlarged.
7. Pistillate flowers with bracts opened, enlarged.
8. Vertical section of fruiting involucre showing nut, x 1.

HABIT. A tree usually 7–10 m in height, but may reach 20 m, with spreading, often drooping branches and ascending branchlets forming a high, open, broad crown.

BARK. Bark brownish, thin, roughened by loose flat scales.

STEMS. Branchlets slender, brownish green and hairy, becoming smooth, shiny, and dark brown; leaf-scars small, flattened, 2-ranked, with 3 small bundle-scars.

WINTER-BUDS. Terminal bud absent; lateral buds ovoid, 2–3 mm long, pointed, reddish brown, smooth and slightly hairy.

LEAVES. Alternate, simple, ovate-oblong, 6–12 cm long, pointed at apex, rounded, wedge-shaped or heart-shaped at base, double-toothed on margin, dull yellowish green above, pale green beneath.

FLOWERS. April–May. Staminate catkins usually in 3's, cylindrical, drooping, to 5 cm long, the scales reddish brown, the stamens 3–14. Pistillate catkins erect, usually in pairs, each flower enclosed in a hairy, sac-like bract.

FRUIT. Fruit a small, flat, spindle-shaped nutlet 6–8 mm long, enclosed in an inflated sac-like bract, the bract covered with long hairs at base; bracts arranged in a hop-like, stalked, hanging cluster or strobile.

DISTRIBUTION. Cape Breton Islands, Ontario and Minnesota to Florida and Texas.

HABITAT. Prefers dry, gravelly slopes and ridges.

CULTIVATION NOTES. The American Hop-Hornbeam produces a valuable wood but it is not an important timber tree due to its small size. As an ornamental tree it is well adapted for planting on lawns and in parks. The tree is not easily transplanted. It grows well in the shade of other trees.

BEECHES
Fagus *(Fagaceae)*

American Beech *(Fagus grandifolia)*

There are about 10 species in the genus *Fagus* distributed in the temperate regions of the northern hemisphere. Only 1 species is native to North America.

The species of the genus are large deciduous trees with smooth bark. The buds are slender and pointed. The toothed or nearly entire-margined leaves are alternate but 2-ranked. The flowers are unisexual, and the staminate and pistillate flowers appear with the leaves on the same tree. The staminate flowers, each with a 4- to 7-lobed perianth and 8–16 stamens, group in large numbers into a slender-stalked head. The pistillate flowers, usually in 2's, are sur- rounded by a 4-part involucre formed by many bracts. The nut is enclosed in a woody 4-valved involucre covered on the outside with prickly or bract-like appendages.

The Beeches are ornamental trees with handsome leaves. The nuts are edible and contain oil. A widely planted species in the eastern states is the Euro- pean Beech, *F. sylvatica* Linnaeus, with many horticultural varieties differing in habit as well as in shape and color of the leaves. The tree is similar to the American Beech but can be distin- guished by the slightly broader, less pointed leaves with fewer veins and fewer prominent teeth on the margin.

American Beech
Fagus grandifolia Ehrhart

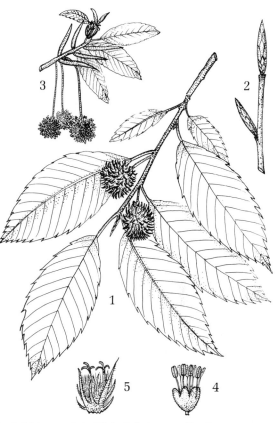

39. Fagus grandifolia
1. Branch with fruits, x ½.
2. Branch with winter-buds, x ½.
3. Branch with staminate and pistillate flower-clusters, x ½.
4. Staminate flower, enlarged.
5. Pistillate flower, enlarged.

HABIT. A large tree to 30 m in height, occasionally reaching to 40 m, forming a dense symmetrical crown.

BARK. Bark close, smooth, light gray, mottled with dark spots.

STEMS. Branchlets slender, dark yellow to gray, hairy, becoming smooth, covered with yellowish lenticels; leaf-scars narrow, almost encircling branchlet, with a few scattered bundle-scars.

WINTER-BUDS. Buds long and slender, 5 times as long as wide, conical, sharply pointed, lustrous, brown, the scales 10–20, smooth and with hairy margins.

LEAVES. Alternate, simple, stiff-leathery, ovate-oblong, 6–12 cm long, sharply pointed at apex, usually wedge-shaped at base, coarsely toothed on margin, silky when unfolding, becoming smooth at maturity, dark bluish green above, light green beneath; petioles 3–8 mm long.

FLOWERS. April–May. Staminate flowers in a stalked round head about 2.5 cm across, yellowish green; calyx bell-shaped, 4- to 7-lobed, hairy; corolla absent; stamens 8–10; stalk long, slender, hairy. Pistillate flowers in 2-flowered clusters on short hairy stalks; calyx urn-shaped, 4–5 lobed; ovary 3-celled.

FRUIT. Fruiting clusters a stalked, prickly burr containing many triangular nuts; involucre with slender straight or recurved prickles about 2 cm long; nuts pale brown, shiny, with sweet edible kernel.

DISTRIBUTION. Nova Scotia to Ontario and Wisconsin, south to Florida and Texas.

HABITAT. Prefers rich, moist, well-drained loam but also does well in gravelly slopes and rich uplands.

CULTIVATION NOTES. The American Beech is a desirable ornamental tree because of its clean trunk and limbs and the deep shade it provides. It is relatively free from insect pests. The tree grows well on a great variety of soils. It has a shallow root system that often sends up many suckers.

CHESTNUTS
Castanea *(Fagaceae)*

American Chestnut *(Castanea dentata)*

There are about 10 species in the genus *Castanea,* distributed in the temperate regions of the northern hemisphere. Three species are native to eastern North America and 1 to Pennsylvania.

The species of *Castanea* are deciduous trees with furrowed bark. The branchlets are without terminal buds and the lateral buds are covered by 3–4 scales. The leaves are alternate and 2-ranked, with toothed margins and many parallel veins. The flowers are unisexual, and the staminate and pistillate ones occur on the same tree. The staminate flowers are arranged in erect cylindrical catkins. The pistillate flowers usually occur on the lower part of those staminate catkins borne at the upper end of the branch. The large brown nuts appear several together in a prickly involucre which splits at maturity into 2–4 valves.

The species of *Castanea* are valuable timber as well as ornamental trees. The large foliage and the long staminate catkins are attractive. The nuts are important food in many countries. The American Chestnut, under the attack of the Chestnut-bark disease commonly known as Chestnut Blight, is threatened with rapid extinction. The more immune species from the Old World, and hybrids between these and the American species, are now commonly cultivated. The two more widely planted species are the Spanish Chestnut, *C. sativa* Miller, of Europe, North Africa and western Asia, and the Chinese Chestnut, *C. mollissima* Blume, of China. These two can be distinguished from the American Chestnut by their leaves, which are hairy beneath, and by the hairy winter-buds. The Spanish Chestnut has leaves rounded to subcordate at base and lepidote-glandular beneath near the veins. The Chinese Chestnut has leaves rounded to truncate at base, without lepidote glands beneath.

American Chestnut
Castanea dentata *(Marshall)* Borkhausen

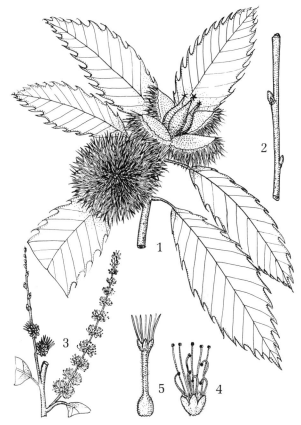

40. Castanea dentata
1. Branch with fruits, x ½.
2. Branch with winter-buds, x ½.
3. Branch with staminate and pistillate flower-clusters, x ½.
4. Staminate flower, enlarged.
5. Pistillate flower, enlarged.

HABIT. A large tree to 30 m, forming a deep wide-spreading crown in open situations.

BARK. Bark on old trunk gray-brown, with shallow fissures and broad flat ridges; smoother on young trunks and older branches.

STEMS. Branchlets stout, smooth or nearly so, shiny, round or angular, green at first becoming dark brown; covered with numerous small, white, raised lenticels; leaf-scars semi-oval, raised with many bundle-scars.

WINTER-BUDS. Terminal bud absent; lateral buds ovoid, about 6 mm long, pointed, brown, the scales 2–3.

LEAVES. Alternate, simple, oblong-lanceolate, 12–24 cm long, sharply pointed at apex, narrowed at base, coarsely toothed on margin, smooth on both surfaces except for minute glands beneath when young.

FLOWERS. June–July. Staminate catkin, long, slender, the flowers arranged in crowded clusters along the axis. Pistillate flowers appear as rounded involucres.

FRUIT. Fruit a burr about 5–6 cm across, covered with many sharp and rigid prickles, containing usually 2–3, rarely 5, nuts; the nuts 1.5–2.5 cm across.

DISTRIBUTION. Maine to Michigan, south to Delaware, and along the mountains to Alabama and Mississippi.

HABITAT. Grows in a great variety of soils except limey or very wet situations.

CULTIVATION NOTES. The American Chestnut, formerly the most common tree of Pennsylvania, is now nearly completely eliminated by Chestnut Bark Disease (caused by *Endothia gyrosa* var. *parasitica*), commonly known as the Chestnut Blight. As there is no means of checking this disease, it is desirable to plant oriental chestnut species or hybrids immune to it.

101

OAKS
Quercus *(Fagaceae)*

The Oak genus is a large one, comprising over 300 species of trees (rarely, shrubs) widely distributed throughout the northern hemisphere. Over 60 species are native to North America and 16 species to Pennsylvania.

The Oaks are generally massive deciduous or evergreen trees. The buds are covered by many imbricate scales. The alternate, simple leaves are toothed or lobed on the margin, rarely entire. They are provided with parallel secondary nerves. The flowers are unisexual, staminate and pistillate borne on the same tree. The staminate flowers, with a small 4- to 7-part calyx and (usually) 6 stamens, are arranged in slender drooping catkins. The pistillate flowers, with a similar calyx and an ovary, usually 3-celled, bearing 3 styles stigmatic on the inner side, occur either singly or few to many in spikes. The fruit is a nut (acorn) subtended by a cup-like involucre made up of many imbricate scales.

The Oaks are divided into two groups. (1) Red Oaks: The leaves have bristle-pointed lobes and apex. The acorns mature in the autumn of the second season. The kernels are bitter. (2) White Oaks: The leaves have rounded lobes and apex. The acorns mature the first season. The kernels are usually sweet.

The Oaks are much planted as ornamental trees because of their especially handsome foliage, brilliantly colored in autumn. Many species are important timber trees. As hybrids occur naturally and as most of the species are quite variable, identification is often difficult.

Besides the 16 species described in detail here the following species occur in the eastern United States south of Pennsylvania.

Turkey Oak, *Quercus laevis* Walter. A small tree with leaves resembling the Spanish Oak, *Q. falcata,* but lighter green in color, more narrowly lobed, with much shorter petioles. Of the southern Coastal Plain north to North Carolina and southeast Virginia.

Laurel Oak, *Quercus laurifolia* Michaux. A distinctive tree with oblong to lanceolate entire leaves which are thin and membranaceous. Of low woods and swamplands in the South, north along the Coastal Plain to Virginia.

Overcup Oak, *Quercus lyrata* Walter. A large tree similar to the Post Oak, *Q. stellata,* differing in the short-stalked fruit, with a rounded depressed-topped acorn nearly covered by the coarsed-scaled cup. A swampland species of the South, north to Indiana and along the Coastal Plain to southern New Jersey.

Basket Oak, *Quercus prinus* Linnaeus. A tree somewhat similar to the Yellow Chestnut Oak, *Q. muehlenbergii,* but with the teeth of the leaves more or less rounded. A swampland species of the South extending north to New Jersey along the coast and to southern Indiana inland.

Water Oak, *Quercus nigra* Linnaeus. A tree with slender branches and distinctly obovate entire leaves sometimes with 3 short rounded lobes at the apex. Of dry woods or bottomlands of the South north to Kentucky and Delaware. It is often planted as a street tree.

Shumard's Red Oak, *Quercus shumardii* Buckley. A tree resembling the Scarlet Oak, *Q. coccinea,* but can be differentiated by the grayish hairy acorn cups. Of rich woods in the South extending north to Maryland, West Virginia and southern Indiana.

Live Oak, *Quercus virginiana* Miller. A distinct evergreen tree with thick firm leaves which are entire-margined or only rarely spiny-toothed. On sandy soils in the South, north to southeastern Virginia. It is often planted in the South as a street tree.

Besides the native species, a number of introduced species are commonly cultivated in the eastern states as ornamentals. Among these are the Turkey Oak, *Q. cerris* Linnaeus, of Europe and western Asia, and the English Oak,

Q. robur Linnaeus, of Europe, North Africa and western Asia. The Turkey Oak is a tall tree with spreading short branches forming a pyramidal head. The dark green foliage turns brown in autumn. The English Oak is also a tall tree but with stout branches forming an open broad head. The dark green foliage stays green late in fall. Both species are very variable with many horticultural forms in cultivation.

QUERCUS
Summer key to the species

A. Leaves entire.
  B. Leaves lanceolate to linear-oblong, to 2 cm broad, the lower surfaces smooth. **Q. phellos**
  B. Leaves oblong to oblong-lanceolate, 2–5 cm broad, the lower surfaces usually hairy. **Q. imbricaria**
A. Leaves pinnately lobed or toothed.
  B. Lobes or teeth of leaves without bristle tips.
    C. Leaves deeply lobed.
      D. Leaves smooth, pale beneath. **Q. alba**
      D. Leaves more or less hairy beneath.
        E. Leaves white-downy beneath, the terminal lobe usually largest. **Q. macrocarpa**
        E. Leaves rusty downy beneath, the middle lobe usually largest. **Q. stellata**
    C. Leaves coarsely toothed.
      D. Leaves with 3–8 teeth on each side.
        E. Leaves 7–15 cm long, with 3–7 more or less rounded or blunt teeth on each side; small tree or shrub. **Q. prinoides**
        E. Leaves 12–15 cm long, with 6–8 irregular rounded teeth on each side; tall tree. **Q. bicolor**
      D. Leaves with 10 or more teeth on each side.
        E. Leaves obovate or obovate-oblong, the teeth rounded. **Q. montana**
        E. Leaves lanceolate, the teeth sharply pointed. **Q. muehlenbergii**
  B. Lobes or teeth of leaves with bristled tips.
    C. Leaves broadly obovate, 3- to 5-lobed at apex, rusty hairy beneath. **Q. marilandica**
    C. Leaves elliptic to oblong, pinnately lobed, green or white to grayish hairy beneath.
      D. Leaves white or grayish hairy beneath.
        E. Leaves 5–10 cm long, with usually 5 short triangular lobes. **Q. ilicifolia**
        E. Leaves 7–17 cm long with 3–7 narrow lobes often sickle-shaped. **Q. falcata**
      D. Leaves green beneath, smooth or hairy.
        E. Leaves more or less hairy beneath. **Q. velutina**
        E. Leaves smooth beneath, except for tufts of hairs in the axils of the veins.
          F. Leaves lobed more than halfway to the midribs, more or less shiny above.
            G. Leaves usually narrowed at base. **Q. palustris**
            G. Leaves usually wedge-shaped at base. **Q. coccinea**
          F. Leaves lobed less than halfway to the midribs, more or less dull above. **Q. borealis maxima**

Winter key to the species

A. Branchlets usually developing wide corky wings.   **Q. macrocarpa**
A. Branchlets not developing corky wings.

  B. Branchlets more or less hairy.

    C. Winter-buds sharply or bluntly pointed, often more than one at a node; shrub.   **Q. ilicifolia**
    C. Winter-buds more or less rounded at tips, often solitary at nodes; tree.

      D. Terminal buds small, less than 3 mm long.   **Q. stellata**
      D. Terminal buds larger, mostly over 3 mm long.

        E. Winter-buds angled, rusty brown hairy.   **Q. marilandica**
        E. Winter-buds not distinctly angled, light brown hairy.   **Q. falcata**

  B. Branchlets smooth.

    C. Terminal buds mostly less than 2 mm long.

      D. Winter-buds narrow, sharply pointed.

        E. Winter-buds angled.

          F. Branchlets stouter, reddish brown; buds strongly angled; acorn-cups saucer-shaped.   **Q. phellos**
          F. Branchlets slender, greenish brown; buds slightly angled; acorn-cups hemispheric.   **Q. imbricaria**

        E. Winter-buds not angled.

          F. Bark flaky; acorns sessile.   **Q. muehlenbergii**
          F. Bark not flaky; acorns stalked.   **Q. palustris**

      D. Winter-buds short, blunt or rounded at tips.

        E. Bark on branchlets peeling off in long dark scales; acorn long-stalked (over 2.5 cm).   **Q. bicolor**
        E. Bark on branchlets not peeling off in long dark scales; acorn sessile or nearly so.

          F. Shrub or small tree; branchlets slender; lateral buds often more than one at a node.   **Q. prinoides**
          F. Large trees; branchlets stout; lateral buds always solitary at a node.   **Q. alba**

    C. Terminal buds mostly over 3 mm long.

      D. Winter-buds sharply pointed.

        E. Buds densely gray-white hairy.   **Q. velutina**
        E. Buds smooth or only slightly hairy toward the tips.

          F. Winter-buds conical, angled; bark with dark prominently angled ridges.   **Q. montana**
          F. Winter-buds ovoid, very slightly angled; bark with light gray, flat-topped ridges.   **Q. borealis maxima**

      D. Winter-buds blunt or rounded at tips.   **Q. coccinea**

Willow Oak
Quercus phellos Linnaeus

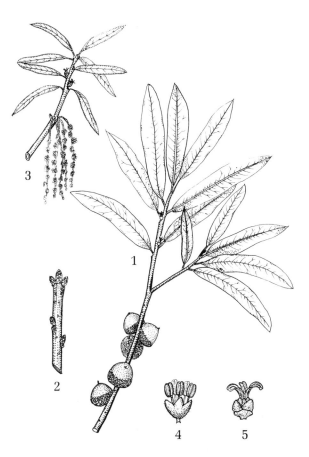

41. Quercus phellos
1. Fruiting branch, x ½.
2. Branch with winter-buds, x ½.
3. Branch with staminate and pistillate inflorescences, x ½.
4. Staminate flower, enlarged.
5. Pistillate flower, enlarged.

HABIT. A tree to 20 m high but sometimes reaching 30 m, with a usually narrow, rather open, pyramidal crown.

BARK. Bark thick, reddish brown, shallowly fissured, separating into irregular plates.

STEMS. Branchlets stout, smooth and shiny, reddish brown to dark brown; leaf-scars raised, concave above, rounded below.

WINTER-BUDS. Buds ovoid, 2–3 mm long, distinctly angular, sharply pointed, dark brown, the scales slightly toothed on margin.

LEAVES. Alternate, simple, linear-oblong to nearly lanceolate, 5–10 cm long, 1.0–2.5 cm wide, bristly and sharply pointed at apex, bluntly pointed at base, entire or slightly wavy on margin, shiny above, hairy beneath when young, becoming smooth and light green.

FLOWERS. May. Staminate flowers in slender, hairy catkins, 5–8 cm long. Pistillate flowers on smooth slender stalks.

FRUIT. Fruit a sessile usually solitary acorn; nut hemispherical, about 1 cm high, yellowish brown, enclosed only at base by the saucer-shaped cup, the scales thin, reddish brown, hairy.

DISTRIBUTION. New York to Florida, west to Missouri and Texas.

HABITAT. Prefers wet sandy soil, along swamps and streams, sometimes also on higher grounds.

CULTIVATION NOTES. The Willow Oak is of little commercial importance as a timber tree but is a desirable ornamental tree for streets and parks. The tree has willow-like leaves turning pale yellow in the fall.

Shingle Oak
Quercus imbricaria Michaux

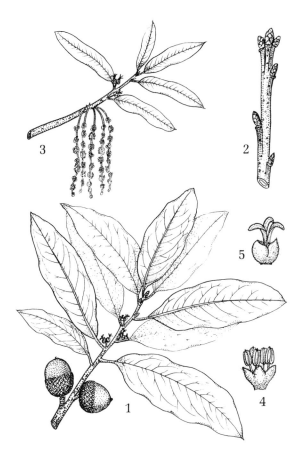

42. Quercus imbricaria
1. Fruiting branch, x ½.
2. Branch with winter-buds, x ½.
3. Branch with staminate and pistillate inflorescences, x ½.
4. Staminate flower, enlarged.
5. Pistillate flower, enlarged.

HABIT. A tree usually to 20 m high, but occasionally reaching 30 m, with an open, shallow crown in mature trees.

BARK. Bark thick, brown, shallowly fissured, separating into low ridges covered by light brown scales.

STEMS. Branchlets slender, smooth, at first green and shiny, soon light brown to dark brown; leaf-scars raised, concave above, rounded beneath.

WINTER-BUDS. Buds ovoid, 2–3 mm long, slightly angular, sharply pointed, the scales shiny, with toothed margins.

LEAVES. Alternate, simple, thin, oblong or oblong-lanceolate, 7–16 cm long, 2.5–5.0 cm wide, bluntly pointed at apex, wedge-shaped or rounded at base, entire or wavy on margin, the margins slightly thickened, rolled downward, dark green and shiny above, pale green and hairy beneath; petioles 5–15 mm long.

FLOWERS. May. Staminate flowers in slender, hairy catkins 5–8 cm long. Pistillate flowers yellow, on slender hairy stalks.

FRUIT. Fruit a short-stalked acorn, solitary or in pairs; nut ovoid, 1.0–1.5 cm high, dark brown, ⅓ to ½ enclosed by the hemispheric cup, the scales reddish brown, hairy.

DISTRIBUTION. Pennsylvania south to Georgia and west to Nebraska.

HABITAT. Prefers rich uplands and fertile bottom lands.

CULTIVATION NOTES. The Shingle Oak is not commercially important as a timber tree but has great attractiveness as an ornamental tree because of its form, which is pyramidal when young and round-topped when old. The lustrous foliage turns russet-red in fall.

White Oak
Quercus alba Linnaeus

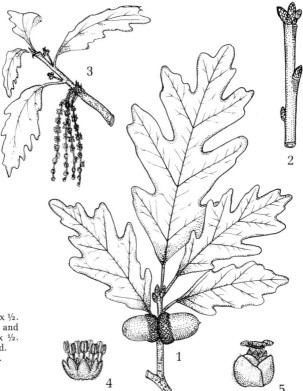

43. Quercus alba
1. Fruiting branch, x ½.
2. Branch with winter-buds, x ½.
3. Branch with staminate and pistillate inflorescences, x ½.
4. Staminate flower, enlarged.
5. Pistillate flower, enlarged.

HABIT. A large tree to 30 m in height, usually with many stout, spreading, twisted branches forming a deep, wide, broad, irregular crown in the open.

BARK. Bark light gray or whitish, shallowly fissured into flat, loosely attached irregular scales.

STEMS. Branchlets light green and hairy at first, soon becoming smooth and light reddish brown; covered with numerous minute, light, raised lenticels; leaf-scars raised, concave above, rounded below.

WINTER-BUDS. Buds broadly ovoid, about 3 mm long, bluntly pointed, the scales smooth, reddish brown.

LEAVES. Alternate, simple, obovate to oblong-obovate in outline, 10–22 cm long, 5–10 cm wide, narrowed at base, with 5–9 usually ascending, oblong lobes, hairy when unfolding, soon smooth, bright green above, bright green and sometimes bloomy beneath, the lobes blunt at apex, usually entire, separated by deep rounded sinuses; petioles 1.5–2.5 cm long.

FLOWERS. May. Staminate flowers in hairy catkins 5–8 cm long. Pistillate flowers yellow, short-stalked, hairy; styles spreading, red.

FRUIT. Fruit a sessile or short-stalked acorn; nut ovoid or rounded, 2.0–2.5 cm high, shiny, light brown, about ¼ enclosed in a bowl-shaped cup, the basal scales of cup much thickened.

DISTRIBUTION. Maine to Minnesota, south to Florida and Texas.

HABITAT. Grows well in many soils, in all open situations.

CULTIVATION NOTES. The White Oak is the most important hardwood species of Pennsylvania. Its noble appearance makes it an outstanding lawn tree; in the fall the bright green foliage turns to deep red or violet purple. It is difficult to transplant and grows slowly. Although tolerant of many soils, it grows best in rich moist soil.

Burr Oak
Quercus macrocarpa Michaux

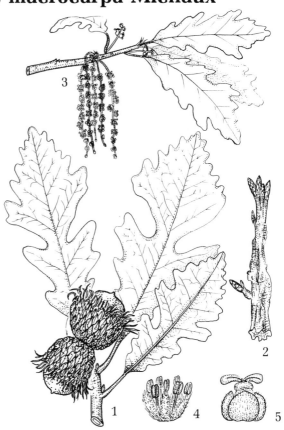

44. Quercus macrocarpa
1. Fruiting branch, x ½.
2. Branch with winter-buds, x ½.
3. Branch with staminate and pistillate inflorescences, x ½.
4. Staminate flower, enlarged.
5. Pistillate flower, enlarged.

HABIT. A medium-sized tree usually to 25 m in height, but occasionally reaching 55 m, with spreading branches forming a broad round-topped crown.

BARK. Bark fissured longitudinally and irregularly into ridges.

STEMS. Branchlets stout, yellowish brown, densely hairy at first, later smooth, with corky wings often 3.5 cm wide; covered with pale, raised and inconspicuous lenticels; leaf-scars raised, concave above, rounded below.

WINTER-BUDS. Buds broadly ovoid or conical, 3–5 mm long, sharply or bluntly pointed, reddish brown, pale hairy; terminal buds often clustered; lateral buds closely appressed.

LEAVES. Alternate, simple, obovate to oblong in outline, 10–24 cm long, 7–12 cm wide, narrowed at base, deeply 5- to 7-lobed, smooth, shiny and dark green above, paler with fine hairs beneath, the lobes very unequal, the lower 2–3 pairs usually separated by wide, deep sinuses from the (usu-ally) very large terminal lobe, pinnately cleft.

FLOWERS. May. Staminate flowers in slender hairy catkins 10–15 cm long. Pistillate flowers short-stalked, reddish, hairy; styles bright red.

FRUIT. Fruit a sessile or short-stalked acorn, usually solitary; nut ovoid or ellipsoid, 2.0–3.5 cm high, covered with down, about half-enclosed by the large cup, the upper scales forming a fringe-like edge, the lower ones much thickened.

DISTRIBUTION. Nova Scotia to Pennsylvania, west to Manitoba, Kansas and Texas.

HABITAT. Prefers low, rich bottom lands, but tolerant of many kinds of soils.

CULTIVATION NOTES. The Burr Oak is a valuable timber tree as well as an attractive ornamental and shade tree. It has a tall trunk and spreading branches forming a broad head. It grows well in moist lowlands, is rather intolerant of shade and is a slow grower.

Post Oak
Quercus stellata Wangenheim

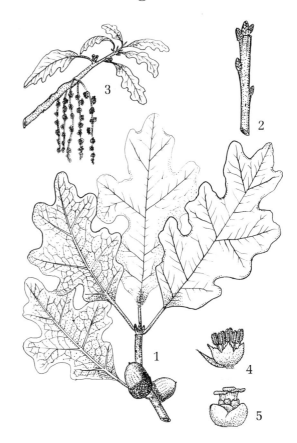

45. Quercus stellata
1. Fruiting branch, x ½.
2. Branch with winter-buds, x ½.
3. Branch with staminate and pistillate inflorescences, x ½.
4. Staminate flower, enlarged.
5. Pistillate flower, enlarged.

HABIT. A medium-sized tree to 20 m, rarely to 30 m in height, with stout, spreading branches forming a dense, broad, round-topped crown in the open.

BARK. Bark light gray, deeply fissured into flat irregular scales.

STEMS. Branchlets stout, light orange and woolly haired at first, becoming dark brown, finally smooth; leaf-scars raised, concave above, rounded below.

WINTER-BUDS. Buds broadly ovoid, about 3 mm long, bluntly pointed, the scales numerous, reddish brown, slightly hairy.

LEAVES. Alternate, simple, obovate in outline, 10–20 cm long, 7–12 cm wide, thick, leathery, narrowed at base, generally deeply 5-lobed, dark green and rough above, pale and rusty hairy beneath, the lobes unequal in size, the middle pair much larger, separated from the other lobes by deep sinuses; petioles 1–2 cm long.

FLOWERS. May. Staminate flowers in slender hairy catkins 10–15 cm long. Pistillate catkins short-stalked, woolly; styles bright red.

FRUIT. Fruit a sessile acorn, solitary, in pairs, or clustered; nut ovoid, 1.5–2.5 cm high, bluntly tipped, enclosed by the thin cup for ⅓–½ of its length, the scales thin, pointed, loosely appressed, hairy.

DISTRIBUTION. Massachusetts to central Pennsylvania, south to Florida and west to Nebraska and Texas.

HABITAT. Grows well on dry rocky soil, on gravelly uplands, limestone hills and sandy plains.

CULTIVATION NOTES. The Post Oak resembles the White Oak, especially in the wood. It is valued as an ornamental tree because of its dense round head and large dark green foliage. It can be grown on poorer soil than the White Oak. It also grows slowly, however, and is difficult to transplant.

Chinquapin Oak
Quercus prinoides Willdenow

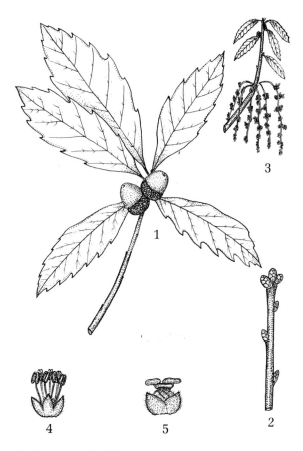

46. Quercus prinoides
1. Fruiting branch, x ½.
2. Branch with winter-buds, x ½.
3. Branch with staminate and pistillate inflorescences, x ½.
4. Staminate flower, enlarged.
5. Pistillate flower, enlarged.

HABIT. Usually a low spreading shrub to 2 m high, but sometimes a slender tree to 6 m in height, usually occurring in clumps.

BARK. Bark thin, light brown with light gray blotches, smooth at first, becoming rough.

STEMS. Young branchlets slender, at first dark green and rusty hairy, soon becoming reddish brown and smooth, marked with inconspicuous pale lenticels; leaf-scars raised, concave above, rounded below.

WINTER-BUDS. Buds broadly ovoid, 2 mm long, light brown, rounded at apex, the scales sometimes hairy on margin.

LEAVES. Alternate, simple, obovate to oblong, 6–12 cm long, 5.0–7.5 cm wide, bluntly pointed at apex, wedge-shaped at base, coarsely toothed with 3–7 pairs of rounded teeth on each margin, bright green and smooth above, grayish hairy beneath; petioles 5–10 mm long.

FLOWERS. May. Staminate flowers yellow, in hairy catkins 4–6 cm long. Pistillate flowers short-stalked; styles bright red.

FRUIT. Fruit a sessile acorn, solitary or in pairs; nut ovoid, 1.0–1.5 cm long, blunt-pointed, often covered with pale down, about ⅓ enclosed by the thin, rather deep cup, the scales indistinct, knobby below and thin at tip.

DISTRIBUTION. Maine to Minnesota, south to North Carolina, Alabama and Texas.

HABITAT. Prefers sandy soils, dry plains and woods, and rocky slopes.

CULTIVATION NOTES. The Chinquapin Oak is a shrub or small tree of no commercial value as a timber tree. It is also of little ornamental value.

Swamp White Oak
Quercus bicolor Willdenow

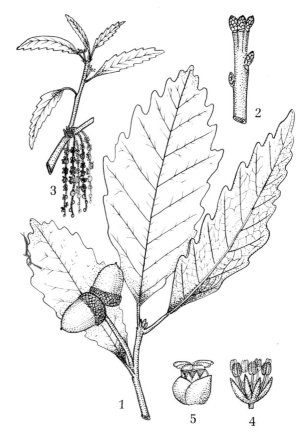

47. Quercus bicolor
1. Fruiting branch, x ½.
2. Branch with winter-buds, x ½.
3. Branch with staminate and
   pistillate inflorescences, x ½.
4. Staminate flower, enlarged.
5. Pistillate flower, enlarged.

HABIT. A medium-sized tree to 20 m in height, rarely to 30 m, with ascending upper branches and often drooping lower branches forming an open round-topped crown in the open.

BARK. Bark light grayish brown, deeply fissured into long flat ridges, breaking up into small gray scales.

STEMS. Branchlets stout, yellowish brown to reddish brown, short-hairy at first, soon becoming smooth, covered with pale raised lenticels; leaf-scars raised, concave above, rounded below.

WINTER-BUDS. Buds broadly ovoid to nearly rounded, 3–5 mm long, bluntly pointed, light brown, often slightly hairy above the middle.

LEAVES. Alternate, simple, obovate in outline, 10–16 cm long, bluntly pointed at apex, narrowed at base, coarsely toothed on margin with 6–10 pairs of entire, bluntly pointed teeth, dark green and shiny above, light green with fine hairs beneath; petioles 1–2 cm long.

FLOWERS. May. Staminate flowers in hairy catkins 8–10 cm long. Pistillate flowers solitary or few in a cluster on long, hairy stalks.

FRUIT. Fruit a long-stalked acorn, solitary or few in a cluster; nut ovoid-oblong, 2–3 cm high, chestnut-brown, usually hairy at apex, about ⅓ enclosed by the deeply saucer-shaped cup, the scales fringed along margin.

DISTRIBUTION. Quebec and Maine to Michigan, south to Georgia and Arkansas.

HABITAT. Prefers moist rich soils bordering swamps and along streams.

CULTIVATION NOTES. The Swamp White Oak is a valuable timber tree but has little ornamental value. The leaves turn yellow-brown, orange or red in fall.

111

Chestnut Oak
Quercus montana Willdenow

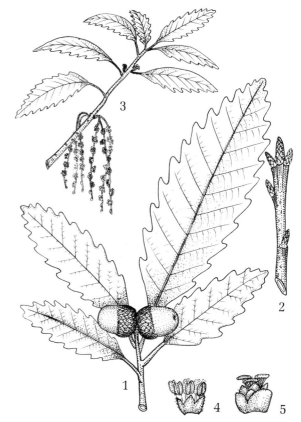

48. Quercus montana
1. Fruiting branch, x ½.
2. Branch with winter-buds, x ½.
3. Branch with staminate and pistillate inflorescences, x ½.
4. Staminate flower, enlarged.
5. Pistillate flower, enlarged.

HABIT. A medium-sized tree to 25 m, or occasionally to 30 m in height; in the open it is usually low and divided, forming a very broad open crown.

BARK. Bark thick, fissured into long, solid ridges.

STEMS. Branchlets stout, at first greenish purple, becoming reddish brown, hairy or smooth at first, later smooth and covered with inconspicuous lenticels; leaf-scars raised, concave above, rounded below.

WINTER-BUDS. Buds ovoid-conical, 6–12 mm long, distinctly sharp-tipped, chestnut-brown, the scales slightly hairy towards apex and on margin.

LEAVES. Alternate, simple, thick, stiff, obovate to lanceolate-oblong, 12–18 cm long, 5–10 cm wide, sharply or bluntly pointed at apex, usually wedge-shaped at base, coarsely toothed with 10–15 pairs of bluntly pointed teeth on margin, bright or yellowish green and smooth and shiny above, pale green and hairy at first beneath, becoming nearly smooth; petioles 1.5–3.0 cm long.

FLOWERS. May. Staminate flowers yellow, in hairy catkins 5–8 cm long. Pistillate flowers short-stalked; styles red.

FRUIT. Fruit an acorn on a short stalk, solitary or in pairs; nut ovoid, 2.5–3.5 cm high, smooth, glossy, ⅓–½ enclosed by the thin hemispheric cup, the scales reddish brown, with knobby bases and thin tips.

DISTRIBUTION. Maine to Ontario, south to South Carolina and Alabama.

HABITAT. Prefers dry rocky situations.

CULTIVATION NOTES. The Chestnut Oak is an important timber tree and its bark is highly valuable for its tannin. This light-demanding tree will grow straight when planted in dense stands but in the open often develops crookedly. It is sensitive to transplanting and best started from seed rather than seedlings.

Yellow Chestnut Oak
Quercus muehlenbergii Englemann

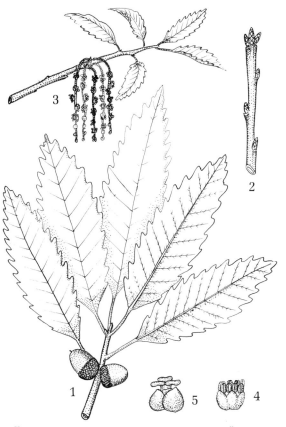

49. Quercus muehlenbergii
1. Fruiting branch, x ½.
2. Branch with winter-buds, x ½.
3. Branch with staminate and pistillate inflorescences, x ½.
4. Staminate flower, enlarged.
5. Pistillate flower, enlarged.

HABIT. A medium-sized tree usually attaining a height of 20 m, occasionally to 50 m, with small lateral branches forming a narrow round-topped crown.

BARK. Bark close, rough, fissured into long irregular ridges, breaking up into brownish or grayish scales.

STEMS. Branchlets slender, reddish brown to grayish brown, hairy at first, soon becoming smooth, covered with pale lenticels; leaf-scars raised, concave above, rounded below.

WINTER-BUDS. Buds broadly ovoid, about 2–3 mm long, sharply pointed, light chestnut-brown, the scales slightly hairy on margin.

LEAVES. Alternate, simple, oblong to oblong-lanceolate in outline, 10–16 cm long, sharply or bluntly pointed at apex, usually rounded at base, coarsely toothed on margin with 8–13 pairs of sharp, abruptly pointed, often incurved teeth, dark or yellowish green above, whitish hairy beneath; petioles 2.0–3.5 cm long.

FLOWERS. May. Staminate flowers in hairy catkins 8–10 cm long. Pistillate flowers sessile or on short stalks; styles bright red.

FRUIT. Fruit a sessile or short-stalked acorn; nut ovoid, 1.5–2.0 cm high, light chestnut-brown, hairy at apex, half-enclosed by the thin cup, the scales small woolly with thickened bases and thin tips.

DISTRIBUTION. Vermont to Virginia, west to Nebraska, New Mexico and Texas.

HABITAT. Prefers limestone soil; found on dry hillsides, rich bottom lands and rocky river banks.

CULTIVATION NOTES. The leaves of the Yellow Chestnut Oak resemble those of the chestnut. It is not as valuable a timber tree as some other species of oaks but it is highly ornamental for lawns and parks: it has an attractive form and handsome foliage.

113

Black-Jack Oak
Quercus marilandica Muenchhausen

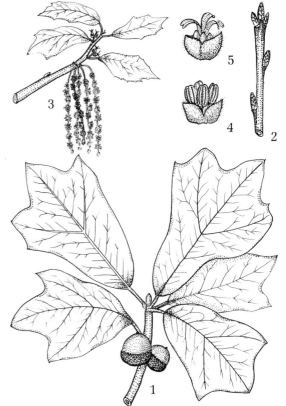

50. Quercus marilandica
1. Fruiting branch, x ½.
2. Branch with winter-buds, x ½.
3. Branch with staminate and pistillate inflorescences, x ½.
4. Staminate flower, enlarged.
5. Pistillate flower, enlarged.

HABIT. A small tree usually to 10 m high, but sometimes reaching 20 m in height, with short branches, ascending above and horizontal below, forming a usually compact, narrow, more or less round-topped crown.

BARK. Bark thick, dark brown to blackish, deeply fissured, separating into broad angular plates covered with blackish scales.

STEMS. Branchlets stout, at first covered by pale woolly hairs, becoming smooth and dark brown or grayish; leaf-scars raised, concave above, rounded below.

WINTER-BUDS. Buds ovoid, 6 mm long, distinctly angular, sharply pointed, reddish brown, the scales rusty hairy.

LEAVES. Alternate, simple, thick and leathery, broadly obovate in outline, 10–20 cm long, often nearly as broad at apex, rounded at base, shallowly 3- to 5-lobed at apex, dark green and smooth above, rusty brown hairy beneath, finally nearly smooth and yellowish green, the lobes very broad, entire or sparingly toothed; petioles 1–2 cm long.

FLOWERS. May. Staminate flowers in slender catkins 5–10 cm long. Pistillate flowers rusty hairy, on short, hairy stalks.

FRUIT. Fruit a short-stalked acorn, solitary or in pairs; nut ovoid-oblong, about 2 cm high, often striated, ⅓ to ⅔ enclosed by the hemispheric cup, the scales reddish brown, large, the upper scales smaller, forming a rim around the margin of the cup.

DISTRIBUTION. New York and Pennsylvania, south to Florida and west to Nebraska and Texas.

HABITAT. Prefers dry, sandy soil.

CULTIVATION NOTES. The Black-Jack Oak is shrubby and of little commercial value in the North although in the South it becomes larger and is used for fuel, charcoal and lumber. With its deep compact crown and large lustrous leaves turning brown or yellow in fall, it is a very attractive tree for ornamental purposes. It grows in a wide variety of soil conditions.

Scrub Oak
Quercus ilicifolia Wangenheim

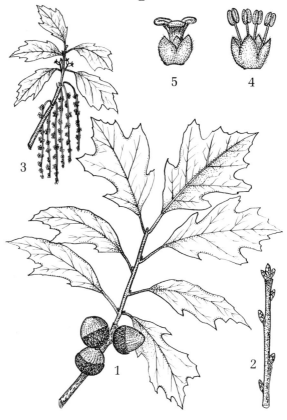

51. Quercus ilicifolia
1. Fruiting branch, x ½.
2. Branch with winter-buds, x ½.
3. Branch with staminate and
   pistillate inflorescences, x ½.
4. Staminate flower, enlarged.
5. Pistillate flower, enlarged.

HABIT. A spreading shrub with intricate crooked and intertwined branches, usually 2–3 m high, occasionally a small tree to 7 m in height.

BARK. Bark thin, gray to dark brown, smooth at first, becoming scaly.

STEMS. Branchlets slender, dark green tinged with red and hoary hairy at first, becoming dark brown and smooth; leaf-scars raised, concave above, rounded below.

WINTER-BUDS. Buds ovoid, 2–3 mm long, blunt at apex, chestnut-brown, the scales dark-margined.

LEAVES. Alternate, simple, thick and leathery, obovate or broadly ovate in outline, 10–20 cm long, 3.5–8.0 cm wide, wedge-shaped to rounded at base, 3- to 5-lobed with sharp- and bristle-pointed lobes separated by shallow sinuses, dark green and shiny above, covered with dense brownish hairs beneath, becoming nearly smooth, the lobes broad, entire or sparingly toothed, the midrib and veins yellow; petioles 1–2 cm long.

FLOWERS. May. Staminate flowers in catkins 10–12 cm long. Pistillate flowers reddish, on stout hairy stalks; styles red.

FRUIT. Fruit a short-stalked or sessile acorn, usually clustered; nut broadly ovoid, about 1 cm high, about half-enclosed by the saucer-shaped cup, the scales reddish brown, their free tips form a fringe around the edge of the cup.

DISTRIBUTION. Maine west to Ohio and south to Virginia and Kentucky.

HABITAT. Prefers rocky hillsides and gravelly or sandy barrens. ⟨

CULTIVATION NOTES. The Scrub Oak is of no commercial value as a timber tree. It often grows as a densely branched spreading shrub. Its gregarious habit and ability to grow in poor soils and exposed situations make it useful for prevention of erosion, sheltering of the forest floor and enrichment of the soil with humus.

115

Spanish Oak
Quercus falcata Michaux

52. Quercus falcata
1. Fruiting branch, x ½.
2. Branch with winter-buds, x ½.
3. Branch with staminate and pistillate inflorescences, x ½.
4. Staminate flower, enlarged.
5. Pistillate flower, enlarged.

HABIT. A medium-sized tree to 25 m, or occasionally to 30 m in height, with an open, broad round-topped crown.

BARK. Bark gray, shallowly fissured, separating into low, brown, scaly ridges.

STEMS. Branchlets stout, at first rusty hairy, becoming nearly smooth and reddish brown to grayish; leaf-scars raised, concave above, rounded below.

WINTER-BUDS. Buds ovoid, 2–3 mm long, sharp-pointed, bright chestnut-brown, the scales hairy.

LEAVES. Alternate, simple, obovate or ovate in outline, 8–20 cm long, 5–12 cm wide, broadly wedge-shaped at base, 5- to 7-lobed with bristly-pointed teeth, separated by broad variable sinuses, dark green and smooth above, covered by grayish down beneath, the lobes broadly triangular, entire or with few bristly teeth on margin; petioles 2.0–3.5 cm long.

FLOWERS. April–May. Staminate flowers in slender, hairy catkins 8–12 cm long. Pistillate flowers reddish, on short, stout stalks; styles short, spreading, dark red.

FRUIT. Fruit a short-stalked acorn; nut ovoid to rounded, 1.0–1.5 cm long, enclosed only at base or sometimes ⅓ by the saucer-shaped cup; the scales thin, reddish, pale hairy especially on margin.

DISTRIBUTION. New Jersey and southeastern Pennsylvania to Florida, west to Missouri and Texas.

HABITAT. Prefers dry gravelly or sandy soil.

CULTIVATION NOTES. The wood of the Spanish Oak is of inferior quality but the bark is rich in tannin. It is rather attractive as an ornamental tree, with its stout spreading branches forming a round-topped crown and dark green deeply cut drooping leaves.

Black Oak
Quercus velutina Lamarck

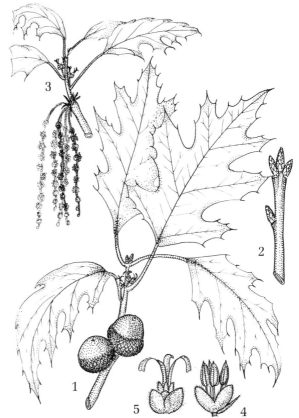

53. Quercus velutina
1. Fruiting branch, x ½.
2. Branch with winter-buds, x ½.
3. Branch with staminate and pistillate inflorescences, x ½.
4. Staminate flower, enlarged.
5. Pistillate flower, enlarged.

HABIT. A large tree usually to 30 m or occasionally to 50 m in height, with lateral branches ascending above and horizontal below, forming a deep, irregular, oblong, narrow or wide crown.

BARK. Bark rough, dark brown, deeply fissured into irregular, thick ridges.

STEMS. Branchlets stout, reddish brown, rusty hairy at first, becoming more or less smooth, covered with inconspicuous pale lenticels.

WINTER-BUDS. Buds large, ovoid, 8–12 mm long, angular, blunt-pointed, the scales yellowish white, hairy.

LEAVES. Alternate, simple, obovate to oblong in outline, 8–20 cm long, 7–10 cm wide, broadly wedge-shaped or rounded at base, deeply 3- to 7-lobed on margin, dark green and shiny above, pale to yellowish green beneath with axillary tufts of rusty hairs, the lobes sharp, bristly-pointed, entire or with few bristly teeth on margin,

gradually narrowed from a broad base; petioles 2.5–5.0 cm long.

FLOWERS. May. Staminate flowers on hairy catkins 10–15 cm long. Pistillate flowers reddish, on short hairy stalks.

FRUIT. Fruit a stalkless or short-stalked acorn, solitary or clustered; nut ovoid, 1.5–2.0 cm high, often hairy or striated, about half-enclosed by the top-shaped cup; the scales sharp-pointed, hairy, the upper scales forming a fringe-like border with their free tips.

DISTRIBUTION. Maine west to Minnesota, south to Florida and Texas.

HABITAT. Prefers dry or gravelly uplands; grows on poor soils or glaciated hills.

CULTIVATION NOTES. The Black Oak is not attractive as an ornamental tree and is of less value as a timber tree than other species of oak. It is sensitive to transplanting and is best planted with seeds than with seedlings.

Pin Oak
Quercus palustris Muenchhausen

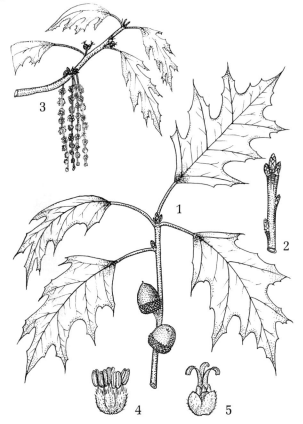

54. Quercus palustris
1. Fruiting branch, x ½.
2. Branch with winter-buds, x ½.
3. Branch with staminate and pistillate inflorescences, x ½.
4. Staminate flower, enlarged.
5. Pistillate flower, enlarged.

HABIT. A medium-sized tree usually to 25 m, or occasionally to 40 m in height, with the upper lateral branches ascending, the middle horizontal, and the lower short and drooping, forming a symmetrical conical crown.

BARK. Bark thick, smooth, shallowly fissured into low ridges covered by small close scales.

STEMS. Branchlets slender, at first hairy and dark red, becoming smooth and grayish brown, covered with inconspicuous pale lenticels; leaf-scars raised, concave above, rounded below.

WINTER-BUDS. Buds small, ovoid, 2–3 mm long, sharply pointed, light chestnut-brown, the scales smooth or very slightly hairy on margin.

LEAVES. Alternate, simple, ovate to elliptic in outline, 8–15 cm long, 5–10 cm wide, broadly wedge-shaped at base, deeply 5- to 9-lobed on margin, dark green and shiny above, pale green and smooth except for small axillary tufts of yellow hairs be-

neath, the lobes few-toothed, bristly-pointed, separated by broad, deep, rounded sinuses.

FLOWERS. May. Staminate flowers in hairy catkins 5–8 cm long. Pistillate flowers short-stalked; styles spreading, bright red.

FRUIT. Fruit a short-stalked or sessile acorn, solitary or in pairs; nut nearly rounded, 1.0–1.5 cm high, light brown, often striped, about ⅓ enclosed by the thin saucer-shaped cup, the scales closely overlapping, hairy.

DISTRIBUTION. Massachusetts west to Michigan and Wisconsin, south to Virginia, Tennessee and Oklahoma.

HABITAT. Prefers moist, rich soil of river bottom lands, borders of streams and swamps.

CULTIVATION NOTES. The Pin Oak is not a commercially important tree but is a valued ornamental. Its rapid growth, ease of transplanting, beautiful form and colorful autumn foliage make it a desirable shade and avenue tree.

Scarlet Oak
Quercus coccinea Muenchhausen

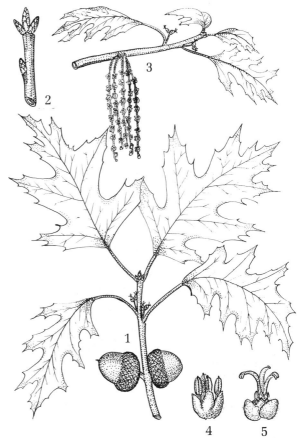

55. Quercus coccinea
1. Fruiting branch, x ½.
2. Branch with winter-buds, x ½.
3. Branch with staminate and pistillate inflorescences, x ½.
4. Staminate flower, enlarged.
5. Pistillate flower, enlarged.

HABIT. A medium-sized tree usually attaining a height of 25 m, with a narrow and shallow crown formed by lateral branches ascending above, horizontal in middle and drooping below.

BARK. Bark gray, deeply fissured into irregular, more or less rough ridges.

STEMS. Branchlets slender, smooth, reddish brown or grayish brown, covered with numerous, small, pale lenticels; leaf-scars raised, concave above, rounded below.

WINTER-BUDS. Buds broadly ovoid, 3–6 mm long, bluntly pointed, dark reddish brown, pale woolly above the middle.

LEAVES. Alternate, simple, ovate to oblong in outline, 10–25 cm long, 6–12 cm wide, broadly wedge-shaped at base, deeply 5- to 9-lobed on margin halfway to the middle of leaf or beyond, dark green and shiny above, brown hairy beneath at first, finally smooth except axillary tufts of hairs, the lobes broad, bristly toothed and separated by deep, rounded sinuses; petioles stout, 3–6 cm long, yellow.

FLOWERS. May. Staminate flowers in slender, hairy catkins 7.5–10.0 cm long. Pistillate flowers reddish, on short hairy stalks; styles recurved, bright red.

FRUIT. Fruit a sessile or short-stalked acorn, solitary or in pairs; nut ovoid, 1.3–2.0 cm high, about ⅓ to ½ enclosed by the thin hemispheric cup, the scales sharply pointed, slightly hairy.

DISTRIBUTION. Maine to Minnesota, south to Florida and Nebraska.

HABITAT. Prefers a light, dry, sandy soil.

CULTIVATION NOTES. A relatively unimportant commercial tree, the Scarlet Oak is highly valued ornamentally for its fast growth, attractive form and beautiful foliage turning brilliant scarlet in fall. It is one of the most desirable street and shade trees.

119

Red Oak
Quercus borealis Michaux f. *(var. maxima Ashe)*

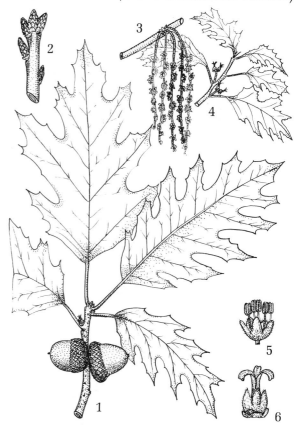

56. Quercus borealis maxima
1. Branch with fruits, x ½.
2. Branch with winter-buds, x ½.
3. Branch with staminate inflorescences, x ½.
4. Branch with pistillate inflorescences, x ½.
5. Staminate flower, enlarged.
6. Pistillate flower, enlarged.

HABIT. A large tree usually to 35 m but occasionally reaching 50 m in height, with a broad round-topped crown in the open.

BARK. Bark thick, dark brown, shallowly fissured into regular, continuous flat-topped ridges.

STEMS. Branchlets slender, smooth, greenish brown at first, becoming dark red; covered with inconspicuous pale lenticels; leaf-scars raised, concave above, rounded below.

WINTER-BUDS. Buds ovoid, 4–8 mm long, sharply pointed, light brown, the scales slightly hairy on margin.

LEAVES. Alternate, simple, firm, ovate to oblong in outline, 12–22 cm long, 10–15 cm wide, usually wedge-shaped at base, deeply 7- to 9-lobed on margin with ascending lobes, dull green above, grayish or whitish and smooth except for axillary tufts of brownish hairs beneath, the lobes with entire margin or a few irregular bristly pointed teeth; petioles 2–5 cm long.

FLOWERS. May. Staminate flowers in slender, hairy catkins 10–12 cm long. Pistillate flowers short-stalked; styles spreading, recurved, light green.

FRUIT. Fruit a short-stalked acorn, solitary or in pairs; nut ovoid, 2.5–3.0 cm high, narrowed at apex, enclosed only at base by the saucer-shaped cup, the scales reddish brown, sometimes hairy.

DISTRIBUTION. Nova Scotia west to Minnesota and south to Florida and Texas.

HABITAT. Prefers porous sandy or gravelly clay soil.

CULTIVATION NOTES. The Red Oak is a valuable timber tree. It makes an attractive shade and avenue tree as well with its straight trunk and stout spreading branches forming a symmetrical round-topped head, its smooth bark, and its large leaves turning dark red in fall. The tree is of rapid growth. It will not grow in wet soil and is intolerant of shade.

120

Willow Oak *(Quercus phellos)*

Shingle Oak *(Quercus imbricaria)*

121

White Oak *(Quercus alba)*

Burr Oak (Quercus macrocarpa)

Post Oak (Quercus stellata)

123

Swamp White Oak *(Quercus bicolor)*

Chestnut Oak *(Quercus montana)*

124

Yellow Chestnut Oak *(Quercus muehlenbergii)*

Black-Jack Oak *(Quercus marilandica)*

125

Scrub Oak (*Quercus ilicifolia*)

Spanish Oak (*Quercus falcata*)

Black Oak *(Quercus velutina)*

Pin Oak
(Quercus palustris)

127

Scarlet Oak (*Quercus coccinea*)

Red Oak *(Quercus borealis)*

ELMS
Ulmus *(Ulmaceae)*

About 18 species of the genus *Ulmus* are known in the temperate regions of the northern hemisphere. Six species are native to North America and 2 to Pennsylvania.

The species of Elms are noble deciduous trees with conspicuous buds. The alternate simple leaves are usually toothed on the margin and oblique at base, full and rounded on one side and more or less wedge-shaped on the other. The flowers are perfect, small and green, appearing in fascicles or racemes. There is a small lobed calyx and no perianth. The fruit, produced in great abundance, is a compressed nutlet surrounded by a broad wing. The fruit matures early and germinates the same season.

The Elms are valuable timber trees. As they are highly ornamental, they are often planted as street or shade trees.

Besides the introduced species, two species extend their range into limited areas in eastern North America. The Winged Elm, *Ulmus alata* Michaux, is so named because of the often corky-winged branches. It is a southern species extending north from Florida and Texas to Virginia, Kentucky, southern Indiana and southern Illinois. It is a small round-topped tree with nearly smooth buds and branchlets and sub-sessile leaves. The tree resembles the White Elm, but the flowers are in elongated instead of clustered racemes. The Cork Elm, *U. thomasii* Sargent, is so named because its older branches are often corky-ridged. It is a round-topped tree with hairy buds and branchlets and petiolate leaves. Its range extends from Quebec, west to Nebraska and south to Tennessee.

Among the introduced species, the following are most commonly planted. The English Elm, *U. procera* Salisbury (*U. campestris* Linnaeus), originally from Europe, is much planted in the northeastern United States in many garden forms. It is a tall tree with deeply fissured bark; the spreading and ascending branches form an oblong head. The Wych Elm, *U. glabra* Hudson, native to Europe and western Asia, having also many garden forms, is a tall tree with bark remaining smooth for many years. The Siberian Elm, *U. pumila* Linnaeus, from eastern Asia, is a medium-sized tree with rough bark and dense green foliage. It has ascending branches and a dense habit. The fourth species is the Smooth-leaved Elm, *U. carpinifolia* Gleditsch, of Europe, North Africa and western Asia. It is a tree with straight trunk, bright green foliage and slender ascending branches forming a pyramidal head.

ULMUS

Summer key to the species

A. Leaves smooth on the upper surface; branchlets and petioles smooth; fruit ovate. **U. americana**

A. Leaves very rough above; branchlets and petioles hairy; fruit round. **U. fulva**

Winter key to the species

A. Inner bark not mucilaginous; buds more or less smooth; branchlets smooth. **U. americana**

A. Inner bark very mucilaginous when chewed; buds densely brown hairy; branchlets hairy. **U. fulva**

White Elm
Ulmus americana Linnaeus

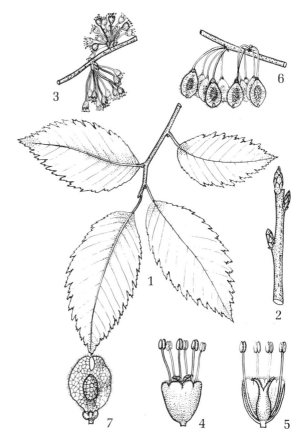

57. Ulmus americana
1. Leafy branch, x ½.
2. Branch with winter-buds, x ½.
3. Branch with flowers, x ½.
4. Flower, enlarged.
5. Vertical section of flower, enlarged.
6. Branch with fruits, x ½.
7. Fruit, x 1.

HABIT. A large tree attaining a height of 40 m, with variable growth forms; the trunk often divides near the ground in trees growing in the open.

BARK. Bark rather thick, light grayish, deeply fissured into rather broad, flat ridges which are firm or scaly.

STEMS. Branchlets slender, at first greenish and hairy, becoming reddish brown and smooth, covered with scattered, inconspicuous, pale lenticels; leaf-scars raised, semicircular, with corky surface.

WINTER-BUDS. Buds ovoid, about 4–5 mm long, sharply or bluntly pointed, reddish brown, smooth to slightly hairy, the scales about 6–10.

LEAVES. Alternate, simple, thick, ovate-oblong, 7–15 cm long, sharply pointed at apex, unequal at base, doubly toothed on margin, rough above, hairy to nearly smooth beneath; petioles 5–8 mm long.

FLOWERS. April. Flowers perfect, 3- to 4-clustered on drooping stalks 1–2 cm long; stamens 7–8; stigmas white.

FRUIT. Fruit a slender-stalked samara, elliptic, about 1 cm long, deeply notched at apex, fringed with hairs on margin.

DISTRIBUTION. Newfoundland to Florida, west to the Rocky Mountains.

HABITAT. Prefers deep, rich, moist soil; bottom lands, stream-banks.

CULTIVATION NOTES. The White Elm has a very extensive natural range. It yields valuable wood but has not been much planted as a timber tree. As an ornamental tree it is especially notable for its large size and magnificent form. The tree has very variable growth forms ranging from those with narrow to broad crowns and ascending to drooping lateral branches.

Slippery Elm
Ulmus fulva Michaux

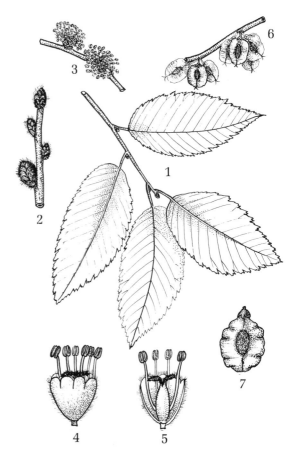

58. Ulmus fulva
1. Leafy branch, x ½.
2. Branch with winter-buds, x ½.
3. Branch with flowers, x ½.
4. Flower, enlarged.
5. Vertical section of flower, enlarged.
6. Branch with fruits, x ½.
7. Fruit, x 1.

HABIT. A small to medium-sized tree attaining a height of 20 m, with stout ascending branches forming a broad flat-topped crown.

BARK. Bark thick, dark reddish brown, longitudinally and shallowly fissured into large loose plates; inner bark mucilaginous and slippery.

STEMS. Branchlets stout, bright green and hairy at first, becoming grayish brown and smooth; covered by raised lenticels; leaf-scars raised, oval.

WINTER-BUDS. Buds large, ovoid, about 6 mm long, dark chestnut-brown, the scales about 12, rusty brown hairy.

LEAVES. Alternate, simple, thick, obovate to oblong, 10–20 cm long, sharp-pointed at apex, rounded and very unequal at base, doubly toothed on margin, very rough above, densely hairy beneath; petioles 4–8 cm long.

FLOWERS. April. Flowers perfect, short-stalked, in dense clusters; stamens 5–9; stigmas pinkish.

FRUIT. Fruit a short-stalked samara, almost circular to broadly elliptic, 1–2 cm long, slightly notched at apex, hairy in the center over the seed.

DISTRIBUTION. Quebec to Florida, west to the Dakotas and Texas.

HABITAT. Prefers low rich situations, along stream-banks and on hillsides; also on rocky ridges and slopes.

CULTIVATION NOTES. The Slippery Elm is not important as a timber tree. It may be used for planting in wet situations, along borders of streams and on limestone outcrops. The tree, with its broad open head and large leaves turning yellow in fall, is useful as an ornamental.

White Elm *(Ulmus americana)*

Slippery Elm *(Ulmus fulva)*

Slippery Elm *(Ulmus fulva)*

HACKBERRIES
Celtis *(Ulmaceae)*

Hackberry *(Celtis occidentalis)*

There are about 70 species in the genus *Celtis* distributed in both the temperate and tropical regions of the northern hemisphere. Nine species are native to North America and 1 to Pennsylvania.

The species of the genus are deciduous trees (evergreen in the tropics), with heavy bark and small winter-buds. The alternate, simple leaves are 3-nerved at base and usually long-stalked. The flowers are polygamo-monoecious, appearing on young branchlets with the staminate flowers fascicled at base and perfect ones above, solitary in the axils of leaves. The fruit is a drupe with a firm outer coat, scanty pulp and a bony stone.

The plants of *Celtis* in eastern North America are difficult to differentiate into their species and varieties. Three species are usually recognized, but they require fully mature fruits for positive identification. Besides the more widely distributed *Celtis occidentalis*, which has larger mature drupes (7–10 mm long), with usually a short beak at the tip, two southern species can be separated by their smaller mature drupes (5–8 mm long) which are beakless or nearly so. These species extend north to Virginia and southern Indiana. *Celtis laevigata* Willdenow is a tree to 30 m high growing in rich bottom lands. It has narrowly lanceolate leaves (4–10 cm long) which are less than half as broad as long. *Celtis tenuifolia* Nuttall is a small tree or shrub inhabiting dry or exposed situations. It has ovate leaves (2–8 cm long) about ½ to ¾ as broad as long.

The Hackberries are used as shade trees but they have no particular ornamental features. While several species, all small trees, are introduced into cultivation, none of them are widely planted.

Hackberry
Celtis occidentalis Linnaeus

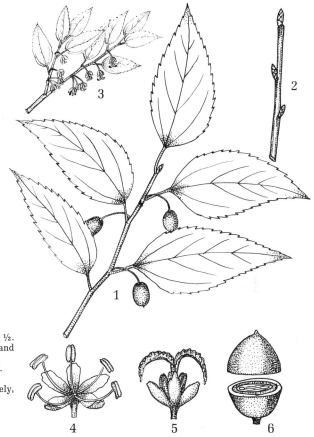

59. Celtis occidentalis
1. Branch with fruits, x ½.
2. Branch with winter-buds, x ½.
3. Branch with staminate and perfect flowers, x ½.
4. Staminate flower, enlarged.
5. Perfect flower, enlarged.
6. Fruit cut open transversely, enlarged.

HABIT. A small tree usually to 10 m high, occasionally attaining a height of 40 m, with a short trunk and a wide-spreading round-topped crown.

BARK. Bark grayish brown, smooth or roughened by warty projections.

STEMS. Branchlets slender, brownish, smooth or slightly downy, covered by scattered, raised, usually longitudinally elongated lenticels; leaf-scars small, semi-oval.

WINTER-BUDS. Buds small, ovoid, 5 mm long, sharply pointed, flattened, the scales 3–4.

LEAVES. Alternate, simple, ovate to ovate-oblong, 5–12 cm long, sharply or bluntly pointed at apex, oblique and rounded at base, toothed on margin except at base, bright green and rough above, paler beneath and smooth or slightly hairy on the veins; petioles 1.0–1.5 cm long.

FLOWERS. May. Three kinds of flowers may be found: staminate, pistillate, and perfect; small, greenish, inconspicuous, on slender stalks. Staminate flowers in clusters at base of shoot. Pistillate and perfect flowers usually solitary in the axils of upper leaves.

FRUIT. Fruit a globose berry-like, dark purple drupe, 7–10 mm thick, on slender stalks longer than the petioles; stone pitted.

DISTRIBUTION. Quebec to Manitoba, south to North Carolina, Alabama and Kansas.

HABITAT. Prefers rich, moist, well-drained soil, but will grow on gravelly uplands.

CULTIVATION NOTES. Although the wood is useful, the Hackberry is of little commercial importance because of its small size. The tree has bright green leaves turning light yellow in fall, but is not of any special attractiveness as an ornamental tree.

MULBERRIES
Morus *(Moraceae)*

Red Mulberry *(Morus rubra)*

The genus *Morus* comprises about 12 species distributed in temperate and semitropical regions of the northern hemisphere, 3 of these native to North America and 1 to Pennsylvania.

The Mulberry species are small trees or shrubs with scaly bark. The alternate simple leaves are sometimes lobed. They are toothed on the margin and 3- to 5-nerved at base, with long, lanceolate, deciduous stipules. The small flowers are unisexual and the staminate and pistillate occur either on the same or different trees. Both sexes appear in stalked, axillary pendulous catkins. There is a 4-part calyx which enlarges in the fruit. The fruit is an ovoid compressed achene covered by the succu-lent white to red and black calyx, aggregating into an ovoid to cylindrical juicy syncarp resembling a black berry.

The Mulberries are planted for ornament and also for the edible fruit. Besides the native species, the White Mulberry, *M. alba* Linnaeus from China, is planted and also naturalized in eastern North America. Its leaves are the chief food of the silkworm. It differs from the native Red Mulberry in the pale yellowish brown bark, in the leaves being glossy and smooth above and with axillary tufts of hairs beneath, and in the white or pinkish syncarp which is sweet to taste. It is a very variable species with many horticultural forms.

Red Mulberry
Morus rubra Linnaeus

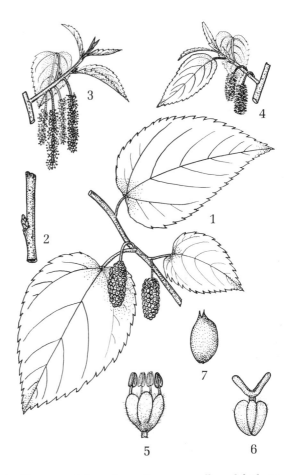

60. Morus rubra
1. Branch with fruits, x ½.
2. Branch with winter-buds, x ½.
3. Branch with staminate flower-
   clusters, x ½.
4. Branch with pistillate flower-
   clusters, x ½.
5. Staminate flower, enlarged.
6. Pistillate flower, enlarged.
7. Nutlet, enlarged.

HABIT. A medium-sized tree to 20 m, with a short trunk and a broad, dense, round-topped crown.

BARK. Bark thin, dark grayish brown, peels off in long narrow flakes.

STEMS. Branchlets stout, smooth, greenish brown tinged with red, covered with a few scattered inconspicuous lenticels; leaf-scars raised, almost circular.

WINTER-BUDS. Terminal bud absent; lateral buds ovoid, about 10 mm long, greenish brown to greenish red, the scales 3–9.

LEAVES. Alternate, simple, broadly ovate to oblong-ovate, 7–12 cm long, bluntly pointed at apex, somewhat heart-shaped at base, usually with 3 primary veins, closely and sharply toothed on margin, slightly rough above, soft hairy beneath; petioles 2–3 cm long. Leaves usually unlobed, occasionally 3-lobed or 5-lobed.

FLOWERS. May. Staminate flowers in slender catkins 2–5 cm long. Pistillate flowers in dense catkins 2.0–2.5 cm long.

FRUIT. Fruit an elongated syncarp 2–3 cm long, green at first, finally dark purple, composed of many small drupes, juicy, sweet and edible.

DISTRIBUTION. Massachusetts to Florida, west to Michigan, Nebraska, Kansas and Texas.

HABITAT. Prefers rich moist soil.

CULTIVATION NOTES. The Red Mulberry is not important as a timber tree but it is an attractive ornamental tree. The rather large dark green foliage turns bright yellow in fall. The fruit is edible and is a good source of food for birds.

OSAGE ORANGE
Maclura *(Moraceae)*

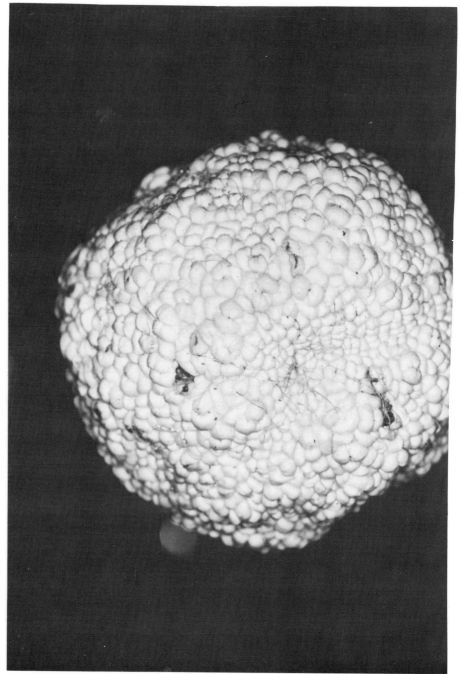

Osage Orange *(Maclura pomifera)*

The genus *Maclura* contains only one
species, exclusively North American.

Osage orange
Maclura pomifera *(Rafinesque)* Schneider

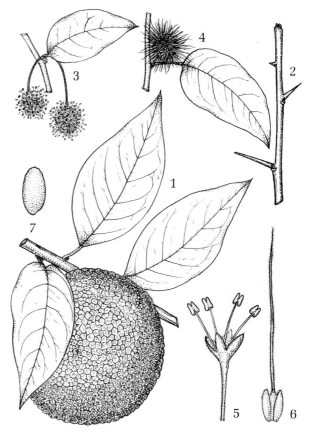

61. Maclura pomifera
1. Branch with fruit, x ½.
2. Branch with winter-buds, x ½.
3. Branch with staminate flower-clusters, x ½.
4. Branch with pistillate flower-clusters, x ½.
5. Staminate flower, enlarged.
6. Pistillate flower, enlarged.
7. Nutlet, enlarged.

HABIT. A small or medium-sized spiny tree usually to 15 m high but may reach 20 m, with a short, stout trunk and a round-topped, often irregular crown.

BARK. Bark rough, dark orange, deeply furrowed, with prominent ridges flaking into thin, close scales.

STEMS. Branchlets greenish and slightly hairy at first, soon smooth and light brown, bearing stout straight axillary spines 1.0–2.5 cm long; branches covered with stiff, spiny, spur-like lateral branchlets; leaf-scars small to medium-sized, triangular to elliptic.

WINTER-BUDS. Terminal bud absent; lateral buds depressed globose, partly hidden in bark, pale brown, the scales 5–7.

LEAVES. Alternate, simple, ovate to oblong-lanceolate, 8–12 cm long, 5–7 cm wide, sharply pointed at apex, wedge-shaped at base, entire on margin, dark green and shiny above, pale green beneath; petioles 3–5 cm long.

FLOWERS. June. Staminate flowers in clusters on long slender drooping stalks 2.5–3.5 cm long. Pistillate flowers in short-stalked dense heads 2.0–2.5 cm across.

FRUIT. Fruit a large, roundish, orange-like syncarp 10–14 cm across, pale green, composed of many small drupes closely grown together, exuding a milky juice when punctured.

DISTRIBUTION. Arkansas to Oklahoma and Texas. Introduced into Pennsylvania.

HABITAT. Grows in nearly all kinds of soils; prefers fertile lowlands.

CULTIVATION NOTES. Although not native to Pennsylvania, the Osage orange has been extensively planted for hedge and ornamental purposes and has often escaped from cultivation to establish itself. The green leaves turn clear yellow in fall and the large orange-like fruits are a conspicuous feature.

141

MAGNOLIAS
Magnolia *(Magnoliaceae)*

There are over 30 species of the genus *Magnolia* distributed in scattered regions in eastern North America and eastern Asia. Three species are native to Pennsylvania.

The species of the genus are deciduous or evergreen trees or shrubs. The buds have a single scale, the terminal bud being much larger than the lateral ones. The large alternate simple leaves are entire-margined, with large stipules whose scars encircle the stem. The large flowers are perfect, regular, terminal and solitary. There are 3 petaloid sepals, 6–15 petals, many stamens, and many carpels adnate to an elongated axis. The latter develops into a cone-like fruit consisting of many dehiscent 1- to 2-seeded carpels. The seeds are suspended at maturity for some time by long thin threads.

Eastern North America is one of the centers of distribution of the genus *Magnolia*. Besides the three species described in detail here, three additional species occur in areas south of Pennsylvania. The Ear-leaved Umbrella Tree, *M. fraserii* Walter, is a slender tree growing along swamps and streams in the South and uplands of Virginia, West Virginia and eastern Kentucky. The oblong leaves, 20–25 cm long, ear-like at base, are in umbrella-like clusters. The leaves, stipules, branchlets, flower buds and fruits are hairless. The flowers are large, creamy white and fragrant. The Great-leaved Cucumber Tree, *M. macrophylla* Michaux, extends from Florida north to Kentucky. The very large leaves, 30–90 cm long, ear-like at base, are also in umbrella-like clusters. The leaves are hairy beneath, and the stipules, young flower buds, and fruits are densely hairy. The large cup-like creamy white flowers are also fragrant. The Bull Bay, *M. grandiflora* Linnaeus, is an evergreen tree with thick leaves 12–20 cm long, shiny above and rusty hairy beneath. The cup-shaped white fragrant flowers are 15–20 cm across. The tree is native from Texas and Florida to North Carolina and is widely planted all over the world in milder temperate regions as an ornamental tree.

The Magnolias are among the showiest flowering trees. Besides the native species, several Asiatic species are cultivated as ornamental trees. These species produce large colorful flowers before the leaves in early spring and are more striking than the American species which all flower with the leaves. The most commonly cultivated introduced Magnolia is a hybrid, *M. x soulangeana* Soulange, originally a cross between two Chinese species, *M. liliflora* Desrouss and *M. denudata* Desrouss. It is a small tree with large purplish flowers—the most gorgeous of the early flowering small trees.

MAGNOLIA
Summer key to the species

A. Large trees; leaves over 12 cm long, not bloomy beneath.
    B. Leaves obovate, 30–60 cm long, crowded at end of flowering branches; flowers white. **M. tripetala**
    B. Leaves ovate, 12–30 cm long, scattered along the branches; flowers green to yellow. **M. acuminata**
A. Small tree or shrub; leaves about 12 cm or less long, white-bloomy beneath. **M. virginiana**

Winter key to the species

A. Large trees; leaves deciduous.
    B. Young branchlets stout; buds smooth, bloomy; leaf-scars large. **M. tripetala**
    B. Young branchlets slender; buds densely hairy; leaf-scars small. **M. acuminata**
A. Small tree or shrub; leaves usually persistent. **M. virginiana**

Umbrella-tree
Magnolia tripetala Linnaeus

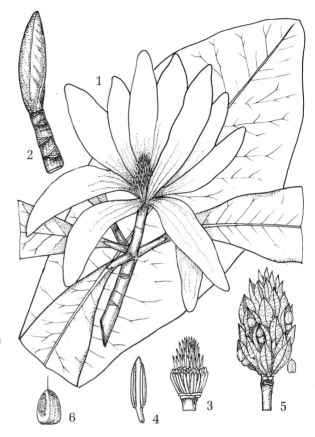

62. Magnolia tripetala
1. Branch with flower, x ½.
2. Branch with winter-bud, x ½.
3. Flower with calyx and corolla removed, x ½.
4. Stamen, enlarged.
5. Fruit clusters, x ½.
6. Seed, x 1.

HABIT. A small tree to 15 m, with a short, slender trunk and stout, spreading branches forming a broad, round-topped crown.

BARK. Bark thick, smooth, light gray, roughened by small scattered projections.

STEMS. Branchlets stout, often swollen at nodes, smooth, shiny, green at first, becoming reddish to greenish brown, covered with a few conspicuous lenticels; leaf-scars large, slightly raised, conspicuous, oval, the bundle-scars numerous, scattered irregularly.

WINTER-BUDS. Buds smooth, purple; terminal bud large, long-conical, to 5 cm long, long-pointed, often curved toward the apex; lateral buds much smaller, to 1 cm, conical.

LEAVES. Deciduous, very large, alternate, simple, oblong-ovate to obovate-lanceolate, 25–60 cm long; pointed at apex, usually wedge-shaped at base, entire on margin, green and smooth above, pale and hairy when young beneath, smooth when old; petioles 1.5–3.0 cm long.

FLOWERS. May–June. Upright, solitary, white, 10–12 cm high, with slight unpleasant odor; petals 6–9, oblong, obovate, 8–12 cm long; sepals shorter, light green, finally reflexed, falling away early.

FRUIT. Fruit cone-like, cylindrical, 5–10 cm long, rose-colored, composed of many closely joined follicles. Seeds red, flattish, suspended at maturity by white threads.

DISTRIBUTION. Pennsylvania south to Alabama, west to Arkansas and Mississippi.

HABITAT. Prefers moist rich soil, along streams, in swamps or ravines.

CULTIVATION NOTES. The Umbrella-tree, with its open crown, large leaves, and large flowers, is an attractive plant. The rose-colored fruit mass is very beautiful in autumn. The tree is shade-tolerant and easily grown. It is often used as stock for related species.

143

Cucumber-tree
Magnolia acuminata Linnaeus

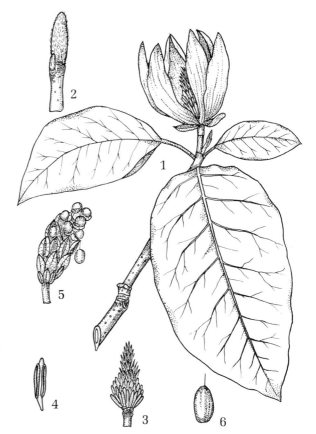

63. Magnolia acuminata
1. Branch with flower, x ½.
2: Branch with winter-bud, x ½.
3. Flower with calyx and corolla removed, x ½.
4. Stamen, enlarged.
5. Fruit clusters, x ½.
6. Seed, x 1.

HABIT. A large tree to 30 m high, with wide-spreading branches all along the trunk from the base forming a pyramidal crown.

BARK. Bark dark brown, furrowed longitudinally into long, loose, scaly ridges.

STEMS. Branchlets slender, reddish brown, shiny, smooth or slightly hairy, covered with a few orange-red inconspicuous lenticels; leaf-scars narrow, crescent-shaped, the bundle-scars 6–9, arranged in a line.

WINTER-BUDS. Buds oblong-ovoid, densely downy, bluntly pointed, the terminal ones larger, 2.0–2.5 cm long, the lateral ones much smaller, 3–5 mm long.

LEAVES. Deciduous. Alternate, simple, thin, ovate to oblong, 10–24 cm long, pointed at apex, tapering or rounded at base, entire on margin, green and smooth above, light green, soft-hairy, with prominent midrib and primary veins beneath; petioles 2.5–3.5 cm long.

FLOWERS. April–June. Upright, solitary, slender, bell-shaped, 6–8 cm high; petals obovate-oblong; greenish yellow, bloomy; sepals much narrower, lanceolate, soon reflexed.

FRUIT. Fruit cone-like, cylindrical, 5–8 cm long, red, composed of many closely joined follicles. Seeds drupe-like, scarlet, suspended at maturity by long, slender white threads.

DISTRIBUTION. New York to Georgia, west to Illinois and Arkansas.

HABITAT. Prefers rich woods, along streams or uplands.

CULTIVATION NOTES. The Cucumber-tree is valued both as a timber tree and an ornamental tree, attractive for its symmetrical crown, large leaves and the large red fruits in late summer. The tree is rapid-growing but demands light.

144

Sweet Bay, Laurel Magnolia
Magnolia virginiana Linnaeus

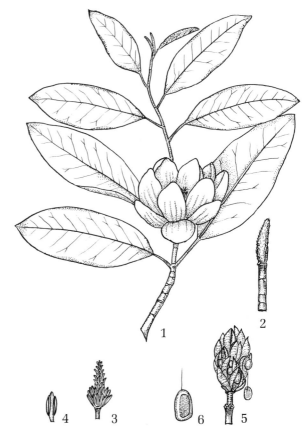

64. Magnolia virginiana
1. Branch with flower, x ½.
2. Branch with winter-bud, x ½.
3. Flower with calyx and corolla removed, x ½.
4. Stamen, enlarged.
5. Fruit clusters, x ½.
6. Seed, x 1.

HABIT. A small half-evergreen tree or shrub to 10 m, with a short trunk and an irregular, broadly conical crown.

BARK. Bark thin, gray, smooth to scaly.

STEMS. Branchlets relatively slender, green, smooth, becoming reddish brown; leaf-scars prominent, narrow, oval to crescent-shaped, the bundle-scars 6–9, arranged in a line.

WINTER-BUDS. Buds conical, 10–17 mm long, pointed at apex, the scales hairy.

LEAVES. Half-evergreen in the South, deciduous in the North. Alternate, simple, elliptic to oblong-lanceolate, 7–12 cm long, pointed or blunt at apex, broadly cuneate at base, rarely rounded, entire on margin, white-bloomy beneath and silky hairy at first; petioles slender, 1–2 cm long, smooth.

FLOWERS. June–July. Upright, solitary, roundish, 5–7 cm long, white, fragrant; calyx and corolla of same color; petals 9–12, obovate; sepals shorter and thinner, spreading.

FRUIT. Fruit cone-like, fleshy to dry, ellipsoid, 4–5 cm long, dark red, composed of closely joined follicles. Seeds drupe-like, red, shiny, suspended at maturity by long, slender, white threads.

DISTRIBUTION. Massachusetts to Florida, west to Texas.

HABITAT. Prefers swamps and wet places.

CULTIVATION NOTES. The Sweet Bay or Laurel Magnolia is a very ornamental small tree with lustrous leaves persisting in the South until spring, very fragrant white flowers and an attractive form. It is one of the choicest species in the native flora. The tree is slow-growing and decidedly moisture-loving.

Umbrella-tree *(Magnolia tripetala)*

Cucumber-tree *(Magnolia acuminata)*

146

Sweet Bay (*Magnolia virginiana*)

TULIP-TREES
Liriodendron *(Magnoliaceae)*

Tulip-tree *(Liriodendron tulipifera)*

The genus *Liriodendron* comprises 2 species only, one distributed in eastern North America and one in central China.

The species are deciduous trees with alternate, simple, long-stalked, characteristically saddle-shaped leaves. The leaves are broadly ovate in outline with a truncate apex and a short-pointed lobe on each side. The flowers are perfect, regular, terminal, solitary, and tulip-like. There are 3 sepals, 6 petals, numerous stamens and carpels spirally and densely arranged on a spindle-like column. The latter develops into a cone-like brown fruit consisting of many carpels, each a 1- to 2-seeded nutlet with a long narrow wing.

The American species, widely distributed in the eastern part of the United States, is an important timber tree. The other species is confined to a small area in central China and little cultivated.

Tulip-tree
Liriodendron tulipifera Linnaeus

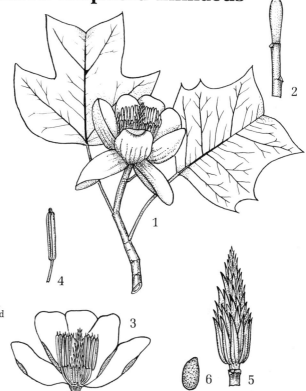

65. Liriodendron tulipifera
1. Branch with flower, x ½.
2. Branch with winter-bud, x ½.
3. Flower with front sepals and petals removed, x ½.
4. Stamen, x 1.
5. Fruit, x ½.
6. Seed, enlarged.

HABIT. A large tree to 50 m, sometimes reaching 60 m in height, with a tall, very straight trunk free of branches for a considerable height and a pyramidal crown in young trees and a broad, spreading crown in older trees.

BARK. Bark thick, brownish, deeply furrowed.

STEMS. Branchlets smooth, lustrous, reddish, becoming gray, covered with conspicuous pale lenticels; leaf-scars large, raised, conspicuous, circular, the bundle-scars small, numerous, scattered uniformly.

WINTER-BUDS. Terminal bud large, oblong, 1.5–2.5 cm long, dark red, covered with a whitish bloom, bluntly pointed, flattish, smooth; lateral buds smaller, divergent.

LEAVES. Alternate, simple, saddle-shaped, 9–12 cm long and about as broad, the apex broadly truncate with a pointed lobe on each side, 1 or 2 (rarely 3 or 4) pointed lobes on each side near the more or less rounded base, bright green above, paler beneath; petioles slender, 5–10 cm long.

FLOWERS. May–June. Large, tulip-shaped, 4–5 cm long, greenish yellow; sepals 3, reflexed, ovate-lanceolate, spreading and deciduous; petals 6, converging, oblong-obovate, with a broad orange band near base; stamens numerous, slightly shorter than the petals.

FRUIT. Fruit an oblong, pointed cone 6–8 cm long, 1.0–1.5 cm wide, consisting of many carpels 2.5–4.0 cm long. Seeds contained in the base of the carpels.

DISTRIBUTION. Massachusetts to Wisconsin, south to Florida and Mississippi.

HABITAT. Prefers rich, moist soil, along streams and at base of mountain slopes.

CULTIVATION NOTES. The majestic and beautiful Tulip-tree is both an important timber tree and an ornamental tree. The unusually shaped leaves turn bright yellow in autumn. The large greenish flowers are conspicuous and attractive. The tree is relatively free from insect and fungus diseases—altogether a most desirable shade, lawn, and street tree. Though moisture-loving, it adapts readily to all situations with good light soil. It is, however, sensitive to transplanting.

149

PAWPAWS
Asimina *(Annonaceae)*

Pawpaw *(Asimina triloba)*

There are 8 species in the genus *Asimina,* a genus confined to the warmer parts of North America. Only 1 species is hardy in the northern states.

The species of *Asimina* are deciduous or evergreen shrubs, rarely trees. The leaves are large, alternate, simple and entire. The flowers are axillary, perfect, solitary or a few, nodding on short stalks. There are 3 caducous sepals, 6 petals, many stamens, and 13–15 carpels. The fruit is a large oval to oblong berry, occurring singly or a few in a cluster, with large compressed seeds in 1 or 2 ranks.

The Custard Apple family, Annonaceae, is primarily tropical in distribution. *Asimina* is the only genus that has a tree species extending north as far as New York.

Pawpaw
Asimina triloba *(Linnaeus)* Dunal

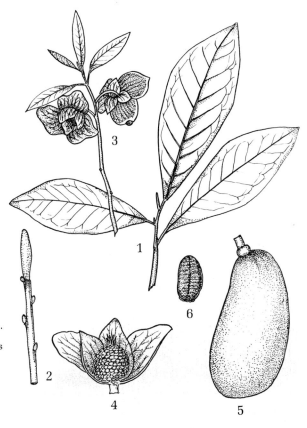

66. Asimina triloba
1. Leafy branch, x ½.
2. Branch with winter-buds, x ½.
3. Branch with flowers, x ½.
4. Flower with sepals and petals
   cut open vertically, x ½.
5. Fruit, x ½.
6. Seed, x ½.

HABIT. A small tree to 12 m, with a short, slender trunk. Spreading, straight branches form a high, broad crown.

BARK. Bark thin, closed, dark brown, covered with scattered white blotches, sometimes slightly fissured.

STEMS. Branchlets slender, hairy when young, becoming smooth, brown, covered with a few fine lenticels; leaf-scars semi-circular in shape, containing usually 5 bundle-scars.

WINTER-BUDS. Buds brown, naked, hairy; terminal bud 8–10 mm long, flattened; lateral buds about 2–3 mm long, appressed.

LEAVES. Alternate, simple, thin, ovate-lanceolate to obovate-oblong, 15–30 cm long, pointed at apex, gradually narrowed at base, entire on margin, dark green above, paler beneath; petioles 5–10 mm long.

FLOWERS. April–May. Solitary, axillary, 4–5 cm across, green at first, becoming reddish purple, on stout hairy stalks about 1 cm long; sepals ovate, rounded and later reflexed at apex; inner petals upright, much smaller, more pointed.

FRUIT. Fruit formed of 1 or more ellipsoid to oblong carpels, 5–7 cm long, green at first, later dark brown, with edible pulp. Seeds numerous, 2.0–2.5 cm long, dark brown, shiny, flattened, scattered throughout the pulp.

DISTRIBUTION. New York to Florida and west to Nebraska and Texas.

HABITAT. Prefers rich, moist soil, in river valleys near streams.

CULTIVATION NOTES. The Pawpaw is an attractive small tree with handsome flowers and peculiar fruits. The somewhat drooping, large leaves have a tropical appearance. The tree grows best in moist situations and is very tolerant of shade.

151

SASSAFRAS
Sassafras *(Lauraceae)*

Sassafras *(Sassafras albidum)*

The Sassafras genus comprises only 2 species, one distributed in eastern North America and the other in eastern Asia.

The species are deciduous trees with alternate, simple, often 2- to 5-lobed leaves. The flowers are unisexual or apparently perfect. The staminate and pistillate flowers occur on different trees. They appear with or before the leaves in umbel-like racemes. The anthers are 4-celled opening with 4 valves, or 2-celled opening with 2 valves. The fruit is an ovoid drupe supported by a club-shaped fleshy stalk.

The Asiatic species of the genus occur in warmer climates and are not cultivated. In the Pennsylvania flora, there is a relative of *Sassafras,* the Spice Bush, belonging to the same Laurel family. *Lindera benzoin* (Linnaeus) Blume is a small shrub with aromatic branches and leaves. It has alternate, simple, entire leaves, small clustered yellow flowers which appear in early spring before the leaves, and scarlet fruits.

Sassafras
Sassafras albidum *(Nuttall)* Nees

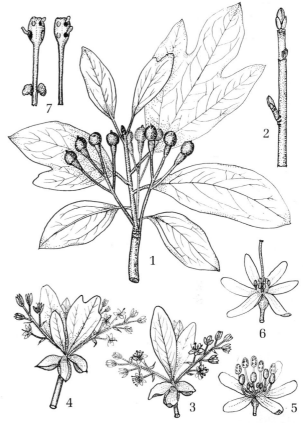

67. Sassafras albidum
1. Branch with fruits, x ½.
2. Branch with winter-buds, x ½.
3. Branch with staminate flowers, x ½.
4. Branch with pistillate flowers, x ½.
5. Staminate flower, enlarged.
6. Pistillate flower, enlarged.
7. Stamens, enlarged.

HABIT. A tree usually to 20 m in height, but occasionally 40 m, with a short trunk bearing more or less contorted branches forming a round or flat-topped crown.

BARK. Bark reddish brown, deeply fissured into flat ridges separating thin appressed scales.

STEMS. Branchlets slender, brittle, yellowish green, smooth, covered with few lenticels; leaf-scars small, raised, concave, with a single, confluent, linear bundle-scar.

WINTER-BUDS. Terminal bud large, 8–15 mm long, ovoid, sharply pointed, the scales few, loose, green, slightly hairy; lateral buds smaller, somewhat divergent.

LEAVES. Alternate, simple, obovate, 8–12 cm long, pointed at apex, wedge-shaped at base, entire or 2- to 5-lobed at apex, bright green above, paler, smoother and bloomy beneath; petioles 1.5–3.0 cm long.

FLOWERS. April–May. Staminate and pistillate flowers separate, yellowish green,

7 mm across, arranged in loose drooping racemes 3–5 cm long. Staminate flowers without staminodes and without rudimentary pistil.

FRUIT. Fruit a dark blue, bloomy, shiny drupe, ovoid, 1 cm long, subtended by an enlarged calyx terminating a fleshy, bright red, club-shaped stalk.

DISTRIBUTION. Massachusetts to South Carolina and Tennessee.

HABITAT. Prefers rich sandy loam; common along fence rows and abandoned fields.

CULTIVATION NOTES. The Sassafras is a handsome tree with bright green leaves turning orange and scarlet in fall. The dark blue fruit on red stalks is very colorful and good food for birds. Most parts of the tree yield an aromatic oil used for flavoring and soap perfume, and the leaves can be used as tea. The tree is easily grown and tolerant of shade and water.

SWEET-GUMS
Liquidambar *(Hamamelidaceae)*

Sweet-Gum *(Liquidambar styraciflua)*

There are 4 species in the genus *Liquidambar,* distributed disjunctively in eastern North America, eastern Asia, and western Asia.

The species of the Sweet-Gum genus are deciduous trees. The simple, alternate leaves are characteristically palmately 3- to 7-lobed, star-shaped with distinctly toothed margins. They are long-stalked, with small stipules. The flowers are small, unisexual, without petals and grouped together in round heads. The staminate and pistillate flowers usually occur on the same tree. The staminate flowers consist of stamens with a few small scales, appearing in small many-flowered heads arranged in a terminal raceme. The pistillate flowers consist of 2-beaked ovaries subtended by minute scales, and these are grouped in long-stalked, many-flowered heads. The fruit-heads, spiny from persisting styles, consist of many dehiscent capsules each containing 1 or 2 seeds.

The Sweet-Gums are highly ornamental trees with foliage that turns brilliantly red in autumn. The foreign species are rarely cultivated.

154

Sweet-Gum
Liquidambar styraciflua Linnaeus

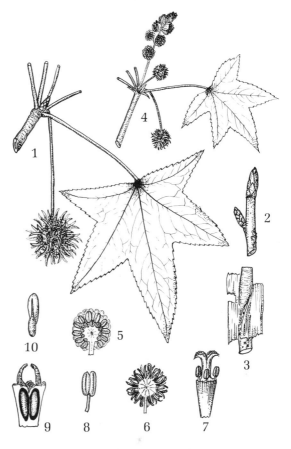

68. Liquidambar styraciflua
1. Branch with fruiting head, x ½.
2. Branch with winter-buds, x 1.
3. Branch with winged bark, x 1.
4. Branch with staminate and pistillate flower-clusters, x 1.
5. Vertical section of head of staminate flowers, x 1.
6. Vertical section of head of pistillate flowers, x 1.
7. Pistillate flower, enlarged.
8. Stamen, enlarged.
9. Vertical section of capsule, enlarged.
10. Seed, x 1.

HABIT. A large tree usually 20–25 m high but may reach a height of 45 m, with spreading branches forming a symmetrical conical crown.

BARK. Bark thick, grayish brown, deeply furrowed into broad scaly ridges.

STEMS. Branchlets rather stout, somewhat angular, brown, rusty hairy at first, becoming smooth, covered by scattered, dark, raised lenticels, after the second year often by corky-winged projections of the bark; leaf-scars raised, crescent-shaped, containing 3 circular bundle-scars.

WINTER-BUDS. Buds ovoid to conical, pointed, glossy, reddish brown; the scales 6, ovate, pointed, with downy margin.

LEAVES. Alternate, simple, heart-shaped at base, 10-18 cm wide and about as long, palmately 5- to 7-lobed, the lobes oblong, triangular, sharply pointed, toothed on margin, dark green and shiny above, paler beneath and smooth except for axillary tufts of hair in the axils of the principal veins; petioles 6–12 cm long.

FLOWERS. May. Flowers green, in many-flowered heads 6–7 mm across; staminate heads in terminal racemes 5–7 cm long; pistillate heads on slender stalks 2.5–5.0 cm long from the axils of upper leaves.

FRUIT. Fruit a long-stalked roundish head about 3 cm across, consisting of many shiny brown capsules surrounded at base by short bluntly pointed scales; fruit persisting on the tree during the winter.

DISTRIBUTION. Connecticut and New York south to Florida, west to Illinois, Missouri and Mexico.

HABITAT. Prefers deep, rich soil.

CULTIVATION NOTES. The Sweet-Gum is a valuable timber tree as well as a highly ornamental tree. Its maple-like leaves turn deep crimson in autumn. It prefers swampy woodlands but is intolerant of shade.

PLANES, SYCAMORES
Platanus *(Platanaceae)*

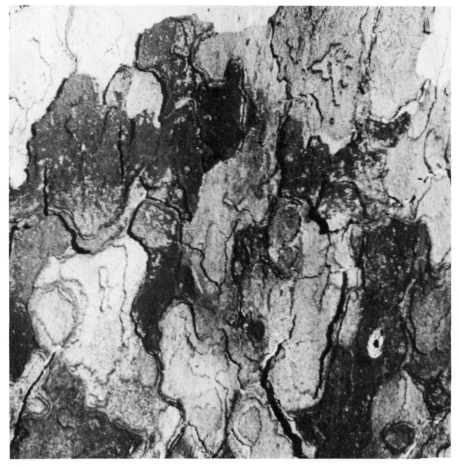

Buttonwood *(Platanus occidentalis)*

There are 6 or 7 species of *Platanus,* the only genus of the family Platanaceae. The species are found in all of North America south to Mexico, in southeastern Europe, western Asia and Indochina.

The Planes are tall, massive, deciduous trees with characteristically pale bark which peels off in thin broad plates. The buds, with a single close scale, are hidden at first by the base of the petiole. The alternate, simple, long-stalked leaves are palmately veined and lobed, and have sheathing stipules with a spreading margin. The small unisexual flowers, appearing on the same tree, are grouped in separate but similar globose heads. The fruit is a syncarp consisting of numerous small angular-conical nut-lets surrounded by long hairs.

The American Plane tree is the most massive deciduous tree of North America. The Plane tree that is much planted as a street tree in the northeastern United States is the London Plane, *P. x acerifolia* Willdenow. The latter is a hybrid between the American Plane and the Oriental Plane, *P. orientalis* Linnaeus, of southeastern Europe and western Asia, a species not hardy in the northeastern United States. The London Plane is very similar to the American Plane in appearance, but it has 2–3 fruit-heads together instead of 1 and the leaves have slightly narrower and longer lobes.

Buttonwood, American Plane
Platanus occidentalis Linnaeus

69. Platanus occidentalis
1. Branch with fruit-head, x ½.
2. Branch with winter-buds, x ½.
3. Branch with pistillate flower-head, x ½.
4. Staminate flower, enlarged.
5. Pistillate flower, enlarged.
6. Achene, enlarged.

HABIT. A large tree to 40 m, occasionally to 50 m in height, with a tall trunk and a wide-spreading, round or ovoid head.

BARK. Bark peels off into large thin plates exposing a whitish mottled inner bark, on old trunks at the base dark brown and fissured into broad ridges covered with thin dark brown scales.

STEMS. Branchlets rather stout, green and hairy at first, becoming brownish to gray and smooth, the nodes enlarged, covered by numerous small, pale lenticels; leaf-scars encircling the bud, with 5 to 10 bundle-scars.

WINTER-BUDS. Terminal bud absent; lateral buds conical, 6–10 mm long, pale brown, bluntly pointed, forming in summer within the petiole of the leaf.

LEAVES. Alternate, simple, broadly ovate, 10–12 cm wide, and often broader than long, usually heart-shaped at base, 3- to 5-lobed with shallow sinuses and broad-triangular lobes, coarsely toothed or entire on margin, bright green above, pale green and white woolly beneath; petioles 4–6 cm long; stipules very conspicuous, 3–4 cm long, encircling the branchlets.

FLOWERS. May. Staminate and pistillate flowers in dense heads on different stalks. Staminate heads axillary, dark red. Pistillate heads 1 or 2, terminal, greenish often tinged with red, hanging on a long stalk.

FRUIT. Fruit-heads usually solitary or rarely in 2's, brown, about 3 cm across, composed of many hairy achenes about 1.5 cm long.

DISTRIBUTION. Maine to Ontario and Minnesota, south to Florida and Texas.

HABITAT. Prefers rich, moist soils.

CULTIVATION NOTES. An important timber tree, the Buttonwood is also planted for ornamental purposes. However, the hybrid London Plane is preferred for cultivation as it is more attractive in form and less subject to fungus diseases. The tree can be propagated from cuttings as well as from seeds.

157

HAWTHORNS
Crataegus *(Rosaceae)*

Dotted Thorn *(Crataegus punctata)*

There are several hundred species in the genus *Crataegus* distributed in the temperate regions of the northern hemisphere.

The species of *Crataegus* are deciduous trees or shrubs, generally low and wide-spreading. The branches are strong, tortuous and usually spiny. The winter-buds are small and shiny brown. The leaves are alternate, simple, generally toothed, often lobed, and stipulate. The perfect regular flowers, usually white, are arranged in simple or compound corymbs. There are 5 sepals, 5 petals, 5–25 stamens and 1–5 carpels which are connate below. The red to yellow fruit is a pome-like drupe with 1–5 bony nutlets, each containing 1 seed.

Some of the species of Hawthorn are desirable ornamentals because of their beautiful flowers and colorful fruits. There have been hundreds of species described in this genus, and although the number has been much reduced by recent authors, their classification is still very complex and confused. Identification is a difficult task, so the following 5 species have been selected as representative of the different groups found in this area. Various manuals and technical publications can be consulted for more detailed information.

CRATAEGUS
Key to the species

A. Nutlets without cavities on the inner surface.
    B. Petioles long and slender, over 2.5 cm in length; leaves often lobed.
        C. Leaves hairy beneath.   **C. mollis**
        C. Leaves smooth or scarcely hairy beneath.   **C. pedicellata**
    B. Petioles usually very short, less than 1 cm in length; leaves not or only very slightly lobed.
        C. Leaves shiny above, smooth, scarcely hairy beneath.   **C. crus-galli**
        C. Leaves dull above, hairy beneath.   **C. punctata**
A. Nutlets with irregular cavities on the inner surface.   **C. calpodendron**

Scarlet Thorn
Crataegus mollis Scheele

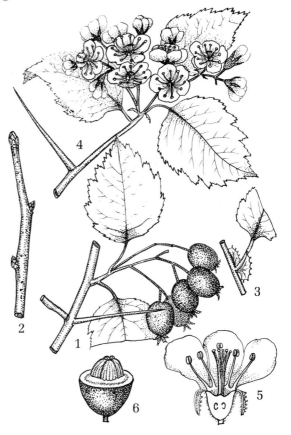

70. Crataegus mollis
1. Branch with fruits, x ½.
2. Branch with winter-buds, x ½.
3. Leaf on a vigorous shoot with stipules, x ½.
4. Branch with flowers, x ½.
5. Vertical section of flower, enlarged.
6. Transverse section of fruit showing nutlets, x 1.

HABIT. A small tree to 12 m with thorny or nearly thornless, spreading, often contorted branches forming a compact round head.

BARK. Bark thick, slightly furrowed and brownish gray on trunk, the surface scaly.

STEMS. Branchlets hairy when young, stout, zigzag, thorny, the thorns short and stout.

WINTER-BUDS. Buds bluntly pointed, about 3 mm long, chestnut-brown.

LEAVES. Leaves of flowering branches relatively large, mostly broad-ovate, 6–10 cm long, sharply and coarsely toothed, with 4–5 pairs of short, pointed lateral lobes, thickly coated with appressed hairs above and densely hairy beneath when young, at maturity yellow-green, firm, smooth above and often slightly hairy beneath chiefly on the veins; leaves of vegetative shoots sometimes deeply cut into narrow, pointed lobes; stipules leaf-like, glandular-toothed; petioles 2.5–5.0 cm long.

FLOWERS. April–May. Flowers white, 1.2–2.5 cm across, in many-flowered, hairy corymbs; calyx densely hairy, lined with a deep red or green disk, the lobes glandular-toothed; stamens about 20, the anthers small, yellowish or rarely pink.

FRUIT. Fruit roundish, oblong, or obovoid, 1.2–1.8 cm across, scarlet or bright crimson, hairy at least toward the ends, with a broad shallow calyx, the flesh thick, sweet, mealy; nutlets 4–5.

DISTRIBUTION. South Ontario to Virginia, west to South Dakota and Kansas.

HABITAT. In open woods; prefers alluvial or fertile grounds.

CULTIVATION NOTES. This is a small, handsome, fast-growing tree cultivated for its bright green foliage, large showy white flowers and conspicuous edible red fruits in the autumn. This is the largest and handsomest species of the Scarlet Hawthorn group in North America.

Scarlet Haw
Crataegus pedicellata Sargent

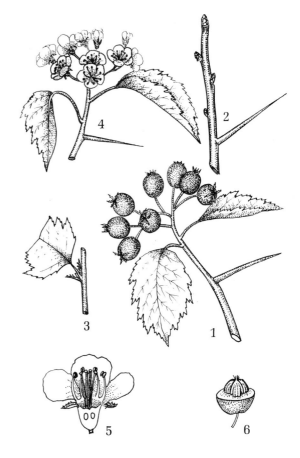

71. Crataegus pedicellata
1. Branch with fruits, x ½.
2. Branch with winter-buds, x ½.
3. Leaf on a vigorous shoot with stipules, x ½.
4. Branch with flowers, x ½.
5. Vertical section of flower, enlarged.
6. Transverse section of fruit showing nutlets, x 1.

HABIT. A small tree to 8 m high with round symmetrical head, sometimes a stout shrub.

BARK. Bark on trunk light brown or ashy gray, slightly fissured, the surface scaly.

STEMS. Branches slender, smooth, with straight or slightly curved thorns 3–5 cm long.

WINTER-BUDS. Buds nearly round, 1–2 mm long, chestnut-brown.

LEAVES. Leaves of flowering branches oblong-ovate, 5–10 cm long, sharp, coarse teeth nearly to the base, with 4–5 pairs of short acute spreading lobes above the middle, dark green and roughened above with hairs while young, paler beneath, smooth thin and firm at maturity; leaves of vegetative shoots often ovate and more deeply divided; stipules linear, glandular-toothed; petioles about 2.5–3.0 cm long.

FLOWERS. May. Flowers white, 1.5–2.0 cm across, many in loose, slightly hairy corymbs; calyx-lobes coarsely glandular-toothed; stamens about 10, the anthers pink or red.

FRUIT. Fruit pear-shaped or ellipsoid, about 1 cm across, bright scarlet, shiny, with a conspicuous broad calyx, the flesh thin, mealy; nutlets 4–5.

DISTRIBUTION. Pennsylvania, New York to Ontario, Indiana and Illinois.

HABITAT. Prefers banks of streams and thickets.

CULTIVATION NOTES. The species and its variety *gloriosa* Sargent, with larger flowers and larger fruits, are sometimes cultivated as ornamentals. This species is known to some authors as *Crataegus coccinea* Linnaeus.

Cockspur Thorn
Crataegus crus-galli Linnaeus

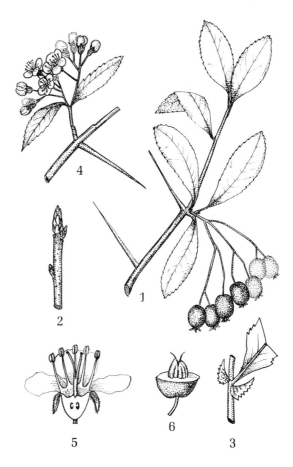

72. Crataegus crus-galli
1. Branch with fruits, x ½.
2. Branch with winter-buds, x ½.
3. Leaf on a vigorous shoot with stipules, x ½.
4. Branch with flowers, x ½.
5. Vertical section of flower, enlarged.
6. Transverse section of fruit showing nutlets, x 1.

HABIT. A small tree to 12 m high, with wide-spreading rigid branches forming a broad flat or round head.

BARK. Bark red-brown or gray, slightly scaly.

STEMS. Branchlets smooth, thorny, stout; the thorns numerous, long, stout, straight or slightly curved, often branched.

WINTER-BUDS. Buds bluntly pointed, about 3 mm long, chestnut-brown.

LEAVES. Leaves of flowering branches obovate, 2–8 cm long, sharply toothed above, entire near the cuneate base, at maturity thick, shiny above, quite smooth; leaves of vegetative shoots often oblong-elliptic, coarsely toothed; stipules linear, glandular, toothed, on vigorous shoots broad and leaf-like; petioles about 2–5 mm long.

FLOWERS. May–June. Flowers white, 1.0–1.5 cm across, in many-flowered smooth corymbs; calyx-lobes linear-lanceolate, entire or minutely glandular-toothed; stamens about 10, the anthers pink or pale yellow.

FRUIT. Fruit short-oblong or obovoid, sometimes roundish, about 1 cm across, often slightly 5-angled, red, with dry thin flesh; nutlets usually 2.

DISTRIBUTION. Quebec to South Carolina, west to Minnesota and eastern Texas.

HABITAT. Thickets and open grounds, in rich soil.

CULTIVATION NOTES. An attractive tree often cultivated for its flowers and the bright red fruits which remain on the tree during the winter. The foliage, changing to orange and scarlet in fall, is also ornamental. This species is more generally cultivated in the United States and Europe than any other American Hawthorn.

161

Dotted Thorn
Crataegus punctata Jacquin

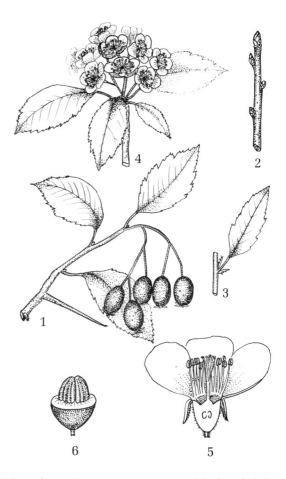

73. Crataegus punctata
1. Branch with fruits, x ½.
2. Branch with winter-buds, x ½.
3. Leaf on a vigorous shoot with stipules, x ½.
4. Branch with flowers, x ½.
5. Vertical section of flower, enlarged.
6. Transverse section of fruit showing nutlets, x 1.

HABIT. A small tree to 10 m high, with stiff horizontal spreading branches forming a broad, round or flat-topped head.

BARK. Bark brownish gray, becoming fissured on the trunk, the surface scaly.

STEMS. Branchlets stout, hairy at first, usually thorny, the thorns stout, short.

WINTER-BUDS. Buds bluntly pointed, about 3 mm long.

LEAVES. Leaves on flowering branches obovate, 5–10 cm long, irregularly toothed above the middle, usually slightly lobed toward the apex, at maturity firm, dull green, with impressed veins above, woolly-haired beneath; leaves of vegetative shoots oblong-elliptic, deeply lobed or laciniate; stipules lanceolate, pointed at apex, glandular-toothed; petioles 5–10 mm long.

FLOWERS. May–June. Flowers white, 1.5–2.0 cm across, several in broad, hairy corymbs; calyx densely grayish hairy, the lobes nearly entire; stamens about 20; the anthers red or yellow.

FRUIT. Fruit globose or pear-shaped, 1.5–2.0 cm long, dull red or yellow, dotted, with thick mellow flesh; nutlets 3–5.

DISTRIBUTION. Quebec to Ontario, Illinois and Georgia.

HABITAT. Open rocky grounds, thickets and pastures, usually in rich moist situations.

CULTIVATION NOTES. The tree is sometimes cultivated as an ornamental. It is especially beautiful in autumn when the leaves turn orange and scarlet and the branches are covered with showy fruits. There are red- and yellow-fruited forms.

162

Urn-tree
Crataegus calpodendron Medicus

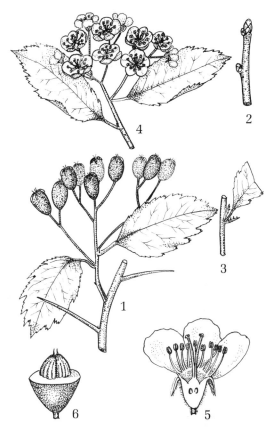

74. Crataegus calpodendron
1. Branch with fruits, x ½.
2. Branch with winter-buds, x ½.
3. Leaf on a vigorous shoot with stipules, x ½.
4. Branch with flowers, x ½.
5. Vertical section of flower, enlarged.
6. Transverse section of fruit showing nutlets, x 1.

HABIT. A small tree to 7 m with spreading, sparingly thorny or nearly thornless branches forming a wide flat head; sometimes a straggling shrub.

BARK. Bark dark brownish gray, becoming thick and furrowed on old trunks, the surface scaly.

STEMS. Young branchlets hairy at first, becoming contorted or zigzag, unarmed or with a few straight, slender sharp spines.

WINTER-BUDS. Buds nearly round, chestnut-brown.

LEAVES. Leaves elliptic to obovate-oblong, 5–12 cm long, pointed at apex, cuneate at base, toothed except near the base, usually with 3–5 pairs of shallow often asymmetrical lateral lobes, hairy when young, at maturity dull green, firm, smooth above, hairy beneath and with veins impressed above; stipules linear, minutely glandular-toothed; petioles 1.0–1.5 cm long.

FLOWERS. May. Flowers white, 1.2–1.5 cm across, in broad hairy corymbs 6–12 cm across; calyx hairy, the lobes glandular-toothed; stamens 15–20, the anthers pink, rarely white.

FRUIT. Fruit oblong or obovoid, sometimes roundish, about 1 cm long, yellowish red or bright red, hairy when young, with thin sweet flesh becoming succulent; nutlets 2–3, deeply pitted with irregular cavities on the inner surface.

DISTRIBUTION. South Ontario to Georgia and Alabama, west to Minnesota and Missouri.

HABITAT. In open woods it grows in low rich soil, usually along small rocky streams.

CULTIVATION NOTES. This tree is called *Crataegus tomentosa* by some authors. It is sometimes cultivated as an ornamental. The leaves turn brilliant orange or scarlet in autumn. The fruit remains on the tree all winter retaining its bright color.

163

Cockspur Thorn (*Crataegus crus-galli*)

Dotted Thorn (*Crataegus punctata*)

Scarlet Thorn (*Crataegus mollis*)

MOUNTAIN-ASHES
Sorbus *(Rosaceae)*

American Mountain-Ash *(Sorbus americana)*

There are over 80 species in the genus *Sorbus* distributed throughout the northern hemisphere.

Most of the species are shrubs or small trees. They are deciduous plants usually with rather large buds. The alternate leaves are toothed and stipulate, either simple or odd-pinnately compound. The perfect flowers are either perigynous or epigynous, with 5 sepals, 5 petals, 15–20 stamens, and a 2- to 5-carpelled ovary which is either half-superior or inferior. The fruit is a small pome with 2–5 cells, each containing 1 or 2 seeds.

Besides the wide-spread species *Sorbus americana,* there is the Mountain-Ash, *S. decora* (Sargent) Hyland, of more northern distribution, extending from Canada south through New England to New York, Ohio and northern Indiana. It differs from the former in the bluish green leaves; shorter, broader, firmer leaflets; broader flowers, and larger, white-bloomy fruits.

The species of *Sorbus* are attractive plants with large clusters of white flowers and showy red fruits in fall. The European Mountain-Ash (or Rowan Tree), *S. aucuparia* Linnaeus, is very generally cultivated and sometimes naturalized in the eastern states. Another European species, the White Beam-tree, *S. aria* (Linnaeus) Crantz, has also been long cultivated. *Sorbus aucuparia* can be distinguished from the American Mountain-Ash by its densely white-villous winter-buds, the hairy branchlets and the smaller leaves with fewer leaflets. *Sorbus aria* can be distinguished by its simple leaves.

American Mountain-Ash
Sorbus americana Marshall

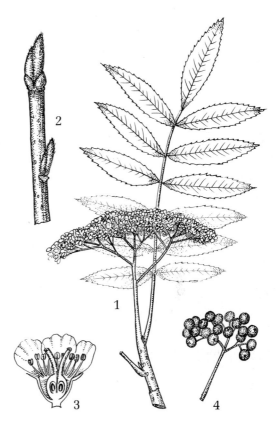

75. Sorbus americana
1. Branch with flower-clusters, x ½.
2. Branch with winter-buds, x ½.
3. Vertical section of flower, enlarged.
4. Cluster of fruits, x ½.

HABIT. A small tree to 10 m, sometimes shrubby, with a short trunk and a narrow, round-topped crown.

BARK. Bark thin, smooth or slightly scaly, grayish.

STEM. Branchlets stout, smooth or nearly so, grayish to reddish brown, covered with conspicuous, pale, oblong lenticels; leaf-scars rather large, raised, broad V-shaped with wavy margin.

WINTER-BUDS. Terminal buds broad-conical, smooth on outside, hairy on inside, about 5–6 mm long, purplish red, sharply pointed and often curved at apex, with 2–3 visible scales; lateral buds smaller, about 2–3 mm long, closely appressed, more or less flattened, with 1–2 visible scales.

LEAVES. Alternate, pinnately compound, about 15–25 cm long, with 11–17 sessile leaflets; leaflets paired, lanceolate, 4-10 cm long, sharply pointed at apex, narrowed to rounded at base, sharply toothed on margin; smooth and dark green above, pale and slightly hairy beneath when young, soon smooth.

FLOWERS. May–June. Perfect, white, 5–6 mm across, densely arranged in flat, smooth cymes 7–14 cm across.

FRUIT. Fruit berry-like, rounded or pear-shaped, 4–6 mm across, bright red, crowned with very small persistent calyx-lobes, arranged in flat-topped clusters.

DISTRIBUTION. Newfoundland to Manitoba, south to Michigan and North Carolina.

HABITAT. Prefers rich, moist soil along streams, rocky hillsides, and mountains.

CULTIVATION NOTES. A small attractive tree, the American Mountain-Ash is particularly showy in fall when its leaves turn yellow and its clusters of fruit ripen into bright red. It is a highly ornamental tree that deserves wide planting.

APPLES
Malus *(Rosaceae)*

American Crab *(Malus coronaria)*

The genus *Malus* comprises some 25 species in the temperate regions of the northern hemisphere.

The species of *Malus* are deciduous trees or shrubs, sometimes with spiny branches. The simple, alternate, stipulate leaves are toothed or lobed. The white to pink perfect flowers are arranged in umbel-like racemes. The flowers are epigynous, with a 5-lobed calyx, 5 roundish or obovate petals, 15–20 stamens, and 3- to 5-celled inferior ovary terminated by 2–5 styles that are connate at base. The fruit is a pome with a persistent or deciduous calyx at top.

In eastern North America the American Crab, *Malus coronaria,* is the most

widespread as well as the largest wild crab. Several other species have been recognized, mostly shrubs or very small trees. Among these is *M. angustifolia* (Aiton) Michaux, a shrub or small tree to 10 m, extending from Florida north to Virginia and Kentucky. It differs from *M. coronaria* in the broader, oblong or elliptic leaves with a tapering base.

This genus includes some important fruit trees and many highly ornamental flowering trees or shrubs. *Malus pumila* Miller is the Common Apple cultivated since ancient times. *Malus coronaria* is a native species that attains tree size. Another, smaller, native species, *M. lancifolia Rehder* is very similar but with slightly smaller and narrower leaves.

168

American Crab, Sweet Crab
Malus coronaria *(Linnaeus)* Miller

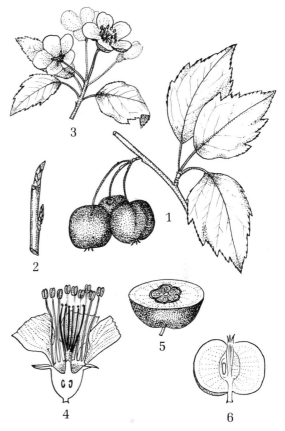

76. Malus coronaria
1. Branch with fruits, x ½.
2. Branch with winter-buds, x ½.
3. Branch with flowers, x ½.
4. Vertical section of flower, enlarged.
5. Transverse section of fruit, x 1.
6. Vertical section of fruit, x 1.

HABIT. A small tree to 10 m, with a short trunk and slender, spreading, often crooked branches forming a broad, round crown.

BARK. Bark thin, reddish brown, fissured longitudinally separating into low, often scaly ridges.

STEM. Branchlets stout, at first white-woolly, becoming smooth, reddish brown, spiny; leaf-scars crescent-shaped, raised.

WINTER-BUDS. Terminal bud 3–6 mm long, bluntly pointed, bright red, with 4–8 scales; lateral buds smaller.

LEAVES. Alternate, simple, thin, ovate to ovate-oblong, 5–10 cm long, sharply pointed at apex, usually rounded at base, sharply and irregularly serrate on margin, usually slightly lobed, short-hairy when young, finally smooth, dark green above, pale green beneath; stipules long, falling early.

FLOWERS. May–June. Perfect, fragrant, rosy-white, about 3–4 cm across, arranged in umbel-like cymes; pedicels smooth.

FRUIT. Fruit apple-like, fragrant, long- and slender-stalked, depressed-globose, about 3 cm across, yellowish green, ribbed at apex and crowned with persistent calyx-lobes and filaments; seeds brown, shiny.

DISTRIBUTION. New York to Alabama, west to Michigan and Missouri.

HABITAT. Prefers rich, moist soil in thickets and open woods, especially on hill-tops along streams and ponds.

CULTIVATION NOTES. The American Crab resembles the cultivated apple except that its leaves are smoother and flowers redder. The fruit is small and very bitter but is used for making jellies and cider. It often persists on the tree far into the winter. The tree, with its abundant showy and fragrant flowers, is a very attractive ornamental. It is also known as *Pyrus coronaria* Linnaeus.

SHAD-BUSHES
Amelanchier *(Rosaceae)*

Shad bush *(Amelanchier canadensis)*

There are about 30 species in the genus *Amelanchier* distributed in temperate regions of the northern hemisphere. Most of the species are found in North America, and 4 are native to Pennsylvania.

The species are deciduous small trees or shrubs with conspicuous pointed buds. The simple alternate leaves have toothed margins, nearly straight veins and small deciduous stipules. The white flowers are borne in terminal racemes. They are perfect and regular, with a 5-toothed calyx, 5 petals, 10–20 stamens and an inferior 4- to 10-celled ovary.

The fruit is a small berry-like pome with 1 seed in each cell and crowned with (usually) reflexed calyx-lobes.

The Shad-bushes are ornamental plants and some have edible fruits. *Amelanchier canadensis* is the largest of the native species; the others are all of low shrubby size. Another species, *A. laevis* Wiegand, is sometimes separated from *A. canadensis*. It is a smaller tree, sometimes shrubby, with smoother leaves and longer pedicels. The flowers and fruits are somewhat larger and are borne in loose, drooping racemes.

Shad-bush, Sarvis
Amelanchier canadensis *(Linnaeus)* Medicus

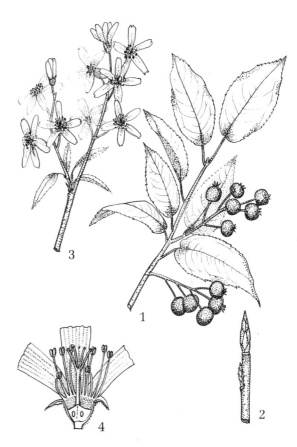

77. Amelanchier canadensis
1. Branch with fruits, x ½.
2. Branch with winter-buds, x ½.
3. Branch with flowers, x ½.
4. Vertical section of flower, enlarged.

HABIT. A small tree to 20 m, with a straight slender trunk and ascending branches, forming a shallow and narrow crown; sometimes shrubby.

BARK. Bark thin, pale reddish brown, smooth or roughened by shallow fissures separating into narrow, longitudinal, scaly ridges.

STEMS. Branchlets slender, light green, turning reddish brown, smooth, covered with a few, pale, scattered lenticels; leaf-scars small, inconspicuous, linear.

WINTER-BUDS. Buds conical, 6–12 mm long, sharply pointed at apex, yellowish brown, smooth or hairy towards apex; terminal bud longer; lateral buds appressed.

LEAVES. Alternate, simple, ovate, obovate or ovate-oblong, 3–8 cm long, sharply pointed at apex, rounded or heart-shaped at base, finely and sharply toothed on margin, densely hairy when young, later less hairy or smooth, dark green above, pale green beneath.

FLOWERS. April–May. Perfect, large, stalked, white, densely arranged in drooping, hairy racemes 7–12 cm long; petals linear to linear-oblong, 1.0–1.5 cm long; ovary smooth or slightly hairy at top.

FRUIT. Fruit berry-like, reddish purple, bloomy when ripe, about 8 mm across; seeds small.

DISTRIBUTION. Maine to Iowa, south to Georgia and Louisiana.

HABITAT. Prefers rich, moist soil, upland woods and hillsides.

CULTIVATION NOTES. The Shad-bush with its conspicuous white flowers is worthy of cultivation as an ornamental tree. Its sweet fruits are good food for birds and animals as well as man. Although it prefers moist situations, it will also grow on sandy sterile soils.

PLUMS, PEACHES and CHERRIES
Prunus *(Rosaceae)*

The genus *Prunus* comprises nearly 200 species distributed over the northern temperate zone with a few in the tropics.

The species of *Prunus* are deciduous or evergreen trees and shrubs. The winter-buds are covered by many imbricate scales. The leaves are alternate, simple, toothed and stipulate. The flowers are perfect, usually white but some pink or red, arranged either singly in fascicles, or in racemes. They are perigynous, with 5 sepals, 5 petals, numerous stamens and a single pistil with a superior, 2-ovuled ovary and an elongated style. The fruit is a 1-seeded drupe.

Many species of the genus are cultivated for their ornamental flowers or edible fruits. The 5 native tree species are not among the more ornamental species or desirable fruit trees. The following species are introduced ones which have been extensively cultivated since very early times, mainly for their fruits:

Apricot, *Prunus armeniaca* Linnaeus, eastern Asia

Peach, *Prunus persica* (Linnaeus) Batsch, China

Plum, *Prunus domestica* Linnaeus, Europe, western Asia

Sour Cherry, *Prunus cerasus* Linnaeus, Europe, western Asia

Sweet Cherry, *prunus avium* Linnaeus, Europe, western Asia

Among those cultivated for their ornamental flowers are 3 species of Japanese flowering cherries:

Prunus serrulata Lindley
Prunus subhirtella Miquel
Prunus yedoensis Matsumura

PRUNUS
Summer key to the species

A. Flowers in elongated racemes terminating the branchlets; bracts small.
  B. Leaves thicker, narrower, oblong to oblong-lanceolate, long-pointed, the teeth short, incurved, stout; calyx persistent in fruit. **P. serotina**
  B. Leaves thinner, broader, ovate to obovate, short-pointed, the teeth sharp, spreading, slender; calyx deciduous in fruit. **P. virginiana**
A. Flowers in few-flowered umbels or short racemes; bracts conspicuous or small.
  B. Leaves obovate to oblong-obovate; flowers larger, 2–3 cm across.
    P. americana
  B. Leaves narrowly elliptic to oblong-lanceolate; flowers smaller, 1.0–1.2 cm across.
    C. Leaves sharply toothed, hairy beneath, at least when young; fruiting stalk short, about 1 cm long. **P. alleghaniensis**
    C. Leaves sharply and finely toothed, smooth, fruiting stalk longer, about 2 cm in length. **P. pennsylvanica**

Winter key to the species

A. Branches not spiny, the branchlets with a small terminal bud.
  B. Branchlets slender, usually less than 3 mm in diameter; buds small, 3–5 mm long.
    C. Buds clustered at tips of the branchlets, bluntly tipped, 3 mm or less long. **P. pennsylvanica**
    C. Buds rarely clustered at tips of the branchlets, sharply pointed, about 5 mm long. **P. serotina**
  B. Branchlets stout, more than 3 mm in diameter; buds larger, about 8 mm long. **P. virginiana**
A. Branches spiny, the branchlets without a terminal bud.
  B. First-year branchlets orange-brown; buds over 3 mm long, light brown. **P. americana**
  B. First-year branchlets dark reddish; buds less than 3 mm long, brown with reddish tips. **P. alleghaniensis**

172

Black Cherry, Rum Cherry
Prunus serotina Ehrhart

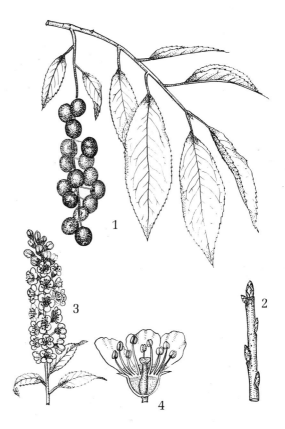

78. Prunus serotina
1. Branch with fruits, x ½.
2. Branch with winter-buds, x ½.
3. Branch with flowers, x ½.
4. Vertical section of flower, enlarged.

HABIT. A tree reaching to 30 m, with a rather irregular oblong crown.

BARK. Bark dark brown, roughened by thick irregular plates with projecting edges.

STEMS. Branchlets smooth, rather slender, reddish brown, marked with numerous pale (generally) rounded lenticels; leaf-scars raised, semielliptical in outline.

WINTER-BUDS. Buds ovate, about 3–4 mm long, reddish brown, smooth, glossy, usually sharply pointed, covered by 4 visible ovate scales.

LEAVES. Alternate, simple, firm to leathery, oblong-ovate to lanceolate-oblong, 5–12 cm long, sharply to bluntly pointed at apex, tapering or rounded at base, finely toothed with short incurved blunt teeth on margin, dark green and shiny above, pale green beneath and often hairy along the broad midrib; petioles 6–25 mm long, glandular.

FLOWERS. May–June. Perfect, white, 8–10 mm across; in slender cylindrical, smooth racemes 6–14 cm long; stalk 3–10 mm long, divergent; calyx-lobes oblong-ovate, often toothed on margin.

FRUIT. Fruit a globose drupe 8–10 mm across, dark red, finally purple-black, arranged in rather open drooping racemes 7–10 cm long.

DISTRIBUTION. Nova Scotia to North Dakota, south to Florida and Texas.

HABITAT. Prefers a rich, moist soil, but grows well on dry, gravelly or sandy slopes.

CULTIVATION NOTES. The Black Cherry is the largest tree among the native cherries. It is an important timber tree and its wood is valuable for furniture and interior finish. It is also often planted for its handsome foliage.

Choke Cherry
Prunus virginiana Linnaeus

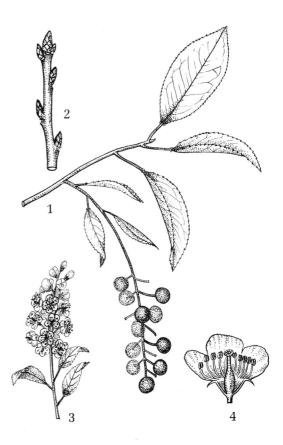

79. Prunus virginiana
1. Branch with fruits, x ½.
2. Branch with winter-buds, x ½.
3. Branch with flowers, x ½.
4. Vertical section of flower, enlarged.

HABIT. A small tree to 10 m, sometimes a large shrub.

BARK. Bark thick, dark grayish, slightly roughened by shallow fissures.

STEMS. Branchlets stout, smooth, brown, covered with numerous conspicuous, dull yellowish, more or less horizontally elongated lenticels; leaf-scars slightly raised, triangular-elliptic in shape.

WINTER-BUDS. Buds conical, 5–10 mm long, sharply pointed at apex, brownish; the scales 6–8, rounded at apex, smooth; lateral buds somewhat divergent.

LEAVES. Alternate, simple, thin, ovate to elliptic or obovate, 4–12 cm long, abruptly sharply pointed at apex, tapering or rounded at base, closely and finely sharp-toothed on margin, bright green and somewhat shiny above, paler beneath, smooth except for axillary tufts of hairs; petioles 1–2 cm long, glandular.

FLOWERS. May–June. Perfect, white, 8–10 mm across, in dense, smooth, many-flowered, drooping racemes 7–15 cm long; calyx-lobes bluntly pointed at apex, the lobes deciduous in fruit.

FRUIT. Fruit a globose drupe about 8 mm across, deep red, becoming red-purple; stone smooth.

DISTRIBUTION. Newfoundland to Manitoba, south to Georgia and Texas.

HABITAT. Prefers deep, rich, moist soils but is common on less favorable sites, along fences, in abandoned fields, along shores or borders of woods.

CULTIVATION NOTES. The Choke Cherry is an attractive plant when cultivated as an ornamental. The tree is propagated by birds dropping the pits along fences and hedgerows. It develops numerous suckers from the roots and often forms extensive thickets difficult to eliminate.

Wild Plum
Prunus americana Marshall

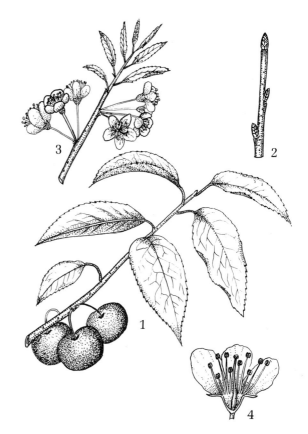

80. Prunus americana
1. Branch with fruits, x ½.
2. Branch with winter-buds, x ½.
3. Branch with flowers, x ½.
4. Vertical section of flower, enlarged.

HABIT. A small tree to 10 m, with a short trunk and many wide-spreading branches forming a deep broad-topped crown.

BARK. Bark thin, dark brown, rough, breaking up into plates.

STEMS. Branchlets rather stout, hairy and light green at first, becoming smooth and reddish brown, covered with scattered roundish lenticels, often spiny; leaf-scars broadly crescent-shaped.

WINTER-BUDS. Buds broadly conical, about 7–8 mm long, brown, sharply pointed at apex, the scales numerous, triangular, pale hairy on margin.

LEAVES. Alternate, simple, firm, obovate to oblong-obovate, 5–12 cm long, long sharp point at apex, more or less rounded at base, sharply and often doubly toothed on margin, dark green and rough above, paler and slightly hairy or smooth beneath; petioles without terminal glands.

FLOWERS. Late April–early June. Per-
fect, white, about 2–3 cm across, on slender smooth stalks arranged in fascicles of 2–5; calyx glandular or nearly so, smooth outside, the lobes promptly reflexed, sharp point at apex, entire on margin; petals white; style 7–12 mm long, often exceeding stamens.

FRUIT. Fruit a roundish drupe, 2–3 cm across, red to yellowish, with a thick tough skin; stone oval, flattened, smooth.

DISTRIBUTION. Massachusetts to Manitoba, south to Georgia, New Mexico and Utah.

HABITAT. Prefers rich, moist soil; common along thickets, borders of woods and banks of streams.

CULTIVATION NOTES. The Wild Plum, attractive in its forms, foliage and showy flowers, is readily cultivated as both an ornamental and a fruit tree. It is used as a stock for grafting the domestic plum. The fruit is used for preserves and jellies.

Sole Plum, Porter's Plum
Prunus alleghaniensis Porter

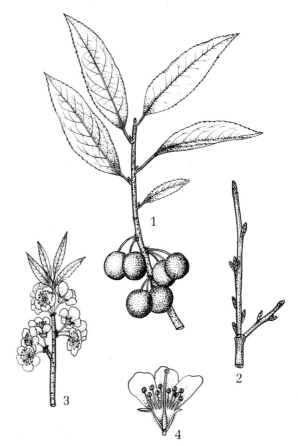

81. Prunus alleghaniensis
1. Branch with fruits, x ½.
2. Branch with winter-buds, x ½.
3. Branch with flowers, x ½.
4. Vertical section of flower, enlarged.

HABIT. A small slender tree to 7 m high with many erect rigid branches or a straggling shrub, often forming thickets.

BARK. Bark dark brown, thick, fissured into thin persistent scales.

STEMS. Young branchlets hairy or nearly so, becoming reddish brown to black, smooth and shiny, unarmed or sometimes with short spine-like lateral branchlets.

WINTER-BUDS. Buds small, pointed or blunt at apex, reddish.

LEAVES. Alternate, simple, lanceolate, oblong-ovate or narrowly obovate, 4–9 cm long, 2.0–4.5 cm wide, sharply pointed at apex, wedge-shaped at base, sharply and finely toothed on margin, smooth or sparingly hairy above, hairy beneath at least when young; petioles 7–12 mm long, hairy, sometimes glandular.

FLOWERS. Late April–May. Perfect, 1.0–1.5 cm across, on slender stalks in fascicles of 2–4; calyx-tube hairy, rarely smooth, the lobes oblong-ovate, bluntly pointed, tardily reflexed, sparingly hairy or smooth within; petals round-obovate, turning pinkish; style 4–7 mm long, usually hidden among stamens.

FRUIT. Fruit a roundish drupe about 1 cm across, dark purple and bloomy; stone hard but not brittle, slightly obovoid, more or less blunt at apex.

DISTRIBUTION. Connecticut to Pennsylvania. In Pennsylvania found near Birmingham, Huntingdon County.

HABITAT. Thickets and borders of woods; prefers moist soil.

CULTIVATION NOTES. The Sole Plum occupies a restricted natural range in a small elevated region in central Pennsylvania, forming thickets of considerable extent in low moist soil and growing sometimes into trees on dry ridges. It is worthy of cultivation as a small ornamental tree for its showy flowers and attractive fruits.

176

Bird-cherry, Fire Cherry
Prunus pennsylvanica Linnaeus

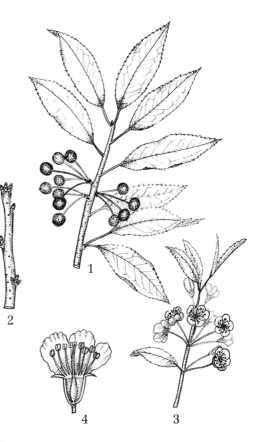

82. Prunus pennsylvanica
1. Branch with fruits, x ½.
2. Branch with winter-buds, x ½.
3. Branch with flowers, x ½.
4. Vertical section of flower,
   enlarged.

HABIT. A small tree to 12 m with a short trunk and somewhat ascending branches forming a narrow rather flat-topped crown.

BARK. Bark thin, reddish brown, somewhat roughened but not fissured, easily removed.

STEMS. Branchlets slender, smooth, reddish, shiny, covered with many conspicuous pale to yellowish horizontally elongated lenticels; leaf-scars slightly raised, semielliptic.

WINTER-BUDS. Buds ovoid, about 2–3 mm long, bluntly pointed at apex, brownish, smooth.

LEAVES. Alternate, simple, membranaceous, ovate to oblong-lanceolate, 6–11 cm long, long sharp point at apex, tapering or rounded at base, finely and sharply toothed on margin, shiny above, smooth and green on both sides; petioles 1–2 cm long.

FLOWERS. May. Perfect, white, 1.2–1.6 cm across, borne on long smooth stalks (1.0–1.5 cm long) in 4- to 5-flowered fascicles; calyx-lobes ovate, blunt at apex, entire on margin, shorter than the calyx-tube.

FRUIT. Fruit a globose juicy drupe 5–7 mm across, bright red, crowned with persistent styles, with thin skin and acid flesh; stone roundish to oblong, 4–5 mm long.

DISTRIBUTION. Newfoundland to British Columbia, south to Georgia, Tennessee and Colorado.

HABITAT. Common on sand-lands, roadsides, recent burned-over lands and clearings and hillsides.

CULTIVATION NOTES. The Bird-cherry is a highly ornamental tree with its showy flowers in spring and numerous red fruits in summer. It is, however, short-lived. In the wild it is an aggressive species, taking over clearings rapidly after fires and lumbering operations, often forming dense thickets. It serves as a shelter for other trees and a source of food for birds and wild animals.

177

Black Cherry *(Prunus serotina)*

Choke Cherry *(Prunus virginiana)*

178

Bird-cherry (*Prunus pennsylvanica*)

HONEY LOCUSTS
Gleditsia *(Leguminosae)*

Honey Locust *(Gleditsia triacanthos)*

There are about 12 species in the genus *Gleditsia,* distributed in North America and central and eastern Asia. Three species are found in the eastern part of North America and 1 is native to Pennsylvania.

The species of *Gleditsia* are deciduous trees with stout often branched spines on the trunk and branches. The alternate leaves are pinnately or bipinnately compound, usually with both types on the same tree. The leaflets are irregularly and slightly round-toothed. The polygamous flowers are usually arranged in racemes or panicles. There are 5 teeth to the calyx-tube and 5 short, nearly equal petals. The staminate flowers contain 6–10 stamens. The pod is usually large and compressed, remaining on the tree for a long time.

Besides the Honey Locust, *Gleditsia triacanthos,* there occurs in the South the Water Locust, *G. aquatica* Marshall, a river-swamp species from Texas and Florida to Kentucky and South Carolina. This is a smaller tree (to 20 m) with fewer leaflets (12–18) more entire and less hairy, longer flower-racemes and much shorter fruit with only 1–3 seeds.

Several introduced species are sometimes cultivated but they are much smaller trees or shrubs.

Honey Locust
Gleditsia triacanthos Linnaeus

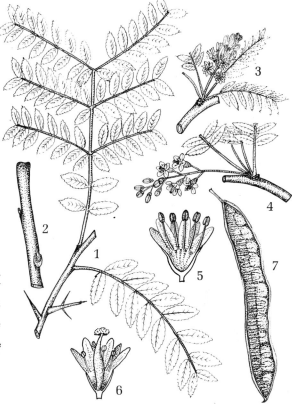

83. Gleditsia triacanthos
1. Leafy branch, x ½.
2. Branch with winter-buds, x ½.
3. Branch with staminate flowers, x ½.
4. Branch with pistillate flowers, x ½.
5. Vertical section of staminate flower, enlarged.
6. Vertical section of pistillate flower, enlarged.
7. Legume, x ¼.

HABIT. A medium-sized tree about 15 m high, but sometimes reaching to 45 m, with a short trunk and long drooping branches forming a broad round-topped crown, usually with stout, simple or branched spines 15–25 cm long on trunk and branches.

BARK. Bark thick, grayish brown, deeply fissured into long, narrow scaly ridges.

STEMS. Branchlets stout, smooth, shiny, with enlarged nodes, greenish red to brown, covered with many conspicuous raised, oblong lenticels; leaf-scars V-shaped.

WINTER-BUDS. Terminal bud absent; lateral buds minute, usually 3–5 at a node, superposed, brownish, smooth.

LEAVES. Alternate, singly or doubly compound, 14–20 cm long; rachis grooved, hairy. Simple-pinnate leaves with 20–30 oblong-lanceolate leaflets, the leaflets 2.0–3.5 cm long. Double-pinnate leaves with 8–14 pinnae each with 18–20 leaflets, the leaflets 8–20 mm long. Leaflets lanceolate-oblong, rounded at apex and base, somewhat toothed on margin.

FLOWERS. June. Flowers unisexual or perfect, small, very short-stalked, the staminate and pistillate on separate trees. Staminate flowers arranged in short, hairy racemes to 5 cm long. Pistillate or perfect flowers in few-flowered solitary racemes to 7 cm long.

FRUIT. Fruit a twisted, thin, flat, reddish brown pod 30–45 cm long; seeds many, ovoid, flat, brown.

DISTRIBUTION. Pennsylvania to Florida, westward to Kansas and Texas.

HABITAT. Prefers deep, rich soil; along moist bottom lands.

CULTIVATION NOTES. The Honey Locust is often planted as an ornamental tree for its attractive form and graceful foliage. The large branched thorns are especially conspicuous in winter. The light-demanding tree grows best in moist situations but will grow on a variety of soils. It is a rapid grower, free from insects and fungus diseases.

181

KENTUCKY COFFEE-TREE
Gymnocladus *(Leguminosae)*

Kentucky Coffee-tree *(Gymnocladus dioicus)*

The genus *Gymnocladus* comprises only two species, one in eastern North America and the other in eastern Asia.

The species of *Gymnocladus* are deciduous trees with stout branches and small winter-buds. The alternate leaves are bipinnately compound, with entire-margined leaflets and deciduous stipules. The unisexual flowers are arranged in terminal panicles, with the staminate and pistillate on different trees. The flowers are regular, with a 5-lobed tubular calyx and 5 short petals. The staminate flowers have 5 stamens. The pistillate flowers have a 4- to 8-ovuled ovary with a short style. The fruit is a broadly oblong, thick, flat pod with several large, flattened seeds.

The Asian species (from China) is not in cultivation in eastern North America.

Kentucky Coffee-tree
Gymnocladus dioicus *(Linnaeus)* K. Koch

84. Gymnocladus dioicus
1. Branch with staminate flowers, x ½.
2. Branch with winter-buds, x ½.
3. Pistillate flowers, x ½.
4. Legume, x ½.

HABIT. A medium-sized tree usually 20 m but sometimes reaching 30 m in height, with a short trunk and a narrow, obovate crown.

BARK. Bark thick, dark gray, deeply fissured into scaly ridges.

STEMS. Branchlets very stout, greenish brown, coated with short dense reddish hairs and covered with large conspicuous lenticels; leaf-scars large, conspicuous, raised, broadly heart-shaped, pale.

WINTER-BUDS. Terminal bud absent; lateral buds small, depressed into the stem, 2 in the axils of each leaf, brown, silky-hairy.

LEAVES. Alternate, twice-compound, 15–35 cm long, with 3–7 pairs of pinnae, the basal ones usually reduced to simple leaf-lets, the upper with 3–7 pairs of leaflets; leaflets ovate to elliptic-ovate, 5–8 cm long, short-stalked, sharply pointed at apex, rounded to wedge-shaped at base, entire to wavy on margin, hairy when young; petioles 4–6 cm long.

FLOWERS. June. Flowers unisexual, regular, about 1.2 cm long, long-stalked, greenish white, hairy, the staminate and pistillate on separate trees. Staminate inflorescence a raceme about 7–10 cm long, more densely flowered. Pistillate inflorescence a terminal raceme to 25 cm long.

FRUIT. Fruit a broad, flat, oblong pod 15–25 cm long, 2.5–5.0 cm wide, thick, brown, sometimes covered with a grayish bloom; seeds more or less rounded, 2.0–2.5 cm across, dark brown, flat.

DISTRIBUTION. New York to Pennsylvania southward to Tennessee and westward to Minnesota, Nebraska, and Oklahoma.

HABITAT. Prefers rich moist soil and bottom lands.

CULTIVATION NOTES. The Kentucky Coffee-tree is extensively planted as an ornamental tree. The large compound leaves are pinkish when unfolding and turn clear yellow in autumn. The large pods are conspicuous and persist through the winter. The tree is grown readily in various situations.

REDBUDS
Cercis *(Leguminosae)*

Redbud *(Cercis canadensis)*

The genus *Cercis* comprises about 8 species distributed in temperate North America, eastern Asia and southeastern Europe. Two species are native to North America and 1 to Pennsylvania.

The species of *Cercis* are deciduous shrubs or small trees with smooth branches and small superposed winter-buds. The leaves are alternate, simple, entire, palmately nerved, petiolate and with caducous stipules. The perfect flowers, in fascicles or racemes, are butterfly-like. There is a broad bell-shaped calyx with short blunt teeth. The 5 rose-colored imbricate petals are unequal, with 3 smaller ones and 2 larger lower ones, the uppermost one being the outermost. The 10 stamens are free, in 2 rows. The ovary is short-stalked. The fruit is a flat, thin, narrow-oblong pod containing several flat seeds.

Besides the native *C. canadensis,* widely planted for its early showy flowers, the Old World Judas-tree, *C. siliquastrum* Linnaeus, of Europe and western Asia, is sometimes also cultivated. The latter species can be distinguished by its leaves, rounded or notched at the apex.

Redbud
Cercis canadensis Linnaeus

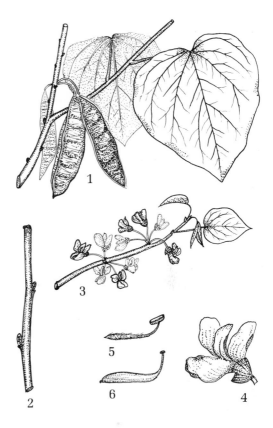

85. Cercis canadensis
1. Branch with fruits, x ½.
2. Branch with winter-buds, x ½.
3. Branch with flowers, x ½.
4. Flower, enlarged.
5. Stamen, enlarged.
6. Pistil, enlarged.

HABIT. A small tree to 12 m, with a short trunk and a broad round crown.

BARK. Bark thin, reddish brown, fissured into scaly ridges.

STEMS. Branchlets slender, smooth, shiny, light brown, becoming grayish brown, covered by many tiny lenticels; leaf-scars slightly raised, inversely triangular in outline.

WINTER-BUDS. Terminal bud absent; lateral buds small, about 3 mm long, bluntly pointed at tip, somewhat flattened and appressed; brownish.

LEAVES. Alternate, simple, broad-ovate to nearly rounded, 7–12 cm long, pointed at apex, heart-shaped at base, entire on margin, hairy to smooth beneath.

FLOWERS. April–May. Flowers perfect, irregular, resembling the pea-flower in form, in clusters of 4–8, rosy-pink, 1.0–1.2 cm long; pedicels 5–12 mm long.

FRUIT. Fruit a small short-stalked pod 6–8 cm long, about 1.2 cm wide, rosy-pink to light brown; seeds about 6 in each pod, broadly ovoid, flattened, light brown.

DISTRIBUTION. Southern Ontario through New York and New Jersey to northern Florida, westward to Minnesota, Arkansas and Texas.

HABITAT. Prefers rich moist soil, along borders of streams, in open woodlands, or in shade of other trees.

CULTIVATION NOTES. The Redbud is an extremely attractive plant for ornamental planting. The beautiful flowers are abundantly and conspicuously produced in spring before the leaves come out. The rapid-growing plant prefers plenty of light but also thrives in shade. There is a white-flowered variety (var. *alba*).

LOCUSTS
Robinia *(Leguminosae)*

Black Locust *(Robinia pseudoacacia)*

The genus *Robinia* is found only in North America. There are about 20 species, of which 1 is native to Pennsylvania.

The species of *Robinia* are deciduous trees or shrubs. The winter-buds, small and naked, are developed inside the base of the petiole. The alternate leaves are pinnately compound with opposite, thin and entire-margined leaflets. The flowers are perfect and butterfly-like, white to pink in color, and arranged in drooping racemes. The calyx is campanulate and 5-toothed but slightly 2-lipped. There are 5 petals, including one almost circular reflexed standard, 2 curved wings, and an incurved keel formed by 2 united petals. The 10 stamens are united except for the upper one which is more or less free. The fruit is an oblong, flat, 2-valved pod with several seeds.

Besides the Black Locust, *R. pseudoacacia,* several shrubby species of the southern states are occasionally cultivated in the northeastern states.

The Yellow Wood genus *Cladrastis* is somewhat related to *Robinia.* There is one American species, the Yellow Wood, *C. lutea* (Michaux) K. Koch, which occurs in North Carolina to Kentucky and Tennessee. It is a medium-sized tree to 15–20 m tall with smooth bark and yellow wood. The once-pinnately compound leaves are composed of 7–11 elliptic, pointed leaflets 7–10 cm in length. The white fragrant butterfly-like flowers appear in panicles 25–40 cm long. The long narrow flattened pod is 7–8 cm long.

Black Locust, Common Locust
Robinia pseudoacacia Linnaeus

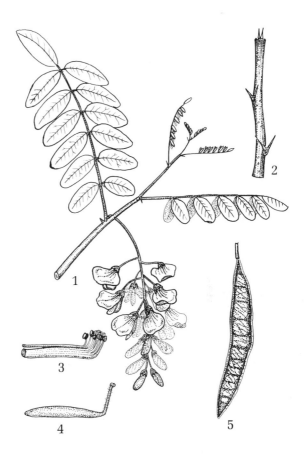

86. Robinia pseudoacacia
1. Branch with flowers, x ½.
2. Branch with winter-buds, x ½.
3. Staminal tube, enlarged.
4. Pistil, enlarged.
5. Legume, x ½.

HABIT. A medium-sized tree to 25 m, with a (usually) narrow, oblong, open crown.

BARK. Bark reddish brown, deeply furrowed with rounded ridges.

STEMS. Branchlets rather stout, brittle, smooth or slightly hairy at first, greenish to reddish brown, covered with a few pale lenticels; leaf-scars large, conspicuous, irregular in outline, covering the bud, often located between two sharp spines which are transformed by the stipules.

WINTER-BUDS. Terminal bud absent; lateral buds minute, 3–4 superposed, imbedded in the stem within the leaf-scar, rusty hairy.

LEAVES. Alternate, pinnately compound, 20–35 cm long, usually rounded at apex and base, entire on margin, smooth beneath or slightly hairy when young; petioles slender, grooved on top, swollen at base.

FLOWERS. June. Flowers perfect, butterfly-like, white, very fragrant, 1.5–2.0 cm long, on slender stalks about 1.2 cm long, arranged in dense drooping racemes 10–20 cm long; standard with yellow spot at base.

FRUIT. Fruit a dark brown, smooth, linear-oblong pod 5–10 cm long, 1.2 cm wide; seeds small, 3–10, dark brown and mottled.

DISTRIBUTION. Pennsylvania to Georgia, west to Iowa, Missouri and Oklahoma; naturalized elsewhere in North America.

HABITAT. Grows on moist rich soil as well as on rocky, dry, sandy situations.

CULTIVATION NOTES. The Black Locust is widely planted in America and Europe as an ornamental tree chiefly for its fragrant attractive flowers and graceful foliage. There are many garden forms. The tree is also used for forestation, shelter plantations, and fence rows. It grows readily in all soil types and situations.

AILANTHUS
Ailanthus *(Simaroubaceae)*

Tree of Heaven *(Ailanthus altissima)*

There are about 10 species in the genus *Ailanthus* in eastern and southern Asia and northern Australia; 1 eastern Asia species is naturalized in the eastern United States.

The species are deciduous trees with stout branchlets. The buds are nearly rounded. The leaves are alternate and odd-pinnately compound. There are 13–41 leaflets near the base, usually with a few large teeth each bearing a large gland beneath. The flowers are small and polygamous, in large terminal panicles. The 5–6 sepals are partly connate, and the 5–6 petals are several times longer than the sepals. The staminate flowers have 10 stamens inserted at the base of the 10-lobed disk and are without a rudimentary pistil. The pistillate flowers have 5–6 carpels with elongated spreading stigmas and 10 rudimentary stamens. The fruit consists of 1–6 free oblong samaras bearing a compressed seed in the middle.

Two or three species native to eastern Asia are cultivated but not naturalized in the eastern United States.

Tree of Heaven
Ailanthus altissima *(Miller)* Swingle

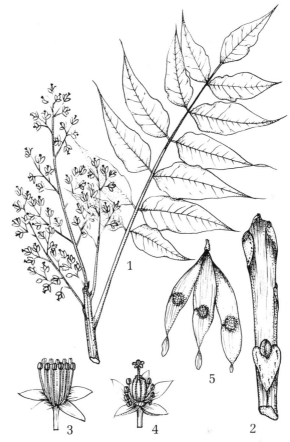

87. Ailanthus altissima
1. Branch with inflorescence, x ½.
2. Branch with winter-buds, x ½.
3. Staminate flower, enlarged.
4. Pistillate flower, enlarged.
5. Fruits, x ½.

HABIT. Tree to 20 m high, with stout as-cending branches forming a round head.

BARK. Bark smooth, with pale stripes.

STEMS. Young branchlets stout, green, minutely hairy becoming dull reddish brown and smooth; leaf-scars very large.

WINTER-BUDS. Terminal bud absent; lateral buds roundish, about 3 mm long, brownish, downy.

LEAVES. Leaves alternate, large, having a disagreeable odor when bruised, odd-pinnately compound, 45–60 cm long; leaf-lets 13–25, short-stalked, ovate-lanceolate, 7–12 cm long, long and sharply pointed at apex, usually unequally truncate at base, wavy on margin and with 2–4 coarse glan-dular teeth near the base, smooth or slightly hairy beneath.

FLOWERS. May–June. Staminate and pistillate flowers on separate trees. Flowers small, 7–8 mm across, greenish white, in many-flowered, large, terminal panicles 10–20 cm long; sepals 5; petals 5; staminate flowers with 10 stamens; pistillate or per-fect flowers with 10 short stamens and 5 carpels with 5 stigmas.

FRUIT. Fruit a samara 3–4 cm long, thinly membranaceous, linear-lanceolate, with a seed in center, light reddish brown.

DISTRIBUTION. Introduced from China, naturalized extensively in eastern North America.

HABITAT. Tolerates any kind of soil.

CULTIVATION NOTES. The Tree of Heaven is planted as an ornamental tree but often becomes an obnoxious weed in a city environment, as it produces suckers and sometimes is difficult to eliminate. It is a rapid-growing and short-lived tree. The staminate tree should not be planted as the pollen has an objectionable odor.

189

SUMACS
Rhus *(Anacardiaceae)*

Shining Sumac *(Rhus copallina)*

The genus *Rhus* is a large one with over 150 species widely distributed in subtropical and temperate regions of both hemispheres. Three species in Pennsylvania attain tree size.

The species of *Rhus* are deciduous or evergreen shrubs and trees. The buds are small and naked. The alternate leaves are trifoliate or pinnately compound, rarely simple. The flowers are small and unisexual, polygamous or dioecious, arranged in axillary or terminal panicles. There are a 5-part calyx, 5 imbricate petals and 5 stamens inserted below a disk. The 1-ovuled ovary is superior, terminated by 3 styles. The fruit is a drupe with a bony kernel.

Besides the 3 native tree species in the genus *Rhus,* there is also the shrubby or climbing Poison Ivy, *R. toxicodendron* Linnaeus, which is readily recognized by its trifoliate leaves.

RHUS

Summer key to the species

A. Petioles winged; margins of leaflets nearly entire.   **R. copallina**
A. Petioles not winged; margins of leaflets entire or toothed.

  B. Leaflets 7–13, the margins entire; branchlets smooth; juice watery, poisonous.   **R. vernix**
  B. Leaflets 11–13, the margins toothed; branchlets densely hairy; juice milky, not poisonous.   **R. typhina**

Winter key to the species

A. Terminal buds present; leaf-scars broad, do not surround buds; juice watery, poisonous.   **R. vernix**
A. Terminal buds absent; leaf-scars crescent-shaped, partly surround buds; juice watery or milky, not poisonous.

  B. Branchlets moderately stout, rust-brown hairy, becoming smooth, with watery juice.   **R. copallina**
  B. Branchlets very stout, densely rusty hairy, with milky juice.
                                                          R. typhina

Shining Sumac
Rhus copallina Linnaeus

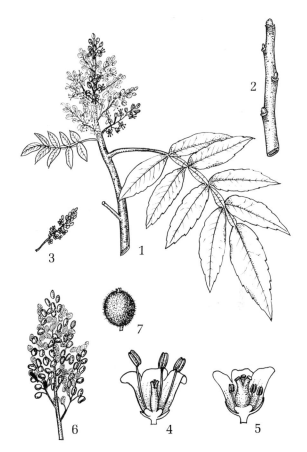

88. Rhus copallina
1. Branch with staminate inflorescence, x ½.
2. Branch with winter-buds, x ½.
3. Portion of pistillate inflorescence, x ½.
4. Vertical section of staminate
   flower, enlarged.
5. Vertical section of pistillate
   flower, enlarged.
6. Portion of fruiting cluster,
   x ½.
7. Fruit, enlarged.

HABIT. A shrub or small tree, occasionally to 10 m.

BARK. Bark thin, light brown to reddish
brown, may peel off into papery layers
when old.

STEMS. Branchlets at first greenish red,
hairy, becoming reddish brown and smooth,
roughened by large elevated dark brown
lenticels and projections; leaf-scars inversely triangular in outline, nearly encircling the bud.

WINTER-BUDS. Terminal bud absent;
lateral buds axillary, small, spherical, rusty
brown hairy.

LEAVES. Alternate, pinnately compound,
15–30 cm long, with winged petioles and
rachis; leaflets 9–21, oblong-ovate to ovate-
lanceolate, pointed at apex, often unequal
and wedge-shaped at base, entire on margin or sometimes with a few teeth near

apex, usually smooth and shiny above,
hairy beneath.

FLOWERS. July–August. Flowers greenish, in dense axillary or terminal panicles,
the staminate and pistillate usually occur on
different plants.

FRUIT. Fruit a small spherical drupe
2–3 mm across, crimson, hairy, arranged in
dense, stout, hairy clusters; seed single,
orange-colored, smooth.

DISTRIBUTION. Maine and Ontario to
Minnesota, south to Florida and Texas.

HABITAT. Common on dry hillsides,
woods and openings, and abandoned fields.

CULTIVATION NOTES. The Shining
Sumac is not poisonous and is planted for
its shiny foliage turning reddish purple in
autumn and for the crimson fruit clusters.
It grows usually into a shrubby plant.

191

Poison Sumac, Poison Oak
Rhus vernix Linnaeus

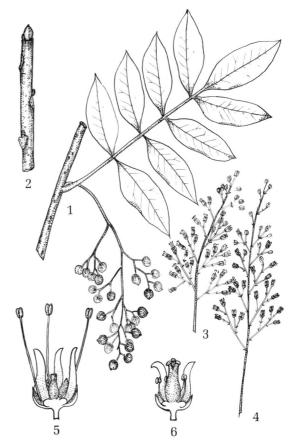

89. Rhus vernix
1. Branch with fruits, x ½.
2. Branch with winter-buds, x ½.
3. Staminate inflorescence, x ½.
4. Pistillate inflorescence, x ½.
5. Vertical section of staminate flower, enlarged.
6. Vertical section of pistillate flower, enlarged.

HABIT. A shrub or small tree to 7 m, with a trunk usually branching near the ground, forming a wide, rounded crown.

BARK. Bark gray, smooth, roughened with horizontally elongated lenticels.

STEMS. Branchlets stout, at first orange-brown, bloomy, becoming gray, smooth, glossy, covered with numerous raised lenticels, with a watery juice; leaf-scars large, conspicuous, broad, the upper margin not encircling the bud.

WINTER-BUDS. Terminal buds larger than lateral buds, purplish, conical, pointed at apex, 5–15 mm long, the scales few, downy.

LEAVES. Alternate, pinnately compound, 18–35 cm long, with a smooth wingless petiole and rachis; leaflets 7–13, short-stalked, elliptic to elliptic-oblong, 4–10 cm long, sharply pointed at apex, wedge-shaped at base, entire on margin, slightly hairy at first, becoming nearly smooth, dark green and shiny above, pale beneath, with 8–12 pairs of veins.

FLOWERS. June–July. Staminate and pistillate flowers borne on different plants, the flowers small, greenish yellow, in long, drooping, slender panicles 8–20 cm long.

FRUIT. Fruit small, spherical, slightly compressed drupes 5–6 mm across, light yellowish gray, arranged in loose drooping panicles.

DISTRIBUTION. Ontario to Minnesota, south to Florida and Louisiana.

HABITAT. Prefers swamps and lowlands; sometimes also found on moist slopes.

CULTIVATION NOTES. The Poison Sumac has leaves turning brilliant orange and scarlet in fall, but it is a highly poisonous plant and never planted. Although some people are immune to its poison, others are affected simply by touching it.

Staghorn Sumac
Rhus typhina Linnaeus

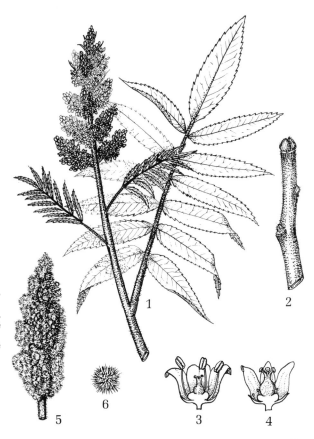

90. Rhus typhina
1. Branch with staminate inflorescence, x ½.
2. Branch with winter-buds, x ½.
3. Vertical section of staminate flower, enlarged.
4. Vertical section of pistillate flower, enlarged.
5. A fruiting cluster, x ¼.
6. Fruit, enlarged.

HABIT. A shrub or small tree to 10 m with a (usually) short trunk and ascending branches forming a broad flat-topped crown.

BARK. Bark rough, dark brown, sometimes scaly, roughened by lenticels.

STEMS. Branchlets stout, densely black velvety-hairy, later smooth, with a milky juice, covered with many conspicuous orange-colored lenticels; leaf-scars large, conspicuous, U-shaped, nearly encircling the bud.

WINTER-BUDS. Terminal bud absent; lateral buds spherical, blunt at apex, covered with dense rusty hairs.

LEAVES. Alternate, pinnately compound, 40–60 cm long, with a stout wingless petiole and rachis; leaflets 11–13, oblong-lanceolate, nearly stalkless, 5–12 cm long, sharply pointed at apex, rounded or wedge-shaped at base, toothed on margin, hairy when young, smooth when mature, dark green above, pale and bloomy beneath.

FLOWERS. June–July. Flowers small, greenish, in dense hairy panicles. Staminate panicles about 20–30 cm long, 12–15 cm broad. Pistillate panicles more compact, 12–20 cm long.

FRUIT. Fruit small, crimson, spherical, densely hairy, drupes arranged densely in erect, cone-like clusters 12–20 cm long, 5–8 cm broad; seed single, hard.

DISTRIBUTION. Quebec to Ontario, south to Georgia, Indiana and Iowa.

HABITAT. Usually found on fertile, dry, rocky or gravelly upland soil; common in fields and abandoned fields.

CULTIVATION NOTES. The Staghorn Sumac is sometimes planted as an ornamental tree for its brilliant scarlet and orange autumn foliage and for the red fruit-clusters persisting far into winter. The bark is rich in tannin. The plant is not poisonous.

Poison Sumac (*Rhus vernix*)

Poison Sumac (*Rhus vernix*)

Staghorn Sumac *(Rhus typhina)*

Staghorn Sumac *(Rhus typhina)*

HOLLIES
Ilex *(Aquifoliaceae)*

American Holly *(Ilex opaca)*

There are over 300 species in the genus *Ilex* widely distributed in temperate and tropical regions of both hemispheres. Five species are native to Pennsylvania, 2 of tree size.

The species of the Holly genus are evergreen or deciduous shrubs or trees. The buds are small, covered by 3 outer scales. The alternate, simple leaves are entire or toothed, often spiny, on the margin. The unisexual, axillary flowers occur singly or in clusters. The staminate and pistillate flowers usually occur on separate trees. They are usually 4-merous, or sometimes 5- to 8-merous. The fruit is a berry-like drupe with 2–8 bony nutlets.

Besides the following 2 tree species, several native shrubby species are also cultivated for their ornamental berries. Among the introduced tree species, the most widely planted one is the English Holly, *Ilex aquifolium* Linnaeus, an evergreen plant like the native *I. opaca*, and with similarly coarsely spiny-toothed leaves. Its leaves, however, are shorter and broader, and the branchlets are smooth instead of being finely hairy. The fruits of the English Holly are usually clustered while those of the American Holly are nearly always solitary.

ILEX
Key to the species
A. Leaves evergreen, coarsely spiny-toothed.   **I. opaca**
A. Leaves deciduous, finely toothed.   **I. montana**

American Holly
Ilex opaca Aiton

91. Ilex opaca
1. Branch with fruits, x ½.
2. Branch with staminate flowers, x ½.
3. Staminate flower, enlarged.
4. Pistillate flower, enlarged.
5. Nutlet, enlarged.

HABIT. A small evergreen tree to 15 m, with a short trunk and spreading, ascending branches forming a narrow pyramidal crown.

BARK. Bark close, thick, grayish to yellowish brown, becoming rough with age.

STEMS. Branchlets slender, at first finely hairy, soon becoming smooth, light brown, covered by a few inconspicuous lenticels; leaf-scars conspicuous, semi-oval, the margin raised.

WINTER-BUDS. Terminal bud pointed; lateral buds shorter, bluntly pointed, somewhat downy.

LEAVES. Alternate, simple, evergreen, thick, elliptic to elliptic-lanceolate, 5–10 cm long, with wavy margin and large widely spaced spiny teeth, rarely nearly entire, dull green above, yellowish green and with very prominent midrib beneath;

petioles short, stout, 6–12 mm long.

FLOWERS. April–June. Flowers small, greenish, the staminate and pistillate usually occurring on different trees. Staminate flowers 3–9 in a stalked cyme. Pistillate flowers usually solitary.

FRUIT. Fruit a smooth, red, spherical drupe 8–10 mm across, usually solitary; seed a light brown nutlet usually 4-ribbed.

DISTRIBUTION. Maine through Pennsylvania to Florida, west to Missouri and Texas.

HABITAT. Prefers moist soil near water, in sheltered and shaded situations.

CULTIVATION NOTES. This handsome tree is planted as an ornamental. The branches, with their attractive leaves and brightly colored fruit, are much used for Christmas decorations. The tree is a slow grower.

Large-leaved Holly
Ilex montana Gray

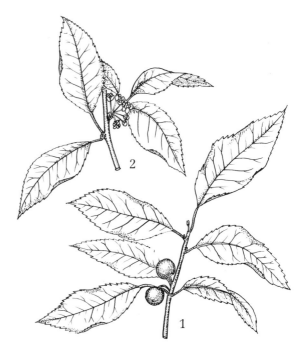

2

1

92. Ilex montana
1. Branch with fruits, x ½.
2. Branch with staminate flowers, x ½.
3. Staminate flower, enlarged.
4. Pistillate flower, enlarged.
5. Nutlet, enlarged.

3   4   5

HABIT. A deciduous shrub or small tree to 12 m, with a short trunk and slender, spreading and ascending branches forming a wide deep crown.

BARK. Bark thin, light brown, rough and warty, marked by many small lenticels.

STEMS. Branchlets smooth, light brown, becoming dark gray, covered with many small conspicuous lenticels; leaf-scars very small, broadly triangular.

WINTER-BUDS. Buds broadly ovoid, small, about 2–3 mm long, pointed, light brown; terminal bud larger; lateral buds smaller, superposed.

LEAVES. Alternate, simple, deciduous, thin, ovate or elliptic-ovate to lanceolate, 6–16 cm long, sharply pointed at apex, wedge-shaped or (rarely) rounded at base, sharply toothed on margin, dark green above, paler and smooth or sparingly hairy along the veins beneath; petioles 1.0–1.5 cm long.

FLOWERS. June. Flowers small, white, about 8 mm across. Staminate flowers clustered on stalks 3–8 mm long; calyx-lobes pointed, fringed with hairs. Pistillate flowers solitary or a few in a cluster, very short-stalked.

FRUIT. Fruit a spherical, orange-red drupe about 8–10 mm across, on stalks 2–6 mm long, with 4–6 nutlets; nutlets pointed at ends, many-ribbed.

DISTRIBUTION. New York to South Carolina, west to Alabama.

HABITAT. Prefers rich, moist, rocky soil, on wooded slopes and mountain sides, in shaded situations under large trees.

CULTIVATION NOTES. The Large-leaved Holly is planted as an ornamental for its attractive foliage and colorful fruit. The tree is slow growing and usually remains shrubby.

198

Large-leaved Holly *(Ilex montana)*

MAPLES
Acer *(Aceraceae)*

The genus *Acer* comprises over 120 species distributed in North America, Asia, Europe and North Africa. About 15 species are native to the United States and 6 are found in Pennsylvania.

The species of Maples are deciduous trees, rarely evergreen or shrub-like. The leaves are opposite, simple and usually palmately lobed, rarely compound. The small staminate and bisexual flowers occur either on the same or different trees and are arranged in racemes, panicles or corymbs. There are usually 5 sepals, sometimes connate, and 5 petals, sometimes missing. The flower mostly has 8 stamens attached to a large annular disk, and there are 2 styles or stigmas. The fruit is characteristically composed of 2 long-winged compressed samaras known as "keys."

Many species of Maples are planted as ornamental trees for their handsome foliage, brilliant in autumn. A number of introduced species are widely cultivated in the northeastern states. Among the most commonly and extensively planted as street and shade trees are the Norway Maple, *A. platanoides* Linnaeus, and the Sycamore Maple, *A. pseudoplatanus* Linnaeus, both originating from Europe and western Asia. The leaves of the Norway Maple are bright green and more or less shiny beneath. The leaves of the Sycamore Maple are more or less bluish white beneath. Among the smaller tree and shrubby Maples, the most widely planted is the Japanese Maple, *A. palmatum* Thunberg, from Japan, a species which appears in numerous cultivated varieties displaying many variations in shape, dissection and coloration of the leaves.

ACER

Summer key to the species

A. Leaves pinnately compound, with 3–5 or sometimes to 9 leaflets.
  A. negundo

A. Leaves simple, lobed, the lobes 3–5.
  B. Leaves whitish or silvery beneath. **A. saccharinum**
  B. Leaves green beneath, sometimes pale or slightly whitened.
    C. Leaves 3-lobed, only sometimes slightly 5-lobed.
      D. Leaves nearly all 3-lobed.
        E. Margins of lobes nearly entire, with usually 3, or sometimes 5 wavy teeth. **A. nigrum**
        E. Margins of lobes finely and sharply double-toothed.
          A. pennsylvanicum
      D. Leaves 3-lobed above the middle or sometimes slightly 5-lobed, coarsely and sharply toothed. **A. spicatum**
    C. Leaves 5-lobed.
      D. Leaves lobed to less than half the depth to the midrib, with pointed sinuses. **A. rubrum**
      D. Leaves lobed to more than half the depth to the midrib, with slightly rounded sinuses. **A. saccharum**

Winter key to the species

A. Buds more or less stalked, with 2 or few exposed scales.

  B. Buds evidently stalked; bark green, with longitudinal white lines.
                                                            A. pennsylvanicum

  B. Buds short-stalked; bark brownish, without longitudinal white lines.

    C. Buds smaller, long-pointed, about 3–4 mm long including the stalk; branchlets reddish brown, not smooth; pith brown.   **A. spicatum**

    C. Buds larger, short-pointed to obtuse, about 7–8 mm long; branchlets green to green-purple, bloomy; pith white or nearly so.   **A. negundo**

A. Buds sessile, with 6 or more exposed scales.

  B. Buds with 6–8 exposed scales, red or green, blunt at apex; bark not deeply furrowed.

    C. Branchlets reddish, shiny, not ill-scented when bruised; bark gray, not flaking in large pieces.   **A. rubrum**

    C. Branchlets chestnut-brown, not shiny, ill-scented when bruised; bark brownish, flaking in large pieces.   **A. saccharinum**

  B. Buds with 8–16 exposed scales, brown, pointed at apex; bark deeply furrowed.

    C. Bark brown; buds smooth or nearly so.   **A. saccharum**

    C. Bark black; buds hairy.   **A. nigrum**

Box Elder
Acer negundo Linnaeus

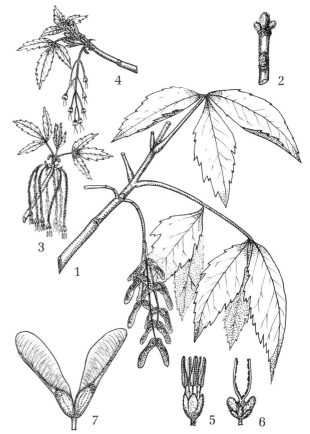

93. Acer negundo
1. Branch with fruits, x ½.
2. Branch with winter-buds, x ½.
3. Branch with staminate flowers, x ½.
4. Branch with pistillate flowers, x ½.
5. Staminate flower, enlarged.
6. Pistillate flower, enlarged.
7. Fruit, x 2.

HABIT. A medium-sized tree to 20 m, with a usually short trunk and stout branches forming a deep broad-topped crown.

BARK. Bark thick, pale gray or light brown, deeply cleft into ridges.

STEMS. Branchlets stout, smooth, green or purplish green, often covered with a whitish bloom and scattered raised lenticels; leaf-scars V-shaped, encircling stem.

WINTER-BUDS. Buds large, ovoid, short-stalked, white woolly, enclosed by 2 outer red scales; terminal bud 3–6 mm long, sharply pointed; lateral buds bluntly pointed, appressed.

LEAVES. Opposite, pinnately compound, with 3–5, rarely 7 or 9 leaflets; leaflets ovate to oblong-lanceolate, 6–10 cm long, about 3–4 cm wide, sharply pointed at apex, wedge-shaped at base, coarsely toothed on margin or the terminal one sometimes 3-lobed, dark green and smooth above, pale green beneath and slightly hairy, or nearly smooth; petioles 5–8 cm long.

FLOWERS. March–April. Flowers greenish yellow, the staminate and pistillate borne on different trees. Staminate flowers on hairy drooping stalks in clusters. Pistillate flowers on slender stalks in narrow drooping racemes.

FRUIT. Fruit a smooth key with wings diverging at an acute angle and usually incurved, 2.5–3.5 cm long with the nutlet, borne in drooping racemes; nutlet thick, somewhat flattened.

DISTRIBUTION. Vermont to Manitoba, south to Florida and Texas.

HABITAT. Prefers deep, moist soil, along banks of streams and borders of swamps, but also grows well in drier situations.

CULTIVATION NOTES. The Box Elder is planted as a shade or ornamental tree. The tree yields a sap from which some maple sugar is made locally. One of the hardiest maples and drought-resistant, it is much used for shelter belts.

202

Silver Maple
Acer saccharinum Linnaeus

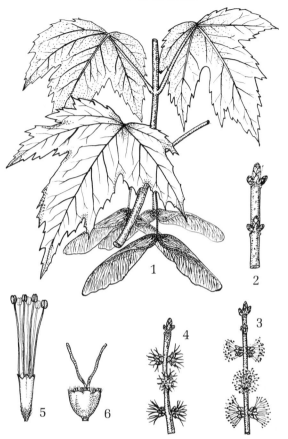

94. Acer saccharinum
1. Branch with fruits, x ½.
2. Branch with winter-buds, x ½.
3. Branch with staminate flowers, x ½.
4. Branch with pistillate flowers, x ½.
5. Staminate flower, enlarged.
6. Pistillate flower, enlarged.

HABIT. A tree usually to 30 m, sometimes attaining 40 m, with a short trunk and slender wide-spreading drooping branches forming a broad-topped crown.

BARK. Bark dark gray, more or less furrowed, separating into thin, loose flakes.

STEMS. Branchlets slender, shiny, green at first, becoming brown, covered with numerous light lenticels; leaf-scars V-shaped, not encircling stem.

WINTER-BUDS. Buds dark red, bluntly pointed, sessile or short-stalked; terminal bud about 6 mm long; flower-buds clustered on side spur-branches, stout, spherical, covered with many overlapping scales.

LEAVES. Opposite, simple, 5-lobed to deeply 5-cleft, roundish in outline, 8–14 cm across, heart-shaped at base, deeply and doubly toothed on margin, bright green above, silvery white beneath and hairy when young, the lobes ovate to broadly triangular, sharply pointed at apex, the middle one often 3-lobed.

FLOWERS. March–April. Flowers small, without petals, greenish, short-stalked, in dense sessile axillary clusters; the staminate and pistillate in separate clusters on the same or different trees.

FRUIT. Fruit a key with divergent wings 3.5–6.0 cm long with the nutlet, borne on slender drooping stalks in clusters along branchlets; nutlet elliptic-oblong.

DISTRIBUTION. New Brunswick to southern Ontario, south to Florida, Kansas and Oklahoma.

HABITAT. Prefers deep moist soil, along stream banks and low bottom lands.

CULTIVATION NOTES. The Silver Maple is planted as an ornamental tree, and the attractive foliage turns clear yellow in the fall. It is a rapid grower except in dry situations, where it does not attain a large size.

Black Maple
Acer nigrum Michaux f.

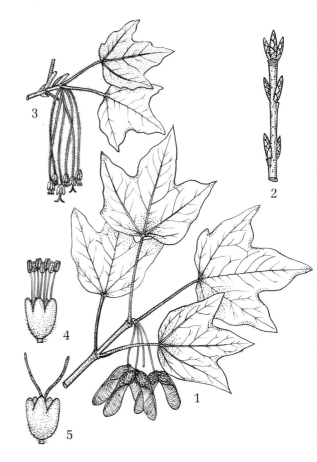

95. Acer nigrum
1. Branch with fruits, x ½.
2. Branch with winter-buds, x ½.
3. Branch with flowers, x ½.
4. Staminate flowers, enlarged.
5. Pistillate flowers, enlarged.

HABIT. A tree to 40 m, with stout spreading or erect branches forming a broad, rounded, symmetrical crown.

BARK. Bark thick, black, deeply furrowed.

STEMS. Branchlets stout, orange-green and hairy at first, soon becoming dull pale grayish brown and smooth, covered with pale oblong lenticels; leaf-scars narrow, nearly encircling stem.

WINTER-BUDS. Buds small, ovoid, 2–3 mm long, pointed at apex, the scales dark reddish brown, hairy on the outer surface.

LEAVES. Opposite, simple, 3-lobed, occasionally 5-lobed, roundish ovate in outline, 10–14 cm across, deeply heart-shaped at base, entire or obtusely toothed on margin and with broad, shallow, usually closed sinuses, the blade with drooping sides, dull green above, yellowish green and soft-hairy beneath, the lobes sharply pointed at apex; petioles stout, 8–12 cm long, usually hairy, much enlarged at base.

FLOWERS. April. Flowers small, yellowish green, without petals, about 6 mm long, in many-flowered, nearly stalkless clusters; the staminate and pistillate in the same cluster.

FRUIT. Fruit a smooth key with nearly upright or diverging wings, 3–4 cm long with the nutlet; nutlet smooth, bright red, 6 mm long.

DISTRIBUTION. Quebec west to South Dakota and Iowa, south to West Virginia, Kentucky and Missouri.

HABITAT. Prefers moist rich soils, river bottoms and lowlands, but also grows well on gravelly soils and uplands.

CULTIVATION NOTES. The Black Maple has duller leaves than other maples. It is not much planted as an ornamental tree and only occasionally as a shade tree.

Moosewood, Striped Maple
Acer pennsylvanicum Linnaeus

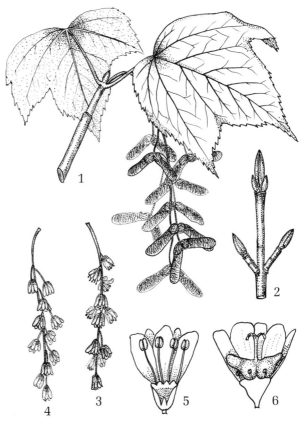

96. Acer pennsylvanicum
1. Branch with fruits, x ½.
2. Branch with winter-buds, x ½.
3. Staminate inflorescence, x ½.
4. Pistillate inflorescence, x ½.
5. Vertical section of staminate flower, enlarged.
6. Vertical section of pistillate flower, enlarged.

HABIT. A small tree, usually 3–8 m, occasionally to 12 m high, with a short trunk and slender straight branches forming a deep broad crown.

BARK. Bark thin, smooth, greenish brown or reddish brown, pale to dark-striped.

STEMS. Branchlets stout, smooth, green, becoming red, with conspicuous longitudinal white lines; leaf-scars V-shaped, nearly encircling stem.

WINTER-BUDS. Buds large, red, glossy, angular, with 2 outer scales; terminal bud about 1 cm long, short-stalked, the bud-scales keeled; lateral buds smaller, closely appressed.

LEAVES. Opposite, simple, 3-lobed at apex, roundish ovate in outline, 12–18 cm long, rounded at base, finely toothed on margin, rusty hairy beneath when young, the lobes pointing forward, sharply pointed at apex; petioles 2–7 cm long, grooved, with enlarged bases, rusty hairy when young.

FLOWERS. May–June. Flowers yellow, about 6 mm across, in drooping terminal racemes 10–15 cm long. Staminate and pistillate flowers occur on same plant but in different clusters.

FRUIT. Fruit a key on stalks 1.0–1.5 cm long, the wings thin, spreading at a wide angle, about 2 cm long with the nutlet.

DISTRIBUTION. Quebec to Minnesota, south along the mountains to Georgia.

HABITAT. Prefers moist, cool, rocky or sandy mountain slopes, usually in the shade of other trees.

CULTIVATION NOTES. The Moosewood's ornamental features are the large green leaves which turn bright yellow in autumn and the striped stems which become conspicuous in winter. It grows best in shaded situations.

Mountain Maple
Acer spicatum Lambert

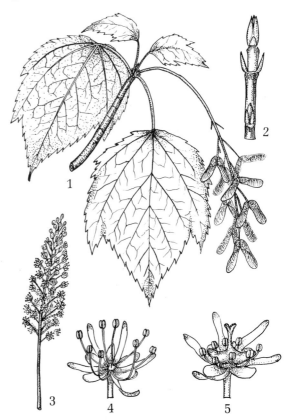

97. Acer spicatum
1. Branch with fruits, x ½.
2. Branch with winter-buds, x ½.
3. Inflorescence, x ½.
4. Staminate flower, enlarged.
5. Pistillate flower, enlarged.

HABIT. A shrub or small tree sometimes to 10 m, with a short trunk bearing slender upright branches.

BARK. Bark thin, brown or grayish brown mottled, flaky or furrowed.

STEMS. Branchlets slightly hairy, reddish purple changing to grayish brown, covered with a few scattered lenticels; leaf-scars V-shaped.

WINTER-BUDS. Buds small, short-stalked, flattish, bright red, pointed, more or less hairy; terminal bud 3–5 mm long; lateral buds smaller, more bluntly pointed, appressed.

LEAVES. Opposite, simple, 3-lobed or sometimes slightly 5-lobed, roundish ovate in outline, 6–12 cm long, heart-shaped at base, coarsely and irregularly toothed on margin, yellowish green above, hairy beneath, the lobes ovate, sharply pointed at apex; petioles long, slender, enlarged at base.

FLOWERS. June. Flowers small, greenish yellow, in terminal upright hairy racemes 8–14 cm long. Staminate and pistillate flowers occur in the same inflorescence, the former usually at the top and the latter at the base.

FRUIT. Fruit a reddish key arranged in drooping racemes, the wings divergent at nearly right angles, about 1.5 cm long with the nutlet, nearly smooth at maturity.

DISTRIBUTION. Newfoundland to Manitoba, south to Iowa and Pennsylvania, and along the mountains to northern Georgia.

HABITAT. Prefers moist, rocky hillsides, in damp forests, bordering ravines and always in the shade of other trees.

CULTIVATION NOTES. The Mountain Maple is much planted as an ornamental tree on account of the attractive foliage, light green in summer and orange and scarlet in autumn, and the bright reddish fruit. Valuable as a soil protector on rocky slopes, the tree is highly shade-demanding.

Red Maple
Acer rubrum Linnaeus

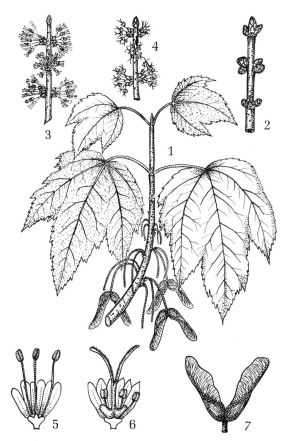

98. Acer rubrum
1. Branch with fruits, x ½.
2. Branch with winter-buds, x ½.
3. Branch with staminate flowers, x ½.
4. Branch with pistillate flowers, x ½.
5. Staminate flower, enlarged.
6. Pistillate flower, enlarged.
7. Fruit, x 1.

HABIT. A tree usually to 20 m, but sometimes to 40 m, with a short trunk and a deep, dense broad-topped crown.

BARK. Bark thick, dark gray, fissured into long ridges separating into platelike scales.

STEMS. Branchlets glossy, green at first, becoming smooth and red, covered with numerous light lenticels; leaf-scars V-shaped, not encircling stem.

WINTER-BUDS. Buds dark red, bluntly pointed; terminal bud about 2–3 mm long, the bud-scales rounded at apex; flower-buds clustered on side spur-branches.

LEAVES. Opposite, simple, 3- to 5-lobed, roundish ovate in outline, 6–10 cm long, heart-shaped at base, unequally and coarsely toothed on margin and with rather shallow sharp sinuses, dark green and shiny above, pale green and whitish bloomy beneath and usually hairy along the veins, the lobes triangular-ovate, short, sharp point at apex; petioles 5–10 cm long, often red.

FLOWERS. March–April. Flowers red, sometimes reddish, with petals, in dense stalkless axillary clusters; the staminate and pistillate in different clusters, on the same or different trees.

FRUIT. Fruit a smooth key with wings spreading at a narrow angle, 1.5–2.0 cm long with the nutlet, red to brown, borne in clusters on drooping stalks.

DISTRIBUTION. Nova Scotia to Manitoba, south to Florida and Texas.

HABITAT. Prefers wet soil, in swamplands and along banks of streams, sometimes on drier hillsides.

CULTIVATION NOTES. The Red Maple is more valuable as an ornamental tree than a timber tree. The tree is attractive with its red flowers in early spring, red fruits in early summer, and bright scarlet and yellow leaves in autumn. It is shade-tolerant.

207

Sugar Maple
Acer saccharum Marshall

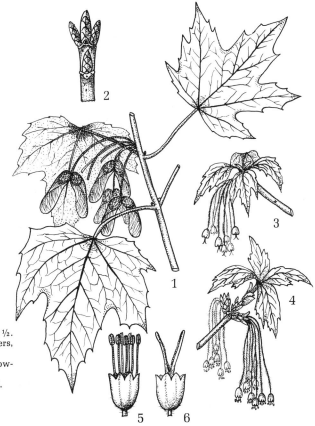

99. Acer saccharum
1. Branch with fruits, x ½.
2. Branch with winter-buds, x ½.
3. Branch with pistillate flowers, x ½.
4. Branch with staminate flowers, x ½.
5. Staminate flower, enlarged.
6. Pistillate flower, enlarged.

HABIT. A large tree to 40 m, with erect branches forming a round-topped crown.

BARK. Bark brown, deeply furrowed into long irregular flakes.

STEMS. Branchlets slender, smooth, brown, covered with many small pale lenticels; leaf-scars V-shaped, nearly encircling stem.

WINTER-BUDS. Buds small, reddish brown, conical, sharply pointed, smooth or somewhat hairy toward apex; terminal bud about 6 mm long; lateral buds smaller, appressed.

LEAVES. Opposite, simple, thin, 3- to 5-lobed, roundish ovate in outline, 8–14 cm across, heart-shaped at base, coarsely toothed on margin and with narrow and deep sinuses, bright green above, pale green and smooth beneath.

FLOWERS. April–May. Flowers small, greenish yellow, bell-shaped, about 5 mm long, on slender hairy drooping stalks 3–7 cm long, 5–10 arranged on nearly stalkless clusters, the staminate and pistillate occurring in different clusters. Staminate flowers with stamens exceeding the calyx-tube.

FRUIT. Fruit a key with slightly divergent or parallel wings, 2.5–4.0 cm long with the nutlet, smooth, borne on drooping stalks in clusters.

DISTRIBUTION. Newfoundland to Manitoba, south to Florida, Georgia and Texas.

HABITAT. Prefers rich, moist soil, in valleys, uplands, and along slopes.

CULTIVATION NOTES. The Sugar Maple is a valuable timber tree, an important food tree yielding maple sugar and maple syrup, and a most attractive ornamental tree, much planted as a street and shade tree. It has a dense regular form with bright green foliage turning yellow, orange or scarlet in fall. It grows best in well-drained rich soil but thrives also in poorer soils.

Box Elder (*Acer negundo*)

Silver Maple (*Acer saccharinum*)

Moosewood *(Acer pennsylvanicum)*

Mountain Maple *(Acer spicatum)*

210

Red Maple *(Acer rubrum)*

Sugar Maple (*Acer saccharum*)

Moosewood *(Acer pennsylvanicum)*

HORSE CHESTNUTS and BUCKEYES
Aesculus *(Hippocastanacae)*

Ohio Buckeye *(Aesculus glabra)*

There are about 25 species in the genus *Aesculus* distributed mainly in the temperate regions of the northern hemisphere. About 10 species are found in North America and 2 are native to Pennsylvania.

The species of *Aesculus* are deciduous trees or shrubs with stout branches and large winter-buds. The opposite leaves are large and digitately compound, with 5–9 toothed leaflets. The leaves are long-stalked and without stipules. The irregular flowers are either staminate or perfect, arranged in large upright many-flowered panicles. The calyx is bell-shaped and 4- to 5-toothed. The 4–5 unequal petals are long-clawed. There are 5–9 distinct stamens and a disk. The ovary is superior and 3-celled. The fruit is a 1-celled, 1-seeded capsule dehiscing into 3 valves.

In addition to the two tree species described in the following pages, there is the southern species, the Red Buckeye, *Aesculus pavia* Linnaeus, which is usually shrubby but may grow into small trees. It occurs Florida to Louisiana north to Virginia and West Virginia. The species has distinctive bright red flowers, comparatively small.

The species of *Aesculus* are ornamental trees grown for their handsome foliage and showy flowers. Besides the native species, the Common Horse chestnut, *A. hippocastanum* Linnaeus, from the Balkan Peninsula, is often planted as a shade and street tree. It differs from the native species in that its winter-buds are resinous, the leaflets are larger and doubly toothed, the petals have shorter claws and the flower clusters are much larger.

AESCULUS

Summer key to the species

A. Branchlets and leaves when bruised emit a bad odor; leaves smaller, the leaflets 7–15 cm long; fruit prickly. **A. glabra**

A. Branchlets and leaves when bruised do not emit a bad odor; leaves larger, the leaflets 10–25 cm long; fruit smooth. **A. octandra**

Winter key to the species

A. Bark thick and warty, furrowed, breaking into plates; buds resinous; bud-scales prominently keeled. **A. glabra**

A. Bark thin and smoother, fissured, breaking into many thin irregular scales; buds nonresinous; bud-scales not distinctly keeled. **A. octandra**

214

Ohio Buckeye, Fetid Buckeye
Aesculus glabra Willdenow

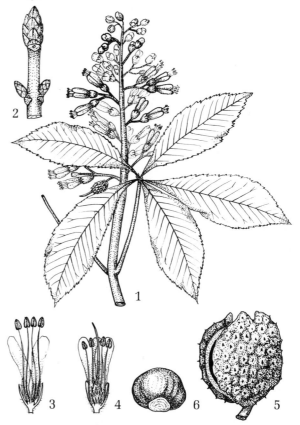

100. Aesculus glabra
1. Branch with flowers, x ½.
2. Branch with winter-buds, x ½.
3. Vertical section of staminate flower, enlarged.
4. Vertical section of perfect flower, enlarged.
5. Fruit, x ½.
6. Seed, x ½.

HABIT. A small tree usually 10–15 m, but sometimes 30 m, with a short slender trunk and a broad, deep round-topped crown.

BARK. Bark thick, gray, furrowed, broken into thick plates.

STEMS. Branchlets stout, downy and brown at first, becoming smooth and reddish brown to ash-gray; leaf-scars large, inversely triangular in shape.

WINTER-BUDS. Terminal buds 1.5–2.0 cm long, pointed, brownish, resinous, covered by triangular keeled scales.

LEAVES. Opposite, palmately compound, with 5 (rarely, 7) stalkless or very short-stalked leaflets; leaflets elliptic to obovate, 8–12 cm long, sharply pointed at apex, wedge-shaped at base, irregularly and finely toothed on margin, hairy when young, becoming nearly smooth at maturity, yellowish green above, paler beneath; petioles stout, 10–15 cm long, hairy at first, later smooth, enlarged at base.

FLOWERS. May. Flowers small, yellowish or greenish yellow, 2–3 cm long, borne in more or less fine-haired panicles 10–15 cm long and 5–8 cm broad; petals 4, of nearly equal length, their claws as long as the calyx; stamens longer than the petals.

FRUIT. Fruit a pale brown, rounded or obovoid, prickly capsule 3–5 cm long, borne on a short stout stalk, containing a single large, smooth, shiny brown seed, round and more or less flattened.

DISTRIBUTION. Western Pennsylvania west to Nebraska, south to Alabama.

HABITAT. Prefers rich, moist soils, river bottoms, banks of streams, ravines.

CULTIVATION NOTES. The Ohio Buckeye occurs naturally in the extreme western part of the state, but is sometimes planted as an ornamental tree elsewhere. The leaves turn yellow in autumn. Although it is usually found growing in moist soils, it will also grow in drier situations. The foliage is ill-smelling when bruised, hence the name "Fetid Buckeye."

215

Sweet Buckeye
Aesculus octandra Marshall

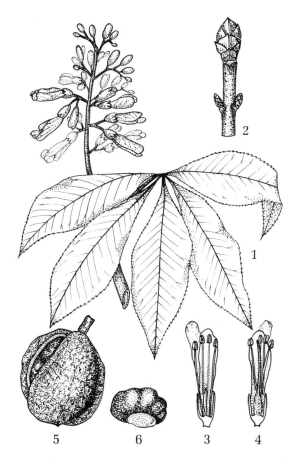

101. Aesculus octandra
1. Branch with flowers, x ½.
2. Branch with winter-buds, x ½.
3. Vertical section of staminate flower, enlarged.
4. Vertical section of perfect flower, enlarged.
5. Fruit, x ½.
6. Seed, x ½.

HABIT. A tree 20–30 m, but may reach 40 m, with a tall straight trunk and small rather drooping branches forming a narrow crown.

BARK. Bark thin, light brown to grayish brown, fissured, broken into many thin irregular scales.

STEMS. Branchlets stout, finely hairy at first, becoming smooth, reddish brown to ash-gray; leaf-scars large, inversely triangular in shape.

WINTER-BUDS. Terminal buds 2–5 cm long, bluntly pointed, reddish brown, non-resinous, covered by triangular keeled scales.

LEAVES. Opposite, palmately compound, with 5 (rarely, 7) sessile or short-stalked leaflets; leaflets narrow-elliptic to oblong-obovate, 10–15 cm long, long sharp point at apex, narrowed at base, hairy beneath when young, nearly smooth at maturity.

FLOWERS. May–June. Flowers small, yellow or purplish, 3 cm long, borne in finely hairy terminal panicles 10–15 cm long; petals very unequal, their claws longer than the calyx; stamens usually 7, shorter than the petals.

FRUIT. Fruit a pale brown, smooth, obovoid capsule 5–6 cm across, with usually 2 seeds; seeds large, smooth, reddish brown, shiny, 2–4 cm broad, somewhat flattened.

DISTRIBUTION. Western Pennsylvania to southern Illinois, south to Georgia and Texas.

HABITAT. Prefers moist rich soil, along streams, in bottom lands and valleys.

CULTIVATION NOTES. The Sweet Buckeye is limited in its distribution to the extreme western part of the state, although sometimes planted as an ornamental tree. It is a rapid grower.

Ohio Buckeye (*Aesculus glabra*)

Sweet Buckeye *(Aesculus octandra)*

Sweet Buckeye (*Aesculus octandra*)

LINDENS
Tilia *(Tiliaceae)*

American Linden *(Tilia americana)*

There are over 30 species in the genus *Tilia* distributed in the temperate regions of the northern hemisphere. Eight species are native to North America and 2 to Pennsylvania.

The species of the Linden genus are deciduous trees, characterized by fascicled hairs. The winter-buds are large and blunt-tipped. The alternate toothed leaves are 2-ranked, with slender petioles and deciduous stipules. The perfect, regular flowers, yellowish or whitish and quite fragrant, are usually arranged in drooping cymes. The stalk of the cyme is adnate about half-way to a large narrow bract. The flower has 5 distinct sepals, 5 distinct petals sometimes with opposite staminodes, many stamens and a pistil. The filaments of the stamens are often forked at the apex. The 5-celled ovary matures into a globose or ovoid nut-like fruit containing 1–3 seeds.

In addition to the two wide-spread species described, there is a southern species, the counterpart of *Tilia americana,* the Florida Linden, *T. floridana* (V. Engler) Small, which occurs from Florida to Texas north to North Carolina, southeastern Virginia and southern Indiana. It is a smaller tree than the American Linden, with leaves hairy when unfolding, soon becoming smooth, and hairy flower-stalks.

Besides the native species, 2 species introduced from Europe are often planted in northeastern North America, the Large-leaved Linden, *T. platyphyllos* Scopoli, the Small-leaved Linden, *T. cordata* Miller, as well as their hybrid, the Common Linden, *T. x europaea* Linnaeus. The European species differ from the American species in that their flowers contain no staminodes, the leaves are smaller and the inflorescences are fewer-flowered.

TILIA
Summer key to the species

A. Leaves nearly smooth beneath, with only tufts of hairs in the axils of the lateral veins, wanting at base, the hairs simple.   **T. americana**

A. Leaves silvery white, densely and thickly hairy beneath, the hairs stellate.   **T. heterophylla**

American Linden, Basswood
Tilia americana Linnaeus

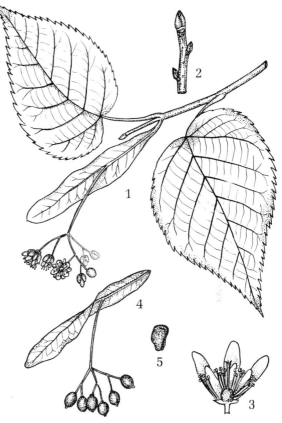

102. Tilia americana
1. Branch with flower, x ½.
2. Branch with winter-buds, x ½.
3. Vertical section of flower, enlarged.
4. Fruiting cluster with bract, x ½.
5. Seed, x 1.

HABIT. A large tree to 40 m, with a straight trunk and a dense, broad, ovoid or round-topped crown.

BARK. Bark thick, dark gray, longitudinally furrowed into flat scaly ridges, the ridge often with transverse secondary furrows.

STEMS. Branchlets smooth, reddish gray, becoming dark gray or brown, covered with scattered dark oblong lenticels; leaf-scars large, conspicuous, raised, broadly triangular.

WINTER-BUDS. Buds ovoid, stout, deep red or greenish, smooth or sometimes slightly hairy toward apex, mucilaginous, the scales rounded at back, usually 3 visible.

LEAVES. Alternate, simple, firm, broadly ovate, 10–20 cm long, long-pointed at apex, unequally truncate to heart-shaped at base, coarsely toothed with long-pointed teeth, dark green and shiny above, light green and smooth beneath except with tufts of hairs in the axils of the lateral veins, wanting at base; petioles slender, 3–5 cm long.

FLOWERS. June–July. Flowers perfect, regular, sweet, fragrant, yellowish white, about 1.5 cm across, in drooping 6- to 20-flowered cymose clusters, the long stalk united for about half its length with a conspicuous green bract, the bract round at apex and narrowed at base.

FRUIT. Fruit a woody ellipsoid to roundish nut-like drupe about 10 mm long, minutely pointed at apex, in small clusters with a common stalk attached to a leafy bract.

DISTRIBUTION. New Brunswick to Manitoba; south to Alabama and Texas.

HABITAT. Prefers rich, well-drained loamy soil.

CULTIVATION NOTES. The American Linden is an important timber tree as well as an ornamental or street tree. Several horticultural forms are recognized. The tree is a rapid grower, very shade-tolerant and fairly free from fungus diseases. Seeds or seedlings may be planted.

White Basswood
Tilia heterophylla Ventenat

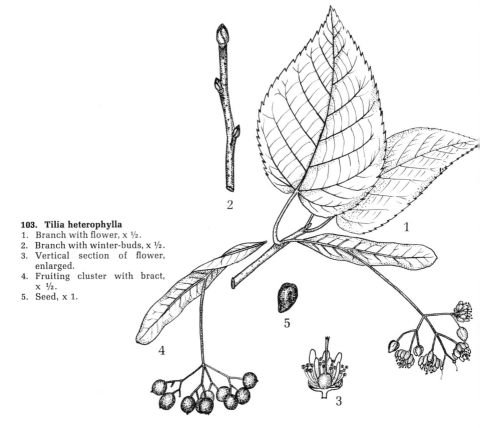

103. Tilia heterophylla
1. Branch with flower, x ½.
2. Branch with winter-buds, x ½.
3. Vertical section of flower, enlarged.
4. Fruiting cluster with bract, x ½.
5. Seed, x 1.

HABIT. A tree usually to 20 m, occasionally 30 m high, with a straight trunk and a dense, broad, more or less round-topped crown.

BARK. Bark thick, dark gray, furrowed longitudinally into flat scaly ridges, the ridges often with transverse secondary furrows.

STEMS. Branchlets smooth, reddish or yellowish brown, covered with scattered dark, oblong lenticels; leaf-scars large, conspicuous, raised, broadly triangular.

WINTER-BUDS. Buds ovoid, stout, deep red or greenish, smooth, mucilaginous, the scales rounded at back, usually 2–3 visible.

LEAVES. Alternate, simple, firm, ovate or oblong-ovate to orbicular-ovate, 12–20 cm long, sharply pointed at apex, obliquely truncate or heart-shaped at base, deeply toothed on margin with sharp teeth, dark green and smooth above and shiny at maturity, silvery white with close thick fine hairs beneath and small tufts of brown hairs; petioles slender, smooth, 3–4 cm long.

FLOWERS. June–July. Flowers perfect, regular, sweet and fragrant, yellowish white, 10–20 in drooping cymose clusters 6–8 cm long, the long stalk united for about half its length with a conspicuous green bract, the bract rounded at apex and narrowed at base.

FRUIT. Fruit a roundish woody nut-like drupe about 8 mm across, rusty hairy, minutely pointed at apex, in small clusters with a common stalk attached to a leafy bract.

DISTRIBUTION. New York to Illinois, south to Florida and Alabama.

HABITAT. Rich woods in mountains; prefers limestone soil.

CULTIVATION NOTES. The White Basswood is, with its attractive form, foliage and fragrant flowers, a very desirable ornamental tree. The tree is tolerant of considerable shade but also thrives in full light. It can be grown with seeds or seedlings transplanted in early spring.

American Linden (*Tilia americana*)

White Basswood (*Tilia heterophylla*)

American Linden (*Tilia americana*)

TUPELO
Nyssa *(Nyssaceae)*

Tupelo *(Nyssa sylvatica)*

Nyssa is a small genus with 6 species, 2 in Asia and 4 in North America, 1 native to Pennsylvania.

The species of *Nyssa* are deciduous trees with imbricate-scaled winter-buds. The alternate leaves, without stipules, are entire or have widely spaced teeth on the margin. The flowers are small, greenish white, and unisexual, with the staminate and pistillate or perfect occurring on separate trees. The staminate flowers are in many-flowered, axillary, stalked clusters; they contain a 5-toothed calyx, 5 small petals inserted on a disk, and 5–12 stamens. The pistillate or perfect flowers, usually sessile and with bractlets at base, are clustered together on a peduncle. They contain a 5-toothed calyx which is adnate to the ovary, 5 small petals, 5–10 short stamens with often sterile anthers, a small epigynous disk, and a 1- to 2-celled inferior ovary. The fruit is an oblong drupe, 1-seeded with a bony stone, and crowned with the remnants of the calyx.

Besides the widely distributed Tupelo, *Nyssa sylvatica* Marshall, there is a southern species, the Cotton Gum, *N. aquatica* Linnaeus, which occurs in inundated swamps from Florida to eastern Texas, north to Virginia and southern Indiana. It is a large tree with leaves 10–16 cm long, with dense, fine hairs beneath. It can also be distinguished from the Tupelo by the solitary instead of clustered pistillate flowers. The fruits are also much larger, 2–3 cm in length.

The Tupelo tree is native to eastern North America and frequently cultivated. Other species of the genus are rarely cultivated in the eastern states.

Tupelo, Black Gum
Nyssa sylvatica Marshall

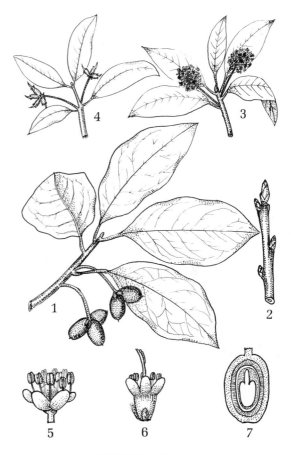

104. Nyssa sylvatica
1. Branch with fruits, x ½.
2. Branch with winter-buds, x ½.
3. Branch with staminate flowers, x ½.
4. Branch with pistillate flowers, x ½.
5. Staminate flower, enlarged.
6. Pistillate flower, enlarged.
7. Vertical section of fruit, enlarged.

HABIT. A tree to 30 m, with a straight trunk and slender spreading branches forming a nearly cylindric flat-topped crown.

BARK. Bark thick, dark brown, deeply furrowed and scaly.

STEMS. Branchlets smooth or downy at first, greenish or light brown, becoming smooth and dark reddish brown; leaf-scars rather large, conspicuous, broadly crescent in shape.

WINTER-BUDS. Buds dark red, ovoid, 3–6 mm long, blunt at apex, with 3–5 scales; lateral buds smaller, superposed.

LEAVES. Alternate, simple, ovate to obovate or elliptic, 5–12 cm long, pointed at apex, wedge-shaped or rounded at base, entire or thickened on margin (rarely, coarsely toothed), dark green and shiny above, often hairy beneath, hairy on veins or smooth at maturity; petioles 6–15 mm long, round or wing-margined.

FLOWERS. May–June. Flowers unisexual, borne on long, slender, hairy stalks 1.0–3.5 cm long, the staminate and pistillate on separate trees. Staminate flowers stalked, in dense, many-flowered heads. Pistillate flowers in open 2- to few-flowered clusters.

FRUIT. Fruit a small, ovoid, blue-black, fleshy drupe 8–12 mm long, borne in clusters of 2–3, with a few remnants of undeveloped pistillate flowers, borne on long stalks.

DISTRIBUTION. Maine, Ontario to Michigan, south to Florida and Texas.

HABITAT. Prefers borders of swamps and wet lowlands, but also common on dry mountain slopes and in abandoned fields.

CULTIVATION NOTES. The Tupelo is a highly ornamental tree with lustrous foliage turning bright red in fall. It is not selective in habit and grows well in a variety of situations.

HERCULES' CLUB
Aralia *(Araliaceae)*

Hercules' Club *(Aralia spinosa)*

Aralia is a small genus with about 20 species distributed in temperate and tropical regions of North America, Asia, Malaysia and Australia. There is only 1 tree species in North America.

The species of *Aralia* are deciduous shrubs or trees. The branches are stout with large pith and armed with very strong prickles. The winter-buds are large and with a few outer scales. The very large leaves are alternate, stalked, without stipules, and pinnately to thrice-pinnately compound. The small, perfect, regular, usually 5-part flowers are arranged in many umbels forming large terminal panicles. The fruit is a small berry-like drupe with 2–5 compressed stones.

The Hercules' Club, native to the eastern United States, is a medium-sized tree. Other native species as well as introduced ones are mostly low shrubs, rarely attaining tree size.

Hercules' Club
Aralia spinosa Linnaeus

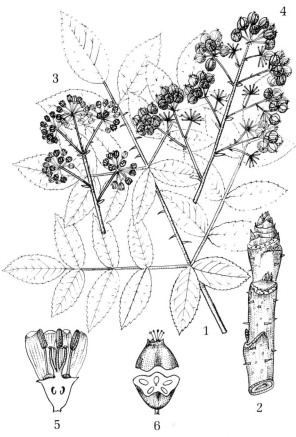

105. Aralia spinosa
1. Leaf, x ½.
2. Branch with winter-buds, x ½.
3. Portion of flowering panicle, x ½.
4. Portion of fruiting panicle, x ½.
5. Vertical section of flower, enlarged.
6. Transverse section of fruit, enlarged.

HABIT. A prickly tree to 15 m, the trunk branchless or sometimes with stout, wide-spreading branches.

BARK. Bark thin, brown, yellow inside, divided into rounded broken ridges.

STEMS. Branchlets very stout, with scattered stout prickles, roughened by narrow, long leaf-scars nearly encircling the stem.

WINTER-BUDS. Terminal bud present, chestnut brown, conical, about 1.2–2.0 cm long, bluntly pointed; lateral buds much smaller, flattened, triangular.

LEAVES. Alternate, pinnately compound or double-compound, 40–80 cm long, 35–70 cm wide; leaflets thick, ovate, 5–8 cm long, sharply pointed at apex, rounded or wedge-shaped at base, toothed on margin, dark green, smooth and usually prickly above, light green, white bloomy and sometimes a little hairy beneath; petioles prickly, to 25 cm long, the base enlarged, sheathing the stem.

FLOWERS. June–August. Flowers usually perfect, small, creamy white, in large, hairy, many-flowered panicles 20–35 cm long, the panicles solitary or 2–3 at end of branches.

FRUIT. Fruit an ovoid black berry about 6 mm across, 5-angled, crowned by the blackened persistent calyx.

DISTRIBUTION. Pennsylvania to Florida, west to Indiana, Texas and Missouri.

HABITAT. Prefers rich, moist bottom lands and moist, fertile woodlands.

CULTIVATION NOTES. The Hercules' Club is often planted for ornament. It has the largest leaves among the native trees. It is a rapid grower and spread by suckers. Often a number of unbranched stems may come up in rather dense clumps.

DOGWOODS
Cornus *(Cornaceae)*

Flowering Dogwood *(Cornus florida)*

There are about 40 species in the genus *Cornus* widely distributed in the temperate regions of the northern hemisphere. Fifteen species are native to North America and 8 to Pennsylvania.

The species of the Dogwood genus are deciduous (rarely, evergreen) trees or shrubs, sometimes herbs. The winter-buds are elongated and with 2 valvate scales. The simple leaves are opposite, rarely alternate, entire-margined and with parallel lateral veins extending along the margin toward the apex of the blade. They usually have 2-armed appressed hairs. The small perfect 4-part flowers are in dense terminal cymes or heads often surrounded by involucral bracts which are commonly mistaken for the corolla. The fruit is a drupe with thin flesh and a 2-celled stone.

The 2 species of native Dogwoods described here are small trees, one with opposite leaves and the other with alternate leaves. The other native species are shrubs or herbs. An introduced small tree frequently cultivated as an ornamental is the Cornelian Cherry, *C. mas* Linnaeus, of Europe and western Asia. The small yellow flowers, appearing in early spring before the leaves, are borne in umbel-like clusters in great profusion. The yellowish involucre of the umbels is small and deciduous early in flowering.

CORNUS

Summer key to the species

A. Branchlets and leaves opposite; flowers in dense heads with 4 large white involucral bracts.　　　**C. florida**

A. Branchlets and leaves alternate, rarely opposite; flowers in terminal cymes.　　　**C. alternifolia**

Winter key to the species

A. Branchlets opposite; bark on older stems broken up into quadrangular scaly blocks.　　　**C. florida**

A. Branchlets alternate; bark on older stems fissured longitudinally.　　　**C. alternifolia**

Flowering Dogwood
Cornus florida Linnaeus

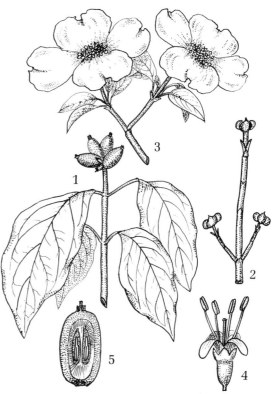

106. Cornus florida
1. Branch with fruits, x ½.
2. Branch with flower-buds, x ½.
3. Branch with inflorescences, x ½.
4. Flower, enlarged.
5. Vertical section of fruit, enlarged.

HABIT. A small tree 5–10 m high with a short trunk and a broad, rather dense crown.

BARK. Bark reddish brown or blackish, separating into quadrangular plate-like scales.

STEMS. Branchlets pale green, changing to red or yellowish green and then to light brown or reddish gray, smooth, shiny, often whitish bloomy, covered with a few small lenticels; leaf-scars V-shaped, raised, sometimes encircling stem.

WINTER-BUDS. Leaf-buds narrow-conical, sharply pointed, greenish, covered by 2 bud-scales; flower-buds spherical or vertically flattened, about 1.0–1.2 cm broad, grayish, covered by 2 opposite pairs of bud-scales.

LEAVES. Opposite, simple, usually crowded toward end of branchlets, ovate, 8–15 cm long, 5–7 cm wide, sharply pointed at apex, wedge-shaped to rounded at base, entire or wavy on margin, bright dark green and nearly smooth above, pale beneath and usually only hairy on the veins, with prominent midrib and 6–7 pairs of veins; petioles 5–15 mm long.

FLOWERS. April. Flowers perfect, small, greenish white or yellowish, arranged in dense heads surrounded by 4 large white or pink bracts, resembling a flower in appearance; bracts obovate, notched or truncate at apex, 4–5 cm long.

FRUIT. Fruit a scarlet ellipsoid drupe about 1 cm long, crowned by the persistent calyx, solitary or 2–5 clustered on a stalk, often with undeveloped pistillate flowers persisting together; stone grooved.

DISTRIBUTION. Massachusetts to Ontario and Michigan, south to Florida and Texas.

HABITAT. Prefers rich, well-drained soil, usually under shade of other trees.

CULTIVATION NOTES. The Flowering Dogwood is one of the most popular ornamental trees. It is extremely attractive both in bloom, in fruit and in foliage. Although the tree thrives best in low, moist, fertile, well-drained and shaded situations, it will grow on other soils and under other conditions.

Alternate-leaved Dogwood
Cornus alternifolia Linnaeus

107. Cornus alternifolia
1. Branch with fruits, x ½.
2. Branch with winter-buds, x ½.
3. Branch with inflorescences, x ½.
4. Flower, enlarged.
5. Vertical section of fruit, enlarged.

HABIT. A small tree to 10 m, with a short trunk and a broad dense, flat-topped crown.

BARK. Bark thin, dark reddish brown, shallowly fissured longitudinally.

STEMS. Branchlets slender, smooth, often shiny, greenish at first, becoming dark green and often striped with white; leaf-scars crescent-shaped.

WINTER-BUDS. Leaf-buds small, sharply pointed, light brown; flower-buds spherical or vertically flattened.

LEAVES. Alternate, simple, usually crowded at end of branchlets, elliptic-ovate, 6–12 cm long, 5–7 cm wide, sharply pointed at apex, wedge-shaped at base, entire or wavy on margin, bright green above, more or less white downy beneath, with 5–6 pairs of veins; petioles 2–5 cm long.

FLOWERS. April–May. Flowers perfect, small, cream-colored, borne in many-flowered terminal cymes 4–6 cm across, the cymes finely and shortly hairy, slender-stalked.

FRUIT. Fruit a bluish-black, bloomy drupe 6–8 mm across, crowned with the remnants of the style, borne on red stalks in cymes.

DISTRIBUTION. New Brunswick to Minnesota, south to Georgia and Alabama.

HABITAT. Prefers moist, well-drained soils, borders of swamps and streams, often under shade of other trees.

CULTIVATION NOTES. The Alternate-leaved Dogwood is the only native *Cornus* with alternate leaves and branches. It is an attractive tree for ornamental planting. The tree is very tolerant of shade and easily transplanted. It prefers a moister situation than the Flowering Dogwood.

Alternate-leaved Dogwood *(Cornus alternifolia)*

RHODODENDRONS
Rhododendron *(Ericaceae)*

Great Laurel *(Rhododendron maximum)*

There are over 600 species in the genus *Rhododendron* distributed through the colder and temperate regions of the northern hemisphere and also on the high mountains of tropical Asia and Australia. Of 26 species in North America, 1 species of tree size is native to Pennsylvania.

The species of *Rhododendron* are evergreen or deciduous shrubs, rarely trees. The leaves are alternate, simple, stalked and entire. The large, perfect, slightly irregular flowers are usually in terminal umbel-like racemes. There are a small 5-part calyx, a large, somewhat

bell-shaped corolla with a (usually) 5-lobed limb, 5–10 stamens and a 5- to 10-celled superior ovary. The anthers open with apical pores. The fruit is an oblong capsule containing numerous minute seeds.

The species of the genus *Rhododendron* are much planted for their beautiful flowers. *R. maximum* is the only native species in eastern North America attaining the height of a small tree. Many other native as well as introduced species are widely cultivated also, but these are nearly all of shrub size.

234

Great Laurel
Rhododendron maximum Linnaeus

108. Rhododendron maximum
1. Branch with flowers, x ½.
2. Branch with flower-bud, x ½.
3. Stamen, enlarged.
4. Pistil, enlarged.
5. Fruits, x ½.
6. Transverse section of fruit, enlarged.

HABIT. A small bushy evergreen tree to 12 m, usually grows as a large shrub to 4–5 m, with often twisted stems and contorted branches forming an irregular round-headed crown.

BARK. Bark thin, reddish brown, close at first, later peeling off in thin scales.

STEMS. Branchlets at first green and rusty hairy, later becoming smooth and bright reddish brown; leaf-scars conspicuous, slightly raised, rounded below, slightly depressed above.

WINTER-BUDS. Leaf-buds usually axillary, sometimes terminal, conical, dark green. Flower-buds usually terminal, conical, about 2.5–3.5 cm long, covered by numerous, overlapping green bracts.

LEAVES. Alternate, simple, persistent, thick and leathery, ovate to oblong or oblong-obovate to oblong-lanceolate, 10–20 cm long, 4.0–6.5 cm wide, pointed to sharply short-pointed at apex, rounded to wedge-shaped at base, entire on margin, dark green and smooth above, paler beneath and covered with close thin hairs (rarely, nearly smooth); petioles 1.5–2.5 cm long, hairy when young.

FLOWERS. June–July. Flowers perfect, large, showy, many arranged in umbel-like clusters about 10–12 cm across, borne on glandular-hairy stalks; calyx 5-lobed; corolla white or rose to purplish pink, upper side spotted olive-green to orange, bell-shaped, 3.5–4.0 cm across, deeply lobed, the lobes ovate, flat; filaments hairy near base; ovary glandular-hairy, the style smooth.

FRUIT. Fruit a dark reddish, elongated, glandular capsule about 1.2 cm long, persisting through winter, splitting open longitudinally; seeds minute, numerous, oblong, flattened.

DISTRIBUTION. Nova Scotia to Ohio, south along the mountains to Georgia and Alabama.

HABITAT. Frequents damp woods, swamps and pond-margins; on mountains but remains along stream-banks in the south.

CULTIVATION NOTES. The Great Laurel is the most attractive shrub in the native flora. It prefers moist locations but will thrive in a variety of situations. However it is an acid-loving plant and will not tolerate soils containing lime.

235

MOUNTAIN LAUREL
Kalmia *(Ericaceae)*

Mountain Laurel *(Kalmia latifolia)*

There are about 8 species in the genus *Kalmia* distributed in eastern North America and the West Indies. Three species are native to Pennsylvania.

The species of *Kalmia* are evergreen shrubs or small trees, rarely deciduous. The leaves are alternate, opposite or irregularly whorled, stalked and entire-margined. The perfect regular flowers are either solitary or in terminal or lateral, simple or compound corymbs. There are a small persistent 5-part calyx, a saucer-shaped 5-lobed corolla, 10 stamens with the anthers opening by apical pores, and a superior 5-celled ovary with a slender style. The anthers, on slender filaments, are held back in little pouches and spring up suddenly by the straightening of the filaments when the corolla expands or is touched. The fruit is a capsule containing numerous minute seeds.

The native Mountain Laurel, *Kalmia latifolia,* attains to the size of a small tree while the other species of the genus are low shrubby plants.

Mountain Laurel
Kalmia latifolia Linnaeus

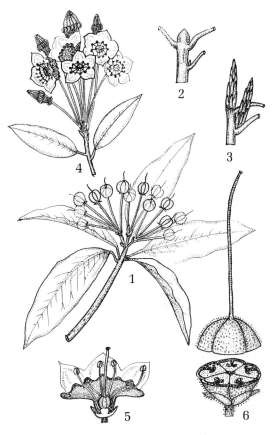

109. Kalmia latifolia
1. Branch with fruits, x ½.
2. Winter-buds, x ½.
3. Flower-buds, x ½.
4. Branch with flowers, x ½.
5. Vertical section of flower, enlarged.
6. Transverse section of fruit, enlarged.

HABIT. An evergreen small tree or shrub, occasionally to 10–12 m, with a stout, usually forked stem bearing wide-spreading branches forming a round compact head.

BARK. Bark very thin, reddish brown, furrowed, peeling off in long narrow thin scales.

STEMS. Branchlets reddish green and covered with viscid hairs, becoming green and finally brown; leaf-scars large, imbedded in branchlets.

WINTER-BUDS. Buds green, ovoid, sharply pointed. Leaf-buds appear below clustered flower-buds. Flower-buds with numerous downy overlapping scales, the scales green, glandular-hairy.

LEAVES. Alternate, simple, persistent, thick and leathery, elliptic to elliptic-lanceolate, 5–10 cm long, 1.0–1.5 cm wide, pointed and sometimes bristly at apex, wedge-shaped at base, entire on margin, dark green and shiny above, yellowish green beneath; petioles 1–2 cm long.

FLOWERS. May–June. Flowers large, showy, borne on red or green sparsely hairy stalks in dense, many-flowered umbel-like clusters about 10 cm across; calyx 5-lobed; corolla white to rose, broad bell-shaped, viscid-hairy.

FRUIT. Fruit a globose woody capsule 5–7 mm across, slightly 5-lobed, covered with viscid hairs, with persistent style and calyx; seeds small, numerous.

DISTRIBUTION. New Brunswick to Ohio, south to Florida and Tennessee.

HABITAT. Common on rocky hilltops, along margins of swamps and in woods.

CULTIVATION NOTES. The Mountain Laurel is the state tree of Pennsylvania. Next to *Rhododendron*, it is the most attractive shrub in the native flora. It thrives in a variety of situations except limestone soils.

SORREL TREE
Oxydendrum *(Ericaceae)*

Sorrel Tree *(Oxydendrum arboreum)*

There is only one species in the genus *Oxydendrum;* it is found in the eastern part of the United States.

This species is a small or medium-sized deciduous tree. It can be recognized by the alternate, bitter, long and narrow toothed shiny leaves somewhat resembling peach leaves. The very small, dark red winter-buds, alternately arranged and partly imbedded in the bark, are also characteristic. In the summer, it bears very distinctive inflorescences, terminal panicles of 6 or more slender one-sided racemes of small whitish flowers resembling the lily-of-the-valley.

Sorrel Tree, Sour-wood
Oxydendrum arboreum *(Linnaeus)* DeCandolle

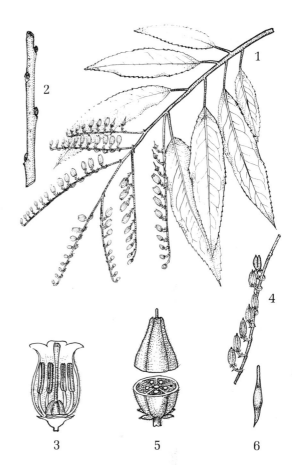

110. Oxydendrum arboreum
1. Branch with flowers, x ½.
2. Branch with winter-buds, x ½.
3. Vertical section of flower, enlarged.
4. Portion of fruit-cluster, x ½.
5. Transverse section of fruit, enlarged.
6. Seed, enlarged.

HABIT. A medium-sized tree to 20 m, with a tall slender trunk and a narrow round-topped crown.

BARK. Bark thick, grayish tinged with red, deeply fissured separating rounded thickly scaly ridges.

STEMS. Branchlets slender, smooth or sparingly fine-haired, yellowish green at first, becoming reddish brown, covered with numerous, oblong, raised lenticels; leaf-scars raised, nearly triangular in shape.

WINTER-BUDS. Terminal bud absent; lateral buds small, pointed at apex, partly imbedded in the bark, the bud-scales dark red, several opposite pairs.

LEAVES. Alternate, simple, elliptic-oblong to oblong-lanceolate, 8–20 cm long, 3–7 cm wide, sharply pointed at apex, broadly wedge-shaped at base, finely toothed on margin, very smooth and shiny above, sparingly hairy on veins beneath; petioles slender, 8–15 mm long.

FLOWERS. July–August. Flowers perfect, white, borne on drooping panicles 10–25 cm long; corolla 6–8 mm long.

FRUIT. Fruit a 5-valved capsule 5 mm long, grayish hairy, terminated by a persistent style, borne in panicles.

DISTRIBUTION. Pennsylvania to Indiana, south to Florida and Louisiana.

HABITAT. Prefers well-drained soils; common on hillsides and in woods.

CULTIVATION NOTES. The Sorrel Tree is native to a limited area of southwestern Pennsylvania but is planted widely as an ornamental tree for its handsome form, late flowers and especially beautiful scarlet leaves in autumn.

239

PERSIMMONS
Diospyros *(Ebenaceae)*

Common Persimmon *(Diospyros virginiana)*

There are about 200 species in the genus *Diospyros,* distributed chiefly in tropical and subtropical regions of the world. Only 1 species is represented in eastern North America.

The species of the Persimmon genus are deciduous or evergreen trees or shrubs. The leaves are alternate, simple and entire-margined. The flowers are regular, whitish and unisexual. The staminate and pistillate flowers occur on separate trees, the staminate in cymes and the pistillate usually solitary. The calyx and corolla are usually 4-lobed. There are 8–16 stamens and a 4- to 12-celled superior ovary. The fruit is a large juicy berry, with the enlarged calyx at base, and containing 1–10 large flattened seeds.

The species *D. virginiana,* the only temperate American species of this primarily tropical genus, is widely cultivated. The other species of the genus are not reliably hardy in the northeastern states.

Common Persimmon
Diospyros virginiana Linnaeus

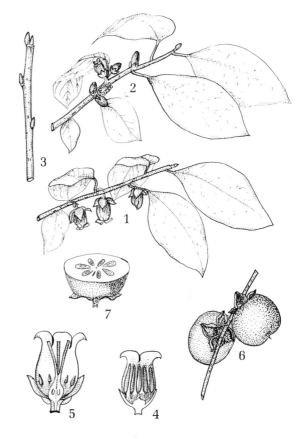

111. Diospyros virginiana
1. Branch with pistillate flowers, x ½.
2. Branch with staminate flowers, x ½.
3. Branch with winter-buds, x ½.
4. Vertical section of staminate flower, enlarged.
5. Vertical section of pistillate flower, enlarged.
6. Branch with fruits, x ½.
7. Transverse section of fruit, x ½.

HABIT. A small tree to 30 m in height, with a (usually) short slender trunk and spreading, often drooping branches forming a round-topped crown.

BARK. Bark thick, hard, dark brown or nearly black, deeply separated into square thick plates peeling off in thin scales.

STEMS. Branchlets slender, hairy when young, grayish brown to reddish brown, covered with a few scattered orange lenticels; leaf-scars raised, flattened.

WINTER-BUDS. Buds small, broadly ovoid, 2–3 mm long, sharply pointed at apex, with 2 dark brown shiny scales.

LEAVES. Alternate, simple, thick, ovate to elliptic, 6–14 cm long, pointed at apex, wedge-shaped to usually rounded at base, entire on margin, dark green and shiny above, paler and hairy beneath, usually smooth at maturity; petioles 1.5–2.5 cm long.

FLOWERS. May–June. Flowers white, the corolla bell-shaped, with 4 reflexed lobes. Staminate flowers usually in 2- to 3-flowered clusters, about 1 cm long, with 16 stamens. Pistillate flowers solitary, about 1.5 cm long, borne on short stalks, with 4 2-lobed styles.

FRUIT. Fruit a fleshy spherical berry 2.0–3.5 cm across, yellowish to pale orange, often with red cheeks, edible but very astringent; seeds usually 4–6, oblong, about 1 cm long.

DISTRIBUTION. Connecticut to Iowa, south to Florida and Texas.

HABITAT. Prefers a light, sandy, well-drained soil; dry woods and clearings.

CULTIVATION NOTES. The Common Persimmon is an ornamental tree with a handsome form, beautiful foliage and interesting and attractive bark. It is sometimes planted for its edible fruit. It is essentially a southern tree and in Pennsylvania rarely exceeds 15 m in height.

ASHES
Fraxinus *(Oleaceae)*

There are about 65 species in the genus *Fraxinus* distributed throughout the northern hemisphere south to Mexico in America and to Java in Asia. About 16 species are native to North America and 3 to Pennsylvania.

The species of the Ash genus are deciduous trees readily recognizable by their opposite compound leaves. The buds, with 1 or 2 pairs of outer scales, are usually brown or black and scurfy. The leaves are pinnately compound (sometimes reduced to 1 leaflet). The small flowers, either perfect or unisexual, occur in crowded panicles. In the flower, there are a small 4-part calyx and a corolla usually of 4 distinct petals, but in some cases the calyx and corolla are missing. There are usually 2 stamens and a 2-celled superior ovary with 2 stigmas. The fruit is a samara formed by a 1-seeded nutlet with a usually elongated wing at the apex.

Besides the 3 widespread species there are 3 additional species extending to the eastern states. *Fraxinus biltmoreana* Beadle closely resembles the White Ash, *F. americana,* but can be distinguished by the hairy leaves and branchlets. It occurs from Georgia, Alabama and Missouri north to New Jersey. The Pumpkin Ash, *F. tomentosa* Michaux

f. is also similar to the Red Ash, *F. pennsylvanica,* distinguished by the leaves green beneath and by the larger leaflets and longer fruits. The branchlets and leaf-stalks are fine-haired instead of hairless. It occurs in swampy areas from Florida to New York, Ohio and Indiana. The Blue Ash, *F. quadrangulata* Michaux is closely related to the Black Ash, *F. nigra,* differing in the angular, usually winged branchlets and the presence of a minute deciduous calyx in the flowers. It occurs from Michigan to Arkansas and Texas. The Water Ash, *F. caroliniana* Miller, is a small shrubby tree also of swamps and wet bottom lands, occurring in the south and along the Coastal Plain to Virginia. It is a most variable species. It can be distinguished from the other species by the fruit, winged to the base.

Besides the native species, many introduced ones are in cultivation in the northeastern states. The most widely planted species is the European Ash, *F. excelsior* Linnaeus, of Europe and Asia Minor. It resembles the native Black Ash, *F. nigra,* but its leaflets are smooth beneath except along the midrib, where it has thick rusty hairs at the base.

FRAXINUS
Summer key to the species
A. Lateral leaflets sessile.   **F. nigra**
A. Lateral leaflets stalked.
> B. Branchlets and leaves smooth or nearly so; fruits usually winged at apex only.   **F. americana**
> B. Branchlets and leaves densely hairy; fruit usually winged at apex and extending down the sides.   **F. pennsylvanica**

Winter key to the species
A. Bark soft, flaky, not furrowed; buds blackish, the terminal ones pointed at apex.   **F. nigra**
A. Bark firm, furrowed; buds brownish, the terminal ones blunt at apex.
> B. Branchlets nearly smooth.   **F. americana**
> B. Branchlets densely hairy.   **F. pennsylvanica**

Black Ash
Fraxinus nigra Marshall

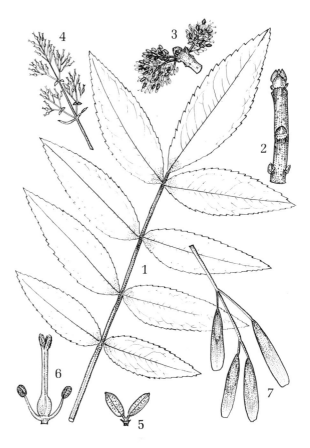

112. Fraxinus nigra
1. Leaf, x ½.
2. Branch with winter-buds, x ½.
3. Branch with staminate panicles, x ½.
4. Pistillate panicle, x ½.
5. Staminate flower, enlarged.
6. Pistil with two staminodes, enlarged.
7. Cluster of fruits, x ½.

HABIT. A medium-sized tree to 25 m, with a tall slender trunk bearing more or less upright branches forming a narrow shallow crown.

BARK. Bark thin, grayish, with shallow irregular fissures separating flaky and scaly ridges.

STEMS. Branchlets stout, at first dark green and somewhat hairy, soon becoming ash-gray or orange and smooth, conspicuous, crescent-shaped.

WINTER-BUDS. Buds black; terminal bud ovoid, sharply pointed; lateral buds smaller, nearly rounded, blunter, closely appressed to stem.

LEAVES. Opposite, pinnately compound, about 30 cm long, with 7–11 stalkless leaflets; leaflets oblong to oblong-lanceolate, sharply pointed at apex, wedge-shaped at base, toothed on margin with small inverted teeth, dark green and smooth above, lighter green beneath, smooth except rusty hairy at base and along midrib beneath.

FLOWERS. May. Staminate and pistillate flowers borne on the same or different trees. Staminate flowers in dense, dark purplish clusters; anthers oblong, with a minute point at apex, on short filaments.

FRUIT. Fruit a samara 2.5–3.5 cm long, the wing completely surrounding the flattened seed-bearing portion, narrow-oblong to oblong-obovate, rounded or notched at apex; samaras in open panicles.

DISTRIBUTION. Newfoundland to Manitoba, south to West Virginia, Iowa and Arkansas.

HABITAT. Prefers cool, moist habitats.

CULTIVATION NOTES. The Black Ash is occasionally planted for ornamental purposes. It decidedly prefers a cool, swampy habitat. It thrives in cooler regions and wet situations but not in dry situations.

243

White Ash
Fraxinus americana Linnaeus

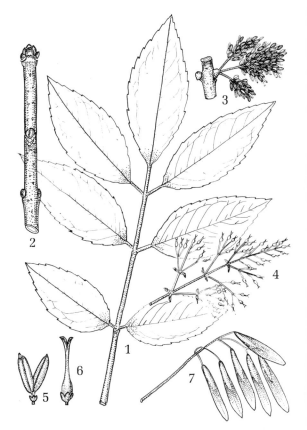

113. Fraxinus americana
1. Leaf, x ½.
2. Branch with winter-buds, x ½.
3. Staminate panicle, x ½.
4. Pistillate panicle, x ½.
5. Stamen, enlarged.
6. Pistil, enlarged.
7. Cluster of fruits, x ½.

HABIT. A tall tree to 40 m, with a tall trunk and a round-topped open crown.

BARK. Bark thick, grayish brown, deeply fissured into narrow flattened ridges, the ridges thinly and closely covered by scales.

STEMS. Branchlets stout, dark green or brownish, smooth and shiny, covered by scattered, large, pale lenticels; leaf-scars conspicuous, raised, crescent-shaped.

WINTER-BUDS. Buds ovoid, bluntly pointed, dark brown or sometimes almost black; terminal bud larger, the scales sharply pointed; lateral buds smaller, the scales blunter.

LEAVES. Opposite, pinnately compound, about 25 cm long, with 5–9 stalked leaflets, usually 7; leaflets ovate to ovate-lanceolate, 6–15 cm long, about 3 cm wide, sharply pointed at apex, rounded to wedge-shaped at base, margin entire or slightly toothed toward apex, dark green above, bloomy and usually smooth beneath, sometimes a few hairs on the veins; stalk of leaflets 5–15 mm long.

FLOWERS. May. Staminate and pistillate flowers borne on different trees. Staminate flowers in dense reddish purple clusters; anthers oblong, with a minute point at apex. Pistillate flowers in open panicles.

FRUIT. Fruit a samara 3–5 cm long, the wing narrow-oblong, notched or bluntly pointed at apex, attached to the apex of the rounded seed-bearing portion; samaras in dense drooping panicles.

DISTRIBUTION. Nova Scotia to Minnesota, south to Florida and Texas.

HABITAT. Prefers rich, fertile, moist soils; along streambeds in moist woods.

CULTIVATION NOTES. The White Ash is an important timber tree and is also planted as an ornamental tree. The leaves turn deep purple and yellow in autumn. It is a vigorous rapid grower, free from insect and fungi diseases. The tree prefers moist habitats but will grow in other rather dry situations.

Red Ash
Fraxinus pennsylvanica Marshall

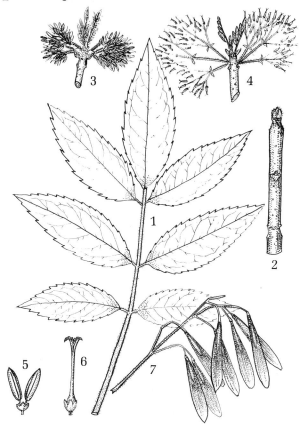

114. Fraxinus pennsylvanica
1. Leaf, x ½.
2. Branch with winter-buds, x ½.
3. Branch with staminate panicles, x ½.
4. Branch with pistillate panicles, x ½.
5. Stamen, enlarged.
6. Pistil, enlarged.
7. Cluster of fruits, x ½.

HABIT. A medium-sized tree to 20 m, with a tall trunk bearing upright branches forming a compact, more or less irregular crown.

BARK. Bark grayish brown, with many longitudinal, shallow fissures separating prominent ridges, the ridges scaly.

STEMS. Branchlets at first hairy, becoming gray or brownish, often white bloomy, covered by large pale lenticels; leaf-scars conspicuous, crescent-shaped.

WINTER-BUDS. Buds small, rounded, brown, the scales in 3 pairs, rounded on the back, hairy.

LEAVES. Opposite, pinnately compound, about 30 cm long, with 5–9 stalked leaflets; leaflets ovate to oblong-lanceolate, 8–14 cm long, 2.5–4.0 cm wide, sharply pointed at apex, wedge-shaped at base, margin slightly toothed or nearly entire, yellowish green above, densely and finely hairy beneath; stalks of leaflets 3–6 mm long, hairy.

FLOWERS. May. Staminate and pistillate flowers usually borne on different trees.

Staminate flowers in compact purplish red, hairy panicles; anthers linear-oblong, on short filaments. Pistillate flowers in open greenish red panicles.

FRUIT. Fruit a samara 3–6 cm long, the wing attached to the seed along its sides and apex, lanceolate to oblong-obovate, rounded, pointed, or sometimes notched at apex; samaras borne in open panicles.

DISTRIBUTION. Nova Scotia to Manitoba, south to Florida and Alabama.

HABITAT. Prefers rich, moist soils, river banks, swampy lowlands and along lakes and ponds.

CULTIVATION NOTES. The Red Ash is a variable species represented also by the variety called the smooth-branched Green Ash (*F. pennsylvanica* var. *lanceolata* [Borkhausen] Sargent). The species is sometimes planted for ornamental purposes. It is hardy, free from attacks of insects and fungi, decidedly moisture-loving and grows in rather wet situations.

Black Ash *(Fraxinus nigra)*

Red Ash *(Fraxinus pennsylvanica)*

White Ash (*Fraxinus americana*)

FRINGE-TREE
Chionanthus *(Oleaceae)*

Fringe-tree *(Chionanthus virginicus)*

There are only 2 species in the genus *Chionanthus,* 1 in eastern North America and the other in eastern Asia.

The species of *Chionanthus* are deciduous small trees or large shrubs with opposite, simple, stalked and entire-margined leaves. The flowers are unisexual, with the staminate and pistillate ones occurring on separate trees. These are white and showy, arranged in loose panicles from lateral buds near the end of the year-old branches. The calyx is 4-cleft and the corolla divided nearly to the base into 4 long, strip-like narrow petals. There are 4 sessile stamens and a 2-celled superior ovary with a very short style and a 2-lobed stigma. The fruit is a 1-seeded dark blue drupe.

Besides the native species, which is cultivated as an ornamental, the Asiatic species, *C. retusus* Lindley, is sometimes also cultivated. It is equally showy but it blooms somewhat later than the American species. It can be distinguished by its shorter and broader leaves.

Fringe-tree
Chionanthus virginicus Linnaeus

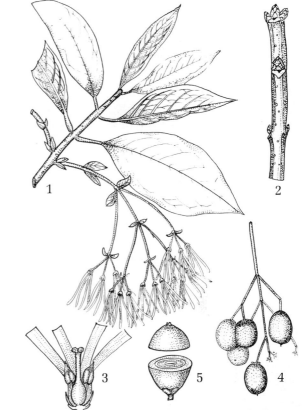

115. Chionanthus virginicus
1. Branch with flowers, x ½.
2. Branch with winter-buds, x ½.
3. Vertical section of flower, enlarged.
4. Cluster of fruits, x ½.
5. Transverse section of fruit, x 1.

HABIT. A small tree to 10 m, with usually a very short trunk and many stout ascending branches forming a deep, narrow crown.

BARK. Bark rather thin, reddish brown, scaly.

STEMS. Branchlets stout, light brown tinged with green, hairy when young, covered by scattered dark lenticels; leaf-scars raised, crescent-shaped, the upper margin surrounding half of the bud.

WINTER-BUDS. Buds ovoid, about 2–3 mm long, sharply pointed, with 5 pairs of scales fringed with hairs on the margin.

LEAVES. Opposite, simple, thickish, narrow-elliptic to oblong or obovate-oblong, 8–20 cm long, 2.5–10 cm wide, pointed or sharply pointed at apex, wedge-shaped at base, entire on margin, dark green and shiny above, pale and smooth except hairy on the veins beneath; petioles 1.0–2.5 cm long, hairy.

FLOWERS. May–June. Flowers white, very showy, slightly fragrant, borne in drooping panicles 10–20 cm long, usually with leafy bracts at base; calyx-lobes triangular; petals 4, ribbon-like, 1.5–3.0 cm long, about 2 mm wide. Staminate flowers larger with sometimes 5 or 6 petals, sterile pistils and borne in larger panicles.

FRUIT. Fruit an ellipsoid berry 1.5–2.0 cm long, dark blue, surrounded at base by a persistent calyx, borne in loose clusters on slender stalks.

DISTRIBUTION. Southern New Jersey, southeastern Pennsylvania to Florida and Texas.

HABITAT. Prefers rich, moist soil, in damp woods, along stream banks, borders of lakes and swamps.

CULTIVATION NOTES. The Fringe-tree is essentially a southern species and in Pennsylvania does not attain a large size. The tree is extensively planted for its beautiful flowers. The leaves turn bright yellow in the fall and the bluish fruits are also ornamental. The plant prefers moist situations but can be grown in drier locations by grafting on species of Ashes.

CATALPAS
Catalpa *(Bignoniaceae)*

Common Catalpa *(Catalpa bignonioides)*

There are about 10 species in the genus *Catalpa* distributed in eastern Asia, North America and the West Indies.

The species of *Catalpa* are usually deciduous trees, rarely evergreen. The large, simple, opposite or sometimes whorled leaves are entire-margined or coarsely toothed, long-stalked, and 3- to 5-nerved at base. They are mostly ill-smelling when crushed. The showy flowers are irregular, arranged in terminal panicles or racemes. There are an irregularly splitting calyx, a 2-lipped bell-shaped 5-lobed corolla, 2 fertile stamens and a superior ovary. The fruit is a very long, narrow, cylindrical capsule which separates into 2 valves, freeing the numerous small seeds bearing a tuft of long white hairs.

The Common Catalpa, *C. bignonioides,* is native to the southeastern states but planted as an ornamental tree and extensively naturalized in Pennsylvania. The Western Catalpa, *C. speciosa* Warder, native to southern Illinois, Indiana to Arkansas and Tennessee, is also planted and is hardier than the eastern species. It has longer-pointed leaves, smaller and fewer-flowered clusters and stouter and thicker-walled fruits.

Common Catalpa
Catalpa bignonioides Walter

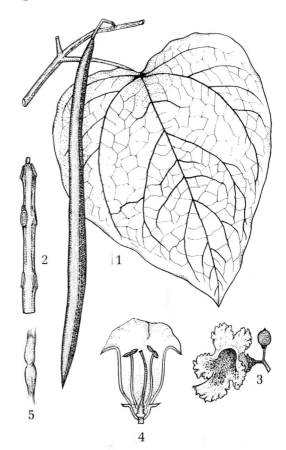

116. Catalpa bignonioides
1. Branch with fruit, x ½.
2. Branch with winter-buds, x ½.
3. Flower and bud, x ½.
4. Vertical section of flower, x 1.
5. Seed, enlarged.

HABIT. A tree to 15 m high, sometimes to 20 m, with usually a short trunk and wide-spreading branches forming a broad roundish crown.

BARK. Bark thin, light brown, shallowly ridged, separating into thin scales.

STEMS. Branchlets stout, smooth or slightly downy, yellowish brown, covered with many large lenticels; leaf-scars large, conspicuous, elliptical in outline.

WINTER-BUDS. Terminal bud usually absent; lateral buds small, brownish, globose, about 2 mm across, almost imbedded in the bark.

LEAVES. Opposite or whorled, simple, ovate, 10–20 cm long, 10–12 cm wide, sharply pointed at apex, truncate to heart-shaped at base, entire or wavy on margin, light green and nearly smooth above, hairy beneath especially on the veins; petioles 8–16 cm long.

FLOWERS. June–July. Flowers perfect, showy, white, about 4–5 cm across, arranged in many-flowered broad-pyramidal panicles 15–20 cm long; corolla white, with 2 yellow stripes and thickly spotted purple brown on inner surface, with oblique limb and entire lower lobes.

FRUIT. Fruit a long, slender, cylindrical capsule 20–40 cm long and 6–8 mm thick, with thin walls; seeds many, flattened, winged, the wings fringed at ends.

DISTRIBUTION. Original range from Georgia to Florida and Mississippi, now found naturalized north to New York.

HABITAT. Prefers rich, moist soils along streams and on bottom lands but also found in drier situations.

CULTIVATION NOTES. The Common Catalpa is now widely naturalized beyond its natural range. The tree, with its showy flowers, is highly ornamental. It grows better in shaded than in open situations.

VIBURNUMS
Viburnum *(Caprifoliaceae)*

Black-haw *(Viburnum prunifolium)*

The genus *Viburnum* is a large one with over 120 species widely distributed in North and Central America, Europe, North Africa and Asia. There are about 20 species native to North America and 11 to Pennsylvania.

The species of *Viburnum* are deciduous or sometimes evergreen shrubs or small trees. The winter-buds are naked or scaly. The leaves are opposite and simple, either with or without small stipules. The blades are entire, toothed or lobed on margin. The small, perfect, whitish or pinkish flowers are arranged in umbel-like or paniculate compound cymes. There are a small, 5-toothed calyx, a 5-lobed corolla, 5 stamens, and a 1-celled inferior ovary.

Many species of the genus are now in cultivation as ornamentals for their handsome foliage, showy flowers, or attractive fruits. Most of these species, however, are shrubby. The Snowballs, *V. tomentosum* Thunberg from Japan, *V. macrocephalum* Fortune from China, and *V. opulus* Linnaeus var. *roseum* Linnaeus from Europe, are among the showiest flowering shrubs.

VIBURNUM

Summer key to the species

A. Leaves sharply pointed at apex, the petioles winged.   **V. lentago**
A. Leaves pointed or blunt at apex, the petioles not winged.
  V. prunifolium

Winter key to the species

A. Buds long-pointed, reddish brown, smooth.   **V. lentago**
A. Buds short-pointed, rusty hairy.   **V. prunifolium**

Sheep-berry, Nanny-berry
Viburnum lentago Linnaeus

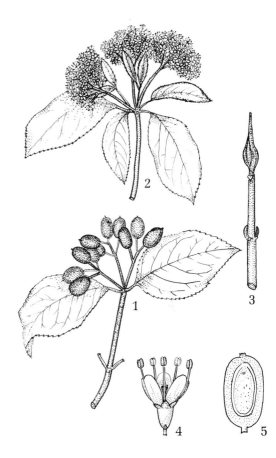

117. Viburnum lentago
1. Branch with fruits, x ½.
2. Branch with flowers, x ½.
3. Branch with winter-buds, x ½.
4. Flower, enlarged.
5. Vertical section of fruit, enlarged.

HABIT. A small tree to 10 m, or sometimes a shrub, with a short trunk and slender, often drooping branches forming a round-topped crown.

BARK. Bark reddish brown, broken into small, thick, scaly plates.

STEMS. Branchlets at first greenish, rusty hairy, becoming dark reddish brown and rather smooth; leaf-scars wide, broadly U-shaped.

WINTER-BUDS. Buds slender, long, gray, scurfy. Terminal buds often are flower-buds, markedly swollen at base, long-pointed, about 2 cm long. Lateral buds are usually leaf-buds, closely appressed to stems.

LEAVES. Opposite, simple, ovate to elliptic-obovate, 5–10 cm long, sharply pointed at apex, broadly wedge-shaped to rounded at base, finely and sharply toothed on margin, bright green, smooth above, smooth or scurfy along veins beneath; petioles 1.0–2.5 cm long, mostly winged and grooved.

FLOWERS. May–June. Flowers small, perfect, white, in dense many-flowered sessile terminal cymes 6–12 cm broad.

FRUIT. Fruit a black or dark blue fleshy, ellipsoid drupe 1.2–1.5 cm long, borne on red stalks and grouped into small clusters borne on slender drooping stalks; stone ovoid, flat.

DISTRIBUTION. Quebec to Manitoba, south to Georgia and Missouri.

HABITAT. Prefers rich, moist soil along banks of streams and borders of forests.

CULTIVATION NOTES. The Sheep-berry is a highly ornamental tree. It has an attractive form, handsome flowers and fruits, and pleasing foliage. It grows best in damp locations.

Black-haw
Viburnum prunifolium Linnaeus

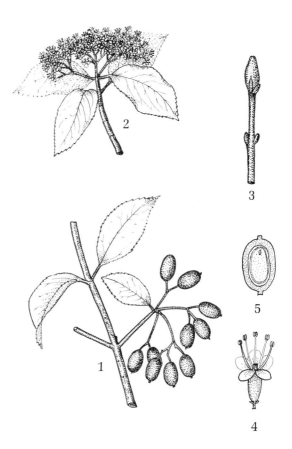

118. Viburnum prunifolium
1. Branch with fruits, x ½.
2. Branch with flowers, x ½.
3. Branch with winter-buds, x ½.
4. Flower, enlarged.
5. Vertical section of fruit, enlarged.

HABIT. A small tree or large shrub, to 5 m, occasionally to 10 m, with a short trunk and rigid spreading branches forming a broad round-topped crown.

BARK. Bark thick, reddish brown, broken into thick plate-like scales.

STEMS. Branchlets smooth, at first green, becoming gray tinged with red, marked with orange-colored lenticels; leaf-scars wide, broadly U-shaped.

WINTER-BUDS. Buds ovoid, 6–12 mm long, short-pointed, reddish hairy; flower-buds swollen near base; lateral buds smaller, flattened, closely appressed to stem.

LEAVES. Opposite, simple, ovate to broadly elliptic, 3–8 cm long, bluntly pointed to slightly pointed at apex, rounded or broadly wedge-shaped at base, finely toothed on margin, smooth or nearly so, dark green above, pale green beneath; petioles 8–16 mm long, usually round, rarely winged.

FLOWERS. April–May. Flowers small, perfect, white, in dense, many-flowered, sessile, terminal cymes 5–10 cm across.

FRUIT. Fruit a dark blue, bloomy, short-ellipsoid to roundish drupe 8–12 mm long, borne on red stalks and grouped in few-fruited clusters; stone ovoid, flat.

DISTRIBUTION. Connecticut to Michigan, south to Florida and Texas.

HABITAT. Prefers dry rocky hillsides, also in moist locations.

CULTIVATION NOTES. The Black-haw is planted for ornamental purposes. The plant often grows along fences and road-sides where seeds are apparently spread by birds.

Sheep-berry (*Viburnum lentago*)

Black-haw (*Viburnum prunifolium*)

Glossary

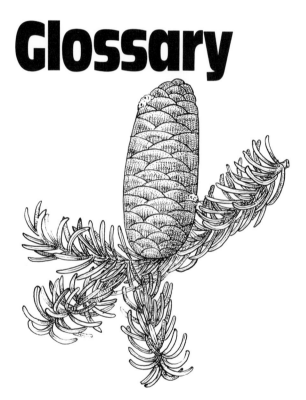

GLOSSARY

Achene. A small, hard, dry, 1-celled indehiscent fruit.

Acorn. The fruit of the oak, consisting of a nut enclosed in a cup of imbricate scales.

Acuminate. Gradually tapering at the end into a long and sharp point.

Acute. Tapering at the end into a sharp point.

Adnate. United to an organ of a different cycle or kind.

Alternate. Not opposite to each other on an axis.

Ament. A scaly spike of unisexual flowers.

-angled. Suffix meaning having corners; e.g., angled means squarish in cross section.

Annular. In the form of a ring.

Anther. The pollen-bearing part of the stamen.

Apex. The tip (of a leaf, bud, or scale).

Apophysis (in Pines). The enlarged exposed part of the cone-scales.

Appressed. Lying close to and flat against.

Aromatic. Fragrant, with a pleasing odor.

Axil. The upper angle formed by a leaf with the stem, by a stem with a branch, or by a main vein with the midrib of a leaf.

Axillary. Situated in an axil.

Bark. The outer covering of a trunk or branch.

Berry. A fruit with the whole fruit wall fleshy or pulpy.

Bifid. Divided into two lobes or parts by a median cleft.

Bipinnate. Twice pinnate.

Blade. The expanded portion of a leaf.

Bloom. A powdery or waxy substance easily rubbed off.

Boss. A knob-like or rounded protuberance.

Bract. A modified or reduced leaf either subtending a flower stalk, or belonging to an inflorescence.

Branchlet. A small branch.

Bud. An undeveloped stem or branch, with or without scales.

Bud-scales. Modified leaves covering a bud.

Bundle-scars. Scars on the surface of a leaf-scar, left by the vascular-bundles which connect the stem and the leaf.

Bur. A spiny fruit.

Caducous. Falling off very early.

Calyx. The outer perianth of a flower, consisting of either united or distinct sepals.

Capsule. A dry dehiscent fruit of more than one carpel.

Carpel. A simple pistil or a member of a compound pistil.

Catkin. A scaly-bracted spike of unisexual flowers.

Cell. A cavity of an anther or an ovary.

Centimeter (cm). 2/5 of an inch.

Chambered. Said of pith which is interrupted by hollow spaces.

Claw. The narrow, stalk-like base of a petal.

Compound. Composed of two or more similar parts, i.e., compound leaves.

Compressed. Flattened laterally.

Cone. A fruit with woody, overlapping scales.

Conical. Cone-shaped.

Conifers. Trees of the pine and related families which usually bear cones.

Coniferous. Cone-bearing.

Connate. United or joined, esp. of structures of the same kind.

Connective. The part of a stamen joining the 2 anther sacs.

Corky. Made of, or like cork.

Corolla. The inner perianth of a flower, consisting of either united or distinct petals.

Corymb. A flat-topped flower-cluster with the outer flowers opening first.

Corymbose. Arranged in corymbs.

Crenate. Toothed with rounded shallow teeth.

Crenulate. Finely crenate.

Crown. The upper part of a tree, also known as the head.

Cuneate. Triangular, with the narrow end at the point of attachment.

Cyme. A flat-topped flower cluster with the central flowers opening first.

Cymose. Arranged in cymes.

Deciduous. Falling, not persistent.

Decurrent. Extending downward; said especially of a leaf which extends down the stem below the insertion.

Dehiscent. Opening to emit the contents.

Dentate. Toothed, with teeth usually pointed and directed outward.

Depressed. Flattened from above.

Dichotomous. Forked regularly in pairs.

Digitate. Finger-shaped; said of a compound leaf in which the leaflets are borne at the apex of the petiole.

Dioecious. Staminate and pistillate flowers on different plants.

Disk. A development of the receptacle around the base of the pistil.

Dissected. Divided into many narrow segments.

Divergent. Pointing away; extending out.

Dormant. Said of parts which are not actively growing or functioning.

Dorsal. Pertaining to the back or outer surface of an organ.

Downy. Covered with fine hairs.

Drupe. A fleshy indehiscent fruit with a bony inner fruit-wall.

Ellipsoid. An elliptic solid.

Elliptic. Oval tapering at both ends to a point.

Entire. Without toothing or division.

Epigynous. Borne on the top of the ovary.

Escaped. Run wild from cultivation.

Evergreen. With green leaves during the winter season.

Exfoliate. Peeling off in thin leaf-like layers.

Exserted. Prolonged beyond the surrounding organs.

Fascicle. A dense cluster.

Fastigiate. With branches erect and near together.

Fertile. Capable of producing fruit or seed.

Filament. The stalk of the stamen.

Filiform. Thread-like.

Fimbriate. *Edged with slender hairs.*

Flora. *The complete system of plants of a particular region or area.*

Fluted. *With rounded ridges.*

Follicle. *A dry dehiscent fruit opening along one suture.*

Frond-like. *Like the leaf of ferns.*

Fruit. *The seed-bearing product of a plant.*

Fruiting cone. *The mature cone in pines or other conifers; bearing seeds.*

Gland. *A secreting structure.*

Glandular. *Bearing glands or gland-like appendages.*

Glandular-hairy, -toothed. *Teeth or hairs with glands.*

Glaucous. *Covered with a bloom.*

Globose. *Ball-like.*

Habit. *The general appearance of a plant.*

Habitat. *The place where a plant naturally grows.*

Hirsute. *With coarse, stiff hairs.*

Imbricate. *Overlapping.*

Indehiscent. *Not opening.*

Inflorescence. *The flowering part of a plant, especially its arrangement.*

Internode. *The portion of the stem between two nodes.*

Involucre. *A whorl of bracts surrounding a flower-cluster.*

Keel. *A central ridge; the lower 2 united petals of a butterfly-like flower.*

Laciniate. *Cut into narrow, pointed lobes.*

Lanceolate. *Lance-shaped.*

Lateral. *Situated on the side.*

Leaflet. *Part of a compound leaf.*

Leaf-base. *The basal part of the leaf-blade.*

Leaf-cushion. *In conifers, the basal part of the leaf decurrent on the stem.*

Leaf-scar. *The scar left by a leaf.*

Legume. *Fruit of the Leguminosae; a single carpel dehiscing by two sutures.*

Lenticel. *A corky growth on the young bark which admits air to the interior of the branch.*

Lepidote. *Provided with small scurfy scales.*

Linear. *Line-like; long and narrow, with parallel edges.*

Lobe. *A segment of an organ.*

Lunate. *Of the shape of a half-moon or crescent.*

Membranaceous. *Thin and rather soft.*

-merous. *A suffix meaning "having parts."*

Meter (m). *About 40 inches, or almost 3½ feet.*

Midrib. *The central vein of a leaf.*

Millimeter (mm). *One-twenty-fifth of an inch.*

Monoecious. *With unisexual flowers of both sexes on the same plant.*

Mucilaginous. *Slimy or gummy.*

Mucronate. *Tipped with a short abrupt point.*

Naked. *A flower without perianth.*

Naturalized. *Said of introduced plants which are reproducing by self-sown seeds.*

Nerve. *A simple or unbranched vein or slender rib (of a leaf).*

Node. *The place on the stem which normally bears leaves and buds.*

Nut. *A one-seeded indehiscent fruit which is hard and bony.*

Nutlet. *A small nut or a small stone of a drupaceous fruit.*

Oblanceolate. *Lanceolate but broadest near the apex.*

Oblique. *Unequal-sided.*

Oblong. *About twice as long as broad, the sides nearly parallel.*

Obovate. *Inversely ovate.*

Obovoid. *Inversely egg-shaped.*

Obtuse. *Blunt-tipped.*

Opposite. *Said of leaves, branches, buds, etc. directly across from each other.*

Orbicular. *Circular in outline.*

Ovary. *The ovule-bearing part of the pistil.*

Ovate. *Having an egg-shaped outline, as in a leaf.*

Ovoid. *An egg-shaped body.*

Ovule. *The body which after fertilization becomes a seed.*

Palmate. *Radiately lobed or*

divided (leaf); *or with 3 or more veins arising from the base of the blade.*

Panicle. *A compound inflorescence of the raceme type.*

Paniculate. *Borne in a panicle.*

Pectinate. *Having narrow projections or divisions suggestive of the teeth of a comb.*

Pedicel. *The stalk of a flower.*

Pedicellate. *Borne on a pedicel.*

Peduncle. *The stalk of a flower-cluster.*

Peltate. *Shield-shaped.*

Pendent. *Hanging downward.*

Pendulous. *More or less hanging or declined.*

Perfect. *A flower with both stamens and pistils.*

Perianth. *The floral envelope.*

Perigynous. *Borne around the ovary and not at its base.*

Persistent. *Remaining attached.*

Petals. *One of the separate parts of the corolla.*

Petiolate. *Having a petiole.*

Petiole. *The stalk of a leaf.*

Petiolulate. *Having a petiolule.*

Petiolule. *The stalk of a leaflet.*

Pilose. *Having long, soft hairs.*

Pinna. *A primary division of a pinnate leaf.*

Pinnate. *Feather-like arrangement of veins in a leaf; in compound leaves, with the leaflets arranged on both sides of the rachis.*

Pistil. *The egg-producing female organ of the flower, consisting of ovary, style and stigma.*

Pistillate. *Having a pistil.*

Pit. *Small depression.*

Pith. *The spongy center of the stem.*

Pod. *A dry dehiscent fruit.*

Pollen. *Spores borne by the anther containing male nuclei.*

Polygamous. *Producing staminate and pistillate and perfect flowers all on the same plant.*

Pome. *A fleshy fruit with a core, such as the apple.*

Pungent. *Acrid.*

Punctate. *Dotted with translucent dots.*

Pyramidal. *Shaped like a pyramid with the broadest part near the base.*

Raceme. *A simple inflorescence of flowers borne on pedicels of equal length arranged on a common elongated axis.*

Racemose. *Resembling a raceme.*

Rachis. *The elongated axis of an inflorescence or of a compound leaf.*

-ranked. *Arranged along a branch in 2 (or 4) regular lines.*

Receptacle. *The more or less expanded tip of the stalk; it bears the organs of a flower.*

Reflexed. *Turning abruptly downward.*

Resin duct. *A passage for the production of resin found in the leaves and wood.*

Reticulate. *Netted.*

Rugose. *Wrinkled.*

Samara. *An indehiscent winged fruit.*

Scales. *Small modified leaves which protect the bud or cone. The flakes into which the outer bark of a tree divides.*

Scarious. *Thin, dry, membranaceous.*

Sculptured. *Having raised or grooved markings on the surface.*

Scurfy. *With scale-like or bran-like particles.*

Seed. *The ripened ovule.*

Sepal. *One of the parts of the calyx.*

Serrate. *Having sharp teeth pointing forward.*

Sessile. *Without a stalk.*

Sheath. *A thin envelope or covering.*

Shrub. *A small woody plant usually branched from the base.*

Simple. *Consisting of one part; not compound.*

Sinuate. *Strongly wavy.*

Sinus. *The cleft or opening between two lobes.*

Spatulate. *Wide and rounded at the apex but gradually narrowed downward, like a spoon.*

Spike. *A simple inflorescence of sessile flowers arranged on a common, elongated axis.*

Stamen. *The pollen-bearing male organ of the flower, consisting of filament and anther.*

Staminate. *Having a stamen.*

Staminode. *A sterile stamen.*

Standard. *The upper broad petal of a butterfly-like flower.*

Stellate. *Star-shaped.*

Sterile. *Not fertile.*

Stigma. *The tip of the style that receives the pollen.*

Stipule. *A pair of appendages at the base of a leaf-stalk.*

Stipule-scar. *Scar on stem after dropping of stipule.*

Stoma. *An opening on the epidermis of the leaf (plural stomata).*

Stomatiferous. *Bearing stomata.*

Strobile. *A small cone.*

Style. *The elongated part of the pistil between the ovary and stigma.*

Sub-. *A prefix, meaning "slightly, somewhat, rather."*

Subulate. *Awl-shaped.*

Superposed. *Said of buds which are arranged one above the other.*

Suture. *A line of splitting.*

Syncarp. *A fleshy, aggregate fruit.*

Terminal. *Pertaining to buds located at end of branches.*

Ternate. *In threes.*

Thorn. *A stiff, woody, sharp-pointed projection.*

Tomentose. *With dense woolly hairs.*

Toothed. *With teeth or sharp projections.*

Tree. *A large woody plant usually with one main stem.*

Tripinnate. *Thrice pinnate.*

Truncate. *Ending abruptly as if cut off.*

Trunk. *The main stem of a tree.*

Umbel. *A flat-topped inflo-rescence with flower-stalks arising from the same point.*

Umbellate. *Borne in umbels.*

Umbo (in Pines). *The bossed center of the apophysis.*

Undulate. *With wavy margin.*

Unisexual. *Of one sex; either staminate or pistillate.*

Valvate. *Opening by valves; meeting by edges without overlapping.*

Vascular bundle. *The strand-like portion of the conduc-tive system of a plant.*

Vein. *The thread of vascular tissue of a leaf or similar organ.*

Ventral. *Pertaining to the front or inner surface of an organ.*

Villous. *Bearing long, soft hairs.*

Viscid. *Glutinous; sticky.*

Whorl. *An arrangement of three or more leaves (or other organs) in a circle around the axis.*

Wing. *A membranaceous ex-pansion of an organ; also one of the lateral petals of a butterfly-like flower.*

Woolly. *Clothed with long, soft hairs.*

264

Bibliography

BIBLIOGRAPHY

This bibliography is offered for those who wish to pursue further studies. It covers the trees of North America in general and the eastern seaboard and Pennsylvania in particular, but the list is not intended to be exhaustive. Some of the items are out of print and available only in larger libraries or libraries specializing in botanical subjects.

Blackburn, B. *Trees and Shrubs in Eastern North America: Keys to the Wild and Cultivated Woody Plants Growing in the Temperate Regions Exclusive of Conifers.* New York: Oxford University Press, 1952.

Blakeslee, A. F., and C. D. Jarvis. *Trees in Winter.* New York: The Macmillan Co., 1931.

Britton, N. L., and J. A. Shafer. *North American Trees.* New York: Henry Holt & Co., 1908.

Brown, H. P. *Trees of Northeastern United States.* Boston: Christopher Publishing House, 1938.

Collingwood, G. H., and W. D. Brush. *Knowing Your Trees.* Washington, D. C.: The American Forestry Association, 1964.

Curtis, C. C., and S. C. Bausor. *The Complete Guide to North American Trees.* New York: New Home Library, 1943.

Emerson, A. I., and C. M. Weed. *Our Trees, How to Know Them.* Garden City, N. Y.: Garden City Publishing Co., 1946.

Fernald, M. L. *Gray's Manual of Botany.* 8th Edition. New York: American Book Co., 1950.

Fowells, H. A. *Sylvics of Forest Trees of the United States.* U. S. D. A. Agriculture Handbook No. 271. Washington, D. C.: U.S. Government Printing Office, 1965.

Grimm, W. C. *The Trees of Pennsylvania.* New York: Stackpole and Heck, Inc., 1950.

Grimm, W. C. *The Book of Trees.* Harrisburg, Pa.: The Stackpole Co., 1962.

Harlow, W. M. *Trees of the Eastern and Central United States and Canada, Their Woodcraft and Wildlife Uses.* New York: McGraw-Hill Book Co., 1942. Reprinted in 1957 by Dover Publications, Inc., New York.

Harlow, W. M., and E. S. Harrar. *Textbook of Dendrology Covering the Important Forest Trees of the United States and Canada.* New York: McGraw-Hill Book Co., 1968.

Illick, J. S. *Pennsylvania Trees.* 4th Edition. Pennsylvania Department of Forestry, 1923.

Illick, J. S. *Tree Habits, How to Know the Hardwoods.* Washington, D. C.: American Nature Association, 1924.

Jacques, H. E. *How to Know the Trees.* Dubuque, Iowa: W. C. Brown Co., 1946.

Keeler, H. L. *Our Native Trees and How to Identify Them.* New York: Charles Scribner's Sons, 1929.

Little, E. L., Jr. *Check List of Native and Naturalized Trees of the United States (Including Alaska).* U. S. D. A. Agriculture Handbook No. 41. Washington, D. C.: U.S. Government Printing Office, 1953.

Matthews, F. S. *Field Book of American Trees and Shrubs.* New York: G. P. Putnam's Sons, 1915.

Peattie, D. C. *A Natural History of Trees of Eastern and Central North America.* Boston: Houghton Mifflin & Co., 1950.

Petrides, G. A. *A Field Guide to Trees and Shrubs.* Boston: Houghton Mifflin & Co., 1958.

Preston, R. J., Jr. *North American Trees.* Cambridge, Mass.: The M.I.T. Press, 1966.

Rehder, A. *Manual of Cultivated Trees and Shrubs Hardy in North America, Exclusive of the Subtropical and Warmer Temperate Regions.* 2nd Edition. New York: The Macmillan Co., 1940.

Rogers, J. E. *The Tree Book.* Garden City, N. Y.: Doubleday, Doran & Co., 1935.

Sargent, C. S. *Silva of North America, a Description of the Trees which Grow Naturally in North America Exclusive of Mexico.* 14 vols. Boston: Houghton Mifflin & Co., 1890–1902.

Sargent, C. S. *Manual of Trees of North America.* 2nd Edition. Boston: Houghton Mifflin & Co., 1922. Reprinted in 2 vols. in 1948 by Dover Publications, Inc., New York.

U. S. D. A. *Trees, Yearbook of Agriculture.* Washington, D. C.: U.S. Government Printing Office, 1949.

Index

INDEX